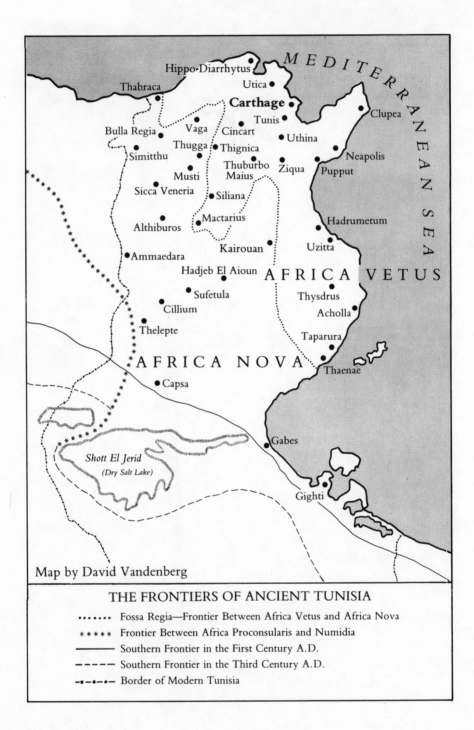

M E D I T E R R A N E A N   S E A

Hippo·Diarrhytus
Thabraca
Utica ●
Carthage ●
Tunis ●
Clupea
Bulla Regia ● Vaga ● Cincart
Uthina ●
Simitthu ●
Thugga ●● Thignica
Neapolis
Thuburbo ● Ziqua
Pupput
Musti ● Maius
Sicca Veneria ●
● Siliana
Hadrumetum
● Mactarius
Althiburos
Uzitta
● Ammaedara Kairouan ●
Hadjeb El Aioun **AFRICA VETUS**
● Sufetula Thysdrus
Cillium ● Acholla
Thelepte Taparura
AFRICA NOVA Thaenae
● Capsa

Shott El Jerid
(Dry Salt Lake)
Gabes

Ghighti

Map by David Vandenberg

THE FRONTIERS OF ANCIENT TUNISIA

······ Fossa Regia—Frontier Between Africa Vetus and Africa Nova
✱✱✱✱✱ Frontier Between Africa Proconsularis and Numidia
——— Southern Frontier in the First Century A.D.
- - - - - Southern Frontier in the Third Century A.D.
-●-●-●- Border of Modern Tunisia

CARTHAGE

Uncovering the Mysteries and Splendors
of Ancient Tunisia

DAVID SOREN

AICHA BEN ABED BEN KHADER

HEDI SLIM

A TOUCHSTONE BOOK

Published by Simon & Schuster

New York   London   Toronto   Sydney   Tokyo   Singapore

Touchstone
Simon & Schuster Building
Rockefeller Center
1230 Avenue of the Americas
New York, New York 10020

1   3   5   7   9   10   8   6   4   2

1   3   5   7   9   10   8   6   4   2   Pbk.

Library of Congress Cataloging in Publication Data
Soren, David.
    Carthage : uncovering the mysteries and splendors of ancient
Tunisia / David Soren, Aicha Ben Abed Ben Khader, Hedi Slim.
    p.   cm.
    Includes bibliographical references.
    1. Carthage (Ancient city)—History.   I. Ben Khader, Aicha Ben
Abed.   II. Slim, Hedi.   III. Title.
DT269.C35S67   1990
939'.73—dc20   89-29984
                                                            CIP

ISBN 0-671-66902-8
ISBN 0-671-73289-7 Pbk.

Acknowledgments

❦

Chapters 1 through 7 and Introduction Author: David Soren; Principal Consultants: Shelby Brown, Richard Jensen, Richard Wilkinson, Samuel Wolff, Norman Yoffee.

Chapters 8 through 11 and Epilogue Authors: Aicha Ben Abed Ben Khader, Hedi Slim; Consultant: Richard Jensen; Editor: David Soren.

The authors wish to thank the consultants but to emphasize that the responsibility for accuracy of information rests with the authors. Special thanks to Thomas Nicholson, former Director of the American Museum of Natural History in New York, and Professor Mohamed Fantar of the Institut national d'archéologie et d'art of Tunis (I.N.A.A.) for making possible the cultural interchanges developed during the recent exhibition "Carthage: A Mosaic of Ancient Tunisia." Azzedine Beschaouch, former director of the I.N.A.A., was to have been a contributor to this volume but was unable to participate due to illness. Thanks to Dr. Margaret Alexander for her pioneering work in the field of Tunisian art history and archaeology.

All photography is by Mohamed Kefi of the Bardo Museum in Tunis, Noelle Soren of the University of Arizona, and Aicha Ben Abed Ben Khader. All plans are by artist David Vandenberg. David Soren wishes to thank Noelle Soren in particular for her many contributions in the area of photography and scientific illustration to this book and many other articles and books. The authors gratefully acknowledge the support of the I.N.A.A. and the Bardo Museum.

This volume is dedicated to
Azzedine Beschaouch and Matthew Wiencke.
You have been an inspiration.
Please get well soon.

Contents

❦

CARTHAGE WAS A CENTER for the creation and dissemination of culture, science and technology. . . . Founded by Easterners from the Lebanese coast, Carthage went beyond its roots to integrate itself into its new environment and transform itself into a metropolis with a major universal influence. . . . Today's Tunisia is proud to be the heir of Carthage in the sense that we wish to remain a land of peace, a meeting place of friendship and culture.

—Zine El Abidine Ben Ali
President of the Republic of Tunisia

Preface

❦

EW COUNTRIES can boast a more colorful past than Tunisia. Situated at the crossroads of the central Mediterranean, within easy sail of Sicily and Italy, it is a country equally tied to its North African roots, nestled as it is between Algeria to the west and Libya to the east. To the south is the seemingly endless expanse of the Sahara desert. There were Berbers, seminomads, in Tunisia from perhaps as early as the eighth millennium B.C., living in simple confederations under tribal leaders.

Most of their adventures throughout prehistory remain unknown to us because there were no historical records kept, no journalists to chronicle their great leaders or impressive achievements. In fact, the Berbers for the most part have passed into modern times with no written language of their own. Only the traces of their bone and flint tools and weapons, lively rock carvings and occasional chamber tombs with their contents bear lively witness to their dominance of the Tunisian landscape.

This pastoral life would come to be seriously affected with the advent of the Phoenician colonizers of the eighth and perhaps even the later ninth centuries B.C. These new settlers were supposedly led by the intrepid Tyrian princess Dido, who founded the city of Carthage (a Phoenician name which meant the New City). The Phoenicians, or as the Greeks and Romans called them, the Punic settlers, gradually established their hegemony over an area roughly equal to that of modern Tunisia, while expanding vigorously throughout the western and central Mediterranean.

Punic Carthage fell definitively to the Romans in 146 B.C., yet by the first century A.D. the city was reborn as the center of a vast Roman agribusiness empire in Africa. In the fifth century A.D., when the vast Roman network broke down, Tunisia endured the rule of the barbarian yet Christianized Vandals for over a century, until the forces of the Byzantine emperor Justinian brought Tunisia under the aegis of Constantinople.

By the mid-seventh century, with Byzantine Tunisia racked by religious dissension, a new force appeared on the horizon to change the appearance of this fertile land forever: Islam. The holy city of Kairouan developed as a center of wealth and knowledge as well as a powerful military headquarters. The ancient cities fell into ruin or were transformed into Arab communities under dynasties such as the Aghlabids (800–910), Fatimids (910–973) and Zirids (973–1050). Tunis, the modern capital city of the country of Tunisia, first became the principal center under the Hafcids in A.D. 1236.

In 1534, Tunis fell to the Turks under Khair ed-Dine, beginning a period of domination which lasted until the French Protectorate was established in 1883—and which is still bitterly resented. Under French rule the country's attractive past became the object of intense investigation, some of it fueled by the passion of the Romantic realist writer Gustave Flaubert, who came to Carthage in 1858, was deeply affected by the ruins and in 1862 wrote his flamboyant novel *Salammbô* about the period between the First and Second Punic wars.

The French fascination with ancient Carthage took the form of significant publications by early giants of the research field such as J. Toutain, Stéphane Gsell, Paul Delattre and Paul Gauckler, then Charles Saumagne and more recent specialists such as Gilbert and Colette Charles-Picard, Paul-Albert Février, Pierre Cintas, Alexandre Lezine and Serge Lancel. With the liberation of Tunisia through the efforts of the Neo-Destour party and courageous freedom fighters such as Habib Bourguiba (who became the country's first president in 1957 and remained in power for thirty years), the fascination with the past continued, and remains a priority in the administration of current President of the Republic, Zine El Abidine Ben Ali.

In the early 1970s the Tunisian government, spearheaded by the Institut national d'archéologie et d'art became increasingly aware of the importance of safeguarding the ruins of Carthage as developers raced to turn the area into an enormous jet-set resort. Sumptuous villas decorated in marine blue sprang up everywhere, along with super-markets, fancy restaurants and snack bars, and large beachfront hotels. Carthage had long been popular with French tourists, but travelers from all over Europe now poured in in ever increasing numbers.

The "Save Carthage" program, cosponsored by UNESCO, brought to Carthage excavators from a wide variety of countries. French archaeologists, to whom the Tunisians felt a longtime special attachment despite the revolution, were given permission to conduct major excavations on the fabled Byrsa hill, alleged site of the original Phoenician settlement of Queen Dido. American teams from the University of Chicago's Oriental Institute and the University of Michigan set to work on such diverse areas as the Precinct of Tanit, the circus and some late Roman to Byzantine domestic areas. The Chicagoans and a team from Cambridge University tried to make sense of the two ancient ports, while a nearby German team found evidence of surprisingly well-made defensive walls and early housing.

By 1975, Carthage looked like a mini-U.N. as Canadians (both the French- and English-speaking), Italians, Danes, Swedes, French, Dutch, Americans and Tunisians all labored in the ruins. For the better part of a decade, excavations produced important results about the history and monuments of the civilizations that affected this legendary metropolis.

These studies helped to provide a more detailed portrait of the nature of the Phoenician settlers of Carthage and have begun to dispel the lingering notion that the Phoenicians were simply disreputable, artless, money-grubbing merchants. The period of Roman high imperial domination in ancient Tunisia is now also better understood and appreciated as a time of both virtually limitless prosperity for the wealthier classes and gradual syncretization of many different social groups.

Despite the efforts of so many countries to bring ancient Tunisia back to life, it is still difficult for the nonarchaeologist to gain an appreciation of the history of the country, just as it is difficult to visualize ancient Carthage when only scattered ruins are visible among the modern resort homes, hotels, restaurants and shops.

The current work is not intended to be a definitive guide to the ruins of Carthage (that work is well under way at the University of Michigan) or even an annotated historical reference work. Its humble goal is to present a general, hopefully readable account to those who may wish to have an introduction to and overview of some of the patterns and problems of ancient Tunisian history and culture. Surrounding areas of North Africa, Sicily, Egypt and Italy have been discussed where absolutely necessary, but the focus remains on the geographical area of Tunisia between the time of the Phoenician arrival and the end of the Roman occupation with the invasions of the fifth through seventh centuries A.D.

Certain material, such as that presented in the discussion of the tophet or sacred place of child sacrifice, represents data gathered from available published sources or dissertations and from conversations with the excavators. The reader is cautioned that, for areas like these, interpretations are apt to change as new data, final reports or new studies come into existence.

Introduction

A PHOENICIAN QUEEN

❦

> The queen herself, Dido, in all her beauty, walked to the temple
> in state. . . . She was like [the goddess] Diana when she keeps
> her dancers dancing on the banks of the Eurotas or along the
> slopes of Cynthus, with a thousand mountain nymphs follow-
> ing in bands on this side and that.[1]

WHEN THE PHOENICIAN PRINCESS known as Dido first set
foot on the northeast coast of ancient Tunisia and named it Carthage,
she set in motion a chain of events that would color the entire fabric of
Western civilization. She would be celebrated in legend and song as the
oikist, the semilegendary founder of the greatest sea empire of the age,
a nation marked as much for its entrepreneurial sagacity as for its
bizarre and horrifying religious practices.

Of course we can never be really sure if she ever lived at all, so
romanticized and distorted has her story become over the centuries.
But she easily could have lived, and the ancient chroniclers of her tragic
life, from Timaeus to Virgil, allow us at least to share their Greek and
Roman perceptions of her and the dynamic and mysterious new city
she created in what would later be the country of Tunisia.

Most scholars agree that Dido must have arrived a little before 800
B.C. By this time the northeast coast of Tunisia had already been
inhabited for many thousands of years by a less culturally advanced
people known to us as Berbers, about whom much more will be said
later.

The precise tribe of Berbers (or Libyans, as they were known to the Greeks and Romans) that Dido met upon her arrival is not known for certain. But whatever the group may have been, it was an extraordinary moment for Western civilization, a first meeting between a primitive and an advanced society—what archaeologists often call a cultural interface.

As to the reason for Dido's selection of this site for a new city . . . Phoenician sailors had long shown a preference for areas with good natural harbors because sea storms were a constant threat. They also needed a natural height suitable for defense, and arable soil in the vicinity. Carthage was ideal. It was in fact almost an island, jutting out from the Tunisian mainland in a hammerheaded promontory and reminiscent of Dido's native city of Tyre in the Lebanon.

The natural harbors just north of the modern town of Le Kram (and just south of Carthage) were adequate until better ones could be made. In 1976 a ship channel created sometime (it is not clear exactly when) before the third century B.C. was discovered in this area. The entire area of Carthage, including the lovely coastal strip, was bordered by the Gulf of Tunis to the east, the Lake of Tunis (El Bahira) to the south and the Sebhka er Riana, a lagoon, to the north. All this left about fifteen square miles, just the right size for a well-protected settlement of the type known to the ancient Greeks and Romans as a *chora,* from a word meaning tract or land area. A quarter of a mile inland from the rocky and sandy shoreline, the rolling hills of Carthage begin, most notably the steep slopes of the Byrsa, where the Phoenicians and their later conquerors, the Romans, would place the heart and citadel of their city.[2]

We cannot be sure how the Libyans felt about the new arrivals. Our sources on this matter only reach back to the third century B.C., at least five hundred years after the event took place. It would be like our estimating now how the Haitians felt when Christopher Columbus first showed up. But several sources are worth quoting. Timaeus was a Sicilian Greek of noble birth, whose family had come from the city Tauromenium now known as Taormina. Considered scholarly and highly reliable by his Greek contemporaries and the later Romans, he fashioned a history of Sicily, which was complete by about 270 B.C.

Timaeus knew Dido also by her Phoenician name Elissa (it might actually be Elisha in Phoenician but the Greeks modified it slightly for their own language).[3] She was able to establish her new city in Carthage, he says, but quickly ran into the disagreeable king of the

Libyans, who insisted that she marry him. Rather than submit to this indignity, since she was in fact a Phoenician widow, she built a funeral pyre as if she were preparing an offering to the gods, and then leaped into the flames and died. So much for cultural interface.

This simple version of the story became much more elaborate in the hands of the Roman poet Virgil. In his epic *The Aeneid*, the Libyan chieftain is said to be Iarbas, the proud son of Jupiter Ammon (Libyan Jupiter) and an African nymph whom the ever-indulgent king of the gods had raped. Iarbas had agreed to give Dido all the land that a bull hide could enclose, and the crafty princess (according to the Greeks and Romans all Phoenicians were supposed to be cunning and dangerous) cut the hide up into strips and stretched it around the Byrsa hill, thus giving it its name, which means hide in Greek. Another school of thought suggests that Byrsa was a Greek corruption of the word for fortress in Phoenician and that Dido used the term to designate her first hilltop settlement.[4]

A view of the Byrsa Hill in Carthage today, from the ancient military port. In the water to the right is part of the central admiral's island within the port; on the hill itself are the nineteenth-century Neo-Byzantine Cathedral of St. Louis and to the right the arches of the Queen Dido Hotel.

In either case it is a matter of much local pride in Carthage today that the hill bears its original name and is still the sacred heart of what has become quite a fashionable jet-set resort. At the hill's summit the newly reopened Queen Dido Hotel (La Reine Didon) offers a chance to survey the traces of Dido's town and enjoy steak *au poivre* at the same time.

Angered that Dido had spurned him in favor of a new lover, the Trojan hero Aeneas, Iarbas protests to his divine father,

> For a woman, a vagrant, who has built a small city on my territory, renting a coastal strip to cultivate under conditions of tenure dictated by me, has rejected my marriage-suit and accepted Aeneas as her master and joint ruler.[5]

Iarbas for Virgil is more than just a sore loser and a grumpy landlord. He is the charismatic *mas* of the "hut-villages of Africa," a Gaetulian leader who can unite the seemingly lawless tribes and sway the opinions of other leaders across northwest Libya.

In this Roman epic/myth Aeneas is a refugee from the Trojan Wars on his way to found the dynasty in Italy that will culminate with the rule of the emperor Augustus in Virgil's own time. His love affair with Dido seems to be a later alteration of the simpler story of Dido told by Timaeus. No doubt Virgil was using, if not inventing, this version to explain the reasons behind Rome's conflicts with Carthage in the third and second centuries B.C. Jupiter, in his aspect as Ammon, the ram-horned Egyptian god of the upper and lower worlds with his headquarters at Siwa in the Libyan desert, hears Iarbas' prayer and sends Mercury, the messenger of the gods, to remind Aeneas that he has more important work to do, such as founding the Roman nation.

The distraught Dido, believing—as Phoenicians did—that sexual intercourse was just as binding as a formal marriage contract, cannot comprehend that Aeneas is really deserting her.[6] She builds a funeral pyre and stabs herself with the very sword that Aeneas had given her. As she prepares to die, she utters those curses against the descendants of Aeneas that would eventually lead Carthage into an inevitable war with Rome. It is to Virgil's credit that we feel sympathy for the wronged Iarbas (to whom Dido refused marriage because she said she wanted to be faithful to her dead Phoenician husband), for Dido (seduced and abandoned) and for the pious but hapless Aeneas (forced to leave the woman he has been made to love by Juno and Venus in order to fulfill his duty). The whole bewildering chain of events is really nobody's fault; it is inscrutable destiny (and entertaining literature).

Who was Dido? A Phoenician royal beauty to be sure, as beautiful as Jezebel, to whom she was related. To Virgil she was a competent, mature and strong woman, a fact which annoyed the male chauvinist Berber Iarbas no end. She first appears, Hollywood-style, in Book I of *The Aeneid* "in all her beauty," walking to the temple of the goddess Juno with a youthful retinue closely attending her.[7] She looks like the goddess Diana, energetic and happy, tall and stately of carriage, a work of art surrounded by other equally stunning masterpieces gracing the temple.

Like a goddess she sits on her central throne, surrounded by armed guards, ministering to her people. She issues decrees right and left, and divides up the work to be done in building up the new city. When we try to conjure up an image of this extraordinary creature in our minds, we think of Elizabeth Taylor as Cleopatra or perhaps even Ursula Andress as H. Rider Haggard's "She Who Must Be Obeyed."[8] But this

Punic coin (stater) *made of electrum (gold and silver mixture). Carthage, third century* B.C. *The identity of the female head is uncertain; suggestions include Queen Dido, goddess Demeter or Persephone, and Tanit. The head type is derived from that of the nymph Arethusa on Syracusan coins.*

may not be a twentieth-century error on our part. Virgil composed his epic in the age of Cleopatra. The story of an exotic foreign queen whose beauty, charm and wiles tempted both Julius Caesar and Mark Antony from their proper duties was still fresh in the Roman mind. Both women were royalty driven by their brothers from their claims to power, both had an effete and ornate court, both shared royal power with a foreigner and both committed suicide. The comparisons go on and on.

Was the image of Dido which has come down to us from Rome colored by the Cleopatra story? It may indeed be so, at least in part, but it is important to realize that the story of Dido allowed this transmutation to take place; it was consistent with the way Romans traditionally thought about her. Since the time of the Greeks, Phoenician women were thought of as beautiful but dangerous, as femmes fatales like Jezebel. They caused scandals and indulged themselves in shameful luxury in their courts. The identification of Dido with Cleopatra played well with the Roman people because it reminded them of current events, of the need for Roman leaders to remember their duty when confronted with a foreign foe.

Virgil's literary patron was the emperor Augustus (through his friend and diplomatic agent Maecenas) and the Dido story would make people think of Mark Antony, Augustus' archenemy and great rival, who forgot his duty to Rome and dallied with Cleopatra. Aeneas, who put duty first, was Augustus' ancestor, a "fact" that the emperor took great pains to promote with his own sculptural program in his expensive new forum in the heart of downtown Rome. In short, the Dido image in Virgil's *Aeneid* is there because it is subtle propaganda for the administration, it is consistent with the Roman people's historical perception of Dido and the Carthaginians, and because it works well within the story as high epic drama.

It must also be remembered that the Romans had an enormous fondness for seduced and abandoned females ranging from Medea to Galatea and Ariadne, and they loved to decorate their walls with such theme paintings.[9] Dido's tragic tale, as recounted by Virgil, would have fit gloriously into this popular folk tradition and she did show up, albeit rarely, on the walls of Pompeii.

But did Virgil invent the liaison between Dido and Aeneas? After all, the Trojan War was probably fought at the end of the thirteenth century B.C., and Dido was most likely living at the end of the ninth century B.C.—if in fact she really lived. Many scholars think that the Dido and Aeneas story did exist in Roman history or legend before Virgil's time. The pioneer epic poet of the Roman Republic was Naevius, who lived in the third century B.C. and actually served on the side of the Romans in the first war with Carthage (264–241 B.C.). His account of the war was the first Roman national epic, and we know that it began with the flight of Aeneas from Troy after its destruction by the mainland Greeks. His work was called the *Bellum Poenicum*, or *The Punic War*, and we know that it mentioned both Aeneas and Dido.[10] But only scattered fragments exist of the epic, and unless we can find more pieces of it we shall never know for sure if Virgil was drawing on an already hoary Roman tradition or making up something new to glorify and clarify the lineage of his emperor. Was Dido a real historical character for Virgil or simply a poet's vehicle and pawn? Perhaps she was both.

Another account of Dido's life and death, written by the historian Pompeius Trogus, a near contemporary of Virgil, survives in an epitome made by Marcus Junianus Justin in the third century A.D. Although Trogus was writing at the time of Augustus, he seems to have kept to an older version of the story of Dido and avoided contamination from Virgil's masterful Aeneas narrative or Augustus' compelling political propaganda.

Trogus may give us a clearer historical picture of Dido because, unlike Virgil, he seems to have had no axe to grind, no emperors to link up with fabled figures of the past and no wars to justify. Instead he seems to be following the same prose tradition as the third-century B.C. writer, Timaeus.

Trogus never doubted for a moment that Dido really lived, and his account fits squarely with what we have come to know of Phoenician culture. The account differs from that of Virgil in a number of points, not the least of which is the utter absence of Aeneas. Dido's brother Pygmalion (the name is the same in Virgil) succeeds King Mattan on the throne of Tyre but has to share power with Dido, known to Trogus as Elissa. Her husband in this version is not the Sychaeus of Virgil but a man named Acherbas, who is the high priest of Hercules (Melqart), the city god of Tyre. For a time Acherbas serves as a moderating force between the new king and Elissa, but gradually Pygmalion becomes jealous of the great wealth which Elissa has inherited and of Acherbas' control of Tyre. Acherbas is murdered.

As the blood feud between brother and sister rages on, Dido decides on a ruse. On the pretext of settling her differences with Pygmalion and surrendering her hidden wealth, she asks to see him. Pygmalion, who controls the fleet of the city-state, agrees to send ships for her people and her gold. The ships are loaded, but while at sea Dido pretends to throw the gold overboard, horrifying Pygmalion's crew, who are now afraid to return to their king with such bad news.

The frightened sailors agree to sail off with Dido, who has secretly hidden the real gold and simply thrown dummy trunks into the sea, and they head for Cyprus. There, just some 120 miles from Tyre, they happen upon eighty maidens about to offer their virginity in the Temple of Astarte at Paphos on the west coast of the island. Somehow the virgins, once they have encountered the frightened and fleeing crew, agree to sail off with them, especially when everyone is told the gold is still on board after all. With ships full of gold, virgins and skilled sailors, the adventure truly begins; they all head for a new land, which will become Carthage.

Trogus' account is not only fun to read, it also takes into consideration a number of Phoenician realities. Palace coups and intrigues were quite characteristic of ninth-century B.C. Phoenicia as well as neighboring Israel, the royal houses of both cultures having become intertwined. The Phoenicians had developed a reputation for getting their way without regard for human life, but with great interest in money and power. In order to get a vineyard for her Israelite husband (the king), the Bible tells us that the Phoenician Jezebel simply disregards the law and has the owner stoned. Her half-Phoenician daughter, Athaliah, witnesses the murder of her own son, the king of Judah, but then reacts by setting out to massacre the entire royal line. She herself falls in a palace coup led by none other than a high priest, Jehoiada.

Although we must be very careful not to evaluate the Phoenicians only by reading the literature of their enemies, it seems clear that palace intrigues led by high priests and rival blood claimants to the throne were well known by Dido's day, and clearly anyone controlling vast sums of capital was of primary importance in this region of the Mediterranean, where profit and trade were the way of life.[11]

The Phoenicians liked Cyprus. It was close at hand and full of rich copper resources and it had excellent harbors and a central location for trading in the eastern Mediterranean. Colonists from Tyre itself had settled at Kition on the east coast in the ninth century B.C., a scant generation before Dido's arrival. An eighth-century-B.C. copper alloy bowl from that major Phoenician center gives the name the ancients used for Kition: Qart Hadasht, or New City, the same name given to Dido's new city (for we translate Qart Hadasht as Carthage). Not surprisingly, Kition's great temple, a superb example of Phoenician architectural craftsmanship, was dedicated to Astarte and it lasted until the fall of the Phoenician city in 312 B.C.[12]

The prominence given to Astarte and to the sanctuary at Paphos in the Dido story also fits well with the archaeological evidence. Paphos was an important cult center on Cyprus from at least the late Bronze Age (circa 1600–1050 B.C.) and Astarte (later to be known to the Greeks as Aphrodite) was worshipped there, a scant fifteen miles from the spot now called Aphrodite's Rock, where she is said to have been born from the sea foam. The ruins of the sanctuary have been under investigation for years by the archaeologist F.G. Maier, but the actual temple complex has not yet been discovered, although it was a symbol frequently used on the coinage of the city.[13]

The rite of sacred prostitution in honor of Astarte, mentioned by Trogus in connection with the Dido story, also has connections with Cyprus. Writers as late as Roman times were shocked at the practice at Paphos, where things went on that were "so abominable that they cannot be described." It is known that processions of people approached the shrine there, and pilgrims fortunate enough to be initiated into the mysteries received a lump of salt (the symbol of the salt sea from which Astarte-Aphrodite was born) and a phallus, her symbol as a deity of fertility. The Greek historian Herodotus reported in the fifth century B.C. that religious prostitution took place on Cyprus, although he failed to go so far as to name Paphos specifically.

> There is one custom amongst these people [the Babylonians]
> which is wholly shameful: every woman who is a native of the
> country must once in her life go and sit in the temple of
> Aphrodite and there give herself to a strange man.[14]

He further describes how rich as well as poor women came in large numbers to the temple and sat with a band of plaited cord around their heads while men passed along various gangways and made their selections. He adds:

Tall, handsome women soon manage to get home again, but
the ugly ones stay a long time before they can fulfill the
condition which the law demands, some of them indeed as
much as three or four years. There is a custom similar to this
in part of Cyprus.

From Kition itself comes a pottery krater that may show not only
the oriental shrine of Astarte as a three-part symmetrical building with
trees outside, but also women inside the temple perched by the windows; these young ladies represent the sacred courtesans. A stunningly
beautiful ivory plaque, now in the Baghdad Museum, was found in the
excavations at Nimrud in Iraq by the archaeologist M.E.L. Mallowan.
Dating virtually to the time of Dido and executed in a Phoenician style,
the plaque shows a woman with a Mona Lisa–type smile looking out
through what appears to be a window. Her hair is braided in the latest
Egyptian manner and her face is beautifully full and round in that
standard of feminine beauty which would prove so popular along the
western coast of ancient Turkey.[15]

She is no doubt a temple girl, part of the cult of what the Greeks
would call Aphrodite Parakyptousa, the "Aphrodite Looking Out the
Window." A cord similar to the one that Herodotus mentions as bound
around the heads of the prostitutes has actually been found in ivory
examples of "The Woman at the Window" from other sites such as
Arslan-Tas and Khorsabad. Anthropologist Norman Yoffee of the
University of Arizona has suggested that such cords may signify a
highborn woman.

Considering that Astarte played such a prominent role in the Dido
legend and in Tyrian society, it would seem logical that her cult on
Carthage would have been of major importance. The historian B.H.
Warmington has noted, however, that the role of Astarte-Aphrodite
seems to have been of minor importance in Carthage and other Phoenician settlements in the west.[16] This might be because in Africa the
Phoenicians seem to have run up against what may have been a great
Libyan mother goddess, whose powers gradually infiltrated the Phoenician religion there. The goddess may have become partially fused
with Tanit, a lesser-known Phoenician divinity so strong by the fourth
century B.C. that she even seems to have replaced Ba'al Hammon as
supreme power. Having said all this, it must still be remembered that
we have a lot to learn about the gods of ancient Carthage. The symbol

of Tanit seems to have been known for many centuries before the fourth in Phoenician and Canaanite lands, upsetting theorists who believe that she is a late arrival on the scene and Libyan in origin.[17]

Astarte may have put in at least a token appearance in Carthage. There is a tantalizing later Roman reference to a town called Eryx in Sicily, where temple prostitution was practiced. The citizens of Eryx erected a temple to Venus, the Roman incarnation of Aphrodite, in the ancient Tunisian town of Sicca near the modern border of Algeria, and there the same Phoenician rites were observed. In the oldest cemeteries of Carthage, located on the hill of Juno or in the area known as Douimès, several statuettes have been found of the so-called Near Eastern Astarte-type: a female figure holding her breasts with both hands as a symbol of fertility and the nourishing of life.[18]

So Astarte apparently reached Carthage, but, according to our current information, in the battle of female divinities for supremacy she seems to have finished a distant second.

Another aspect of the Dido story, which has its roots in the actual history of Phoenician culture, is the notion of sailors setting out to found a new colony to the west. In the later ninth century, when Dido "lived," the Phoenicians had already embarked on an age of exploration and on the bare beginnings of the colonization that would lead to their monopolizing many of the natural resources throughout the Mediterranean. The success of such expeditions was due to the need for Phoenician products (particularly Lebanese timber), the quality of the Phoenician ships and sailors, and the entrepreneurial spirit that enabled Phoenicians to be middlemen trading such goods as Cypriote copper. Also, the perfection of the keel ship so superior to its flat-bottomed predecessor allowed for better controlled steering in rough seas and prevented easy capsizing.

Of course, we don't know if Dido's band sailed off in a warship or a merchant vessel, but both were available by her time. The warship could have been a bireme, meaning that there were two levels in which rowers could sit, even though sails could also be employed as needed. A relief from the Assyrian palace at Nineveh dating to about 700 B.C. shows Phoenician-style warships not too long after Dido's time. The banks of oars are staggered in arrangement, and the stern of the ship curves up dramatically and elegantly. There is a battering ram attached to the bow to impale other ships at sea, and the deck seems to be exceptionally high.[19] Merchant vessels might swoop up at bow and stern but lack the ram. Such highdecked vessels could be quite diverse, ranging from short and broad with a large sail and fewer banks for oars to vessels resembling the war galleys and used to sail into pirate-infested waters where quick oar work might be necessary.

The popular practice of building warships of light fir made rotting a constant problem, necessitating the Phoenician practice of storing the ships on land in specially built shipsheds during any prolonged stays in port. When the port of Carthage was excavated by a British team in the 1970s, it was found that the ships were all pulled up out of the harbor for long-term storage.[20]

Dido's arrival in Carthage also introduced to North Africa another custom that seemed to foreign peoples even more barbaric than the practices of the Berbers themselves: human sacrifice. Although the Phoenician practice of offering small children as an animistic sacrifice to the gods is not mentioned as part of the Dido story, the sources still agree that Dido placed death before dishonor and sacrificed herself on the funeral pyre. Virgil wrote, "In a mad dash she climbed the high funeral pile, and unsheathed the Trojan sword, a gift never meant for such a use as this."[21] Again, Virgil may have had in mind an actual event that occurred during the final Roman invasion and destruction of Carthage in 146 B.C. As the crippled citadel struggled to resist the superior invading force, the wife of the Carthaginian commander killed herself in a manner worthy of Dido rather than see her city fall to the hated Romans.[22]

Whatever the real Dido may have been like, she stands as a symbol of the proud and mysterious people who founded and colonized Carthage and brought civilization to North Africa, even though her story became increasingly garbled and confused as it was told and retold over the centuries and deftly dovetailed into apparently unrelated traditions like the Aeneas story. But through it all we are able not only to catch glimpses of what Dido's real character may have been like. We can also grasp something of the values of Dido's countrymen, the Phoenicians, whose civilization dramatically altered the face of Carthage. Apart from the suggestions of glamorous, strong-willed women, the Dido story reveals much of the culture of her people: great wealth and building skills, a tradition of human sacrifice in times of personal or national stress, duplicity of character, dynastic upheavals and an incredible knowledge of seafaring.

That these ideas should find their way down to Roman times can be no accident; they were ancient perceptions of Phoenicia that a Roman audience would immediately recognize in an epic like *The Aeneid*. Of course not every stereotype is completely true, but there are often pieces of truth in many stereotypes. The scholar's game is to find those pieces, separate them from the extraneous material, and put the whole puzzle together into a believable story. It may not be the correct story, but it will have to serve until new evidence appears.

In 1894 a unique and tantalizing piece of evidence was found in Carthage in a necropolis of the Douimès area.[23] It was a small gold pendant inscribed in Phoenician, possibly an heirloom from a Tyrian soldier. It contained the name of Pygmalion—but was it really Dido's brother and rival? Another name found on the pendant might be Bitias, mentioned by Virgil centuries later as a member of Dido's original expedition. This may be the earliest Punic artifact ever found in Carthage (the Latin *punicus* and Greek *poenos* refer to a person from Phoenicia and, more particularly, a Carthaginian). Hopefully future discoveries will tell us more about the possible historicity of the enigmatic Phoenician queen.

❦ I ❦

Canaanites and Phoenicians

T HE TRADITIONS that the seafaring Phoenicians brought with them to barbarous Carthage were already many centuries old. The Phoenicians were the descendants of a people who occupied the coastal strip of the eastern Mediterranean in an area that now consists of northern Israel, Lebanon and southern Syria. These Canaanites, as they are known to modern biblical archaeologists and historians, gradually felt the civilizing influences of Egypt and Mesopotamia, the great cultural and military centers of the Near East.[1] They were what linguists call Semites, meaning that their roots went back at least into the fourth millennium before Christ, when languages with a possible common origin began to spread through Europe and the Near East.

Until a decade ago the following scenario was taught as gospel: Somewhere near the end of the third millennium a powerful group of Berbers (or Bedouin, as they are sometimes known) was supposed to have come out of the Sinai desert speaking a Semitic language. As they headed north they splintered off, the northernmost branch becoming known as Amorites. The branch that split off into the coastal plain of southern Syria, Lebanon and Palestine became known as the Canaanites. This entire event, which was supposed to have occurred around 2200 B.C., came to be termed, with typical scholarly formality, as the Amorite-Canaanite Influx. Why the nomads felt the need to settle in an area more suited to permanent settlement and seafaring (about which they apparently knew next to nothing) is anyone's guess, and for a long time the question didn't seem to bother scholars very much.[2] But settle they allegedly did, and set

31

out to exploit the enormous timber reserves and trading possibilities all around them.

Over the past ten years a number of scholars have severely challenged this perhaps overly simple invasion theory embraced in various forms by specialists such as W.F. Albright, Kathleen Kenyon and Paul Lapp. Now anthropologists such as Norman Yoffee argue that there was no Amorite invasion and that the whole understanding of what constituted an Amorite needs revision.[3] By the time these people were supposed to have invaded, they were already well integrated into Mesopotamian cities, villages and pastoral life in a wide diversity of professions.

It now seems (but things can always change tomorrow) that the development of the area of Palestine, which archaeologist William Dever has called "a pastoral backwater populated largely by indigenous village peasants, herders and itinerant traders," began between 1900 and 1800 B.C., although Yoffee insists that there were at least some large towns there in the early third millennium.[4] Communication and trade increased with more sophisticated communities in Syria, Anatolia and western Mesopotamia, bringing about a fundamental upgrading in the overall standard of civilization in the areas which were to become known as Canaanite.

The Lebanon was a seemingly endless source of fir, cypress and cedar trees—the famous Cedars of Lebanon. From these trees long and strong beams could be cut and these were soon in tremendous demand in places like Egypt, where, with the desert climate, good wood was extremely difficult to find.

According to Gerhard Herm, the people of Byblos in Syria gradually learned about seafaring and were influenced in their dress, art, religion and writing by the Egyptians, who swarmed all over the port communities to maintain a sphere of influence and monopolize trade.[5] But Egypt was not able to dominate the developing Canaanite region indefinitely. In fact, recent scholarship has attempted to see Egypt falling increasingly under the control of powerful, sophisticated Palestinian Canaanites in the eighteenth and seventeenth centuries B.C. These invaders either became or merged with a group known as the Hyksos, or Princes of the Foreign Uplands. (The Hyksos question is still controversial, and terms such as Canaanite and Amorite evoke complex theories about movements and cultural relations of peoples well beyond the scope of this book.)

A good deal of our information about the relations between Egypt and the Canaanite areas in the fourteenth century B.C. comes from documents known as the Amarna Letters.[6] These are clay tablets, written in cuneiform script and mainly in Akkadian (the international diplomatic language of the day). They first came to light in 1887 and now total well over five hundred in number. They were discovered in the royal archives of the Egyptian pharaoh Amenhotep III and his son Amenhotep IV and are of extraordinary value because they were written by the rulers of other city-states and kingdoms that traded with Egypt, including centers in northern Syria and Canaan. Both the extensive influence of Egypt in the region and the impending danger from the powerful Hittites of Anatolia come through strongly in the letters. The threat of a Hittite takeover put a severe strain on the ability of the Egyptians to control this important region. Much-needed money for keeping up the Egyptian front was siphoned away from the treasury by the otherworldly pharaoh Amenhotep IV, who called himself Akhenaton, and who, in about 1373 B.C., began pouring huge sums into the building of his new city at Amarna, dedicated to the sun god Aton.

As Egypt turned its thoughts heavenward and ignored the Hittites, Canaan became a major bone of contention. The Battle of Kadesh between Egyptians and Hittites did little to further Egypt's claims in the area, but the real death knell to Egypt's sphere of influence was to come about 1200 B.C.

By this time the people of Canaan had already developed the areas of expertise that their descendants, the Phoenicians, would take up (in fact, many scholars see no real difference between Canaanites and Phoenicians). The great cities of Byblos, Tyre and Sidon were already able to function as important commercial centers in Canaanite times.[7] Byblos, just twenty-five miles north of modern Beirut, was exploited for the adjacent timber forests. Shipbuilding became a major industry, but up until 1984, most scholars believed that the ships produced were still simple and lacked the ability to sail very far out into the Mediterranean. Flat-bottomed, coast-hugging vessels seemed the rule of the day, but a thriving import-export business could still develop with city-states throughout the eastern Mediterranean and eastern North Africa.

It was widely believed that the mainland Greeks, known as the Myceneans, along with the skilled sailors of Crete were the main peoples dominating trade throughout the central and eastern Mediterranean. But an extraordinary shipwreck only recently found off the southern coast of Turkey at Ulu Burun has revealed the astonishing diversity of late Bronze Age trade in this area.[8] Dating perhaps to the later fourteenth century B.C., the vessel may have been of Canaanite origin, although artifacts and art objects from seven different cultures were abundantly represented. The ship's hull (the upper part has been lost) was sturdily made of fir, and the cargo included everything from huge ingots of copper to amber from the Baltic. There were bronze tools and weapons, small cymbals like those found later in so many Carthaginian tombs, ostrich shells and glass beads. Popular transport jars, known to archaeologists as Canaanite amphorae, were found in great abundance, and there was even a plaque of the Egyptian god Ptah, patron of metalsmiths and a major protective divinity later on in Phoenician Carthage. From this wreck, superbly excavated by the renowned underwater archaeologist George Bass and his team from the Texas A&M Institute of Nautical Archaeology, it is possible to argue that the Canaanites played a major role in the commerce of the eastern Mediterranean. (Incidentally, Bass has become so well known as a result of his pioneering efforts in the excavations of undersea wrecks that he was last seen making television commercials for waterproof watches.)

Another wreck, found at Cape Gelidonya in southwest Turkey in 1960, was of a more modest nature and probably belonged to an independent and rather poor trader or itinerant metalworker. So the evidence suggests that, whether rich or poor, a number of Mediterranean peoples—including especially Canaanites—were out trying to turn a profit on the high seas. Attendant industries such as logging, woodworking and shipping grew rapidly too, and the skilled craftsmen of Canaan gradually gained international prestige as far away as Egypt and the Sinai.

To speed up the harnessing of the abundant natural resources and their shipment abroad, some enterprising Canaanite seems to have invented—or at least developed—a sort of shorthand writing system that would be less cumbersome than the known written languages of the area, such as Akkadian cuneiform and Egyptian hieroglyphs (in some circles the term hieroglyphics is no longer considered proper). The latter were a difficult combination of ideograms, or pictorial symbols, and partly phonetic arrangements of signs, that is, symbols which could be read roughly like letters of an alphabet. Knowledge of such writing was considered a sacred gift from the god Thoth, consequently not everyone was permitted to know how to use it. The Canaanites seem to have begun to transform hieroglyphs into a simpler, more useful phonetic language, which could be used to make shorthand notations for their inventories. Since they were great traders, such a shorthand system—one that large numbers of Canaanites could use quickly—was absolutely necessary.

By a phonetic language, or perhaps more properly put, an alphabetic script, we mean one in which each symbol or letter corresponds to a single sound—as opposed to a syllabic or even a logographic script (where a letter, character or symbol is used to stand for an entire word). The modification of Akkadian cuneiform into an alphabet featured vowel and consonantal forms—writing had finally become the graphic counterpart of speech. This discovery, easy to take for granted today, revolutionized recordkeeping and not only streamlined Canaanite overseas and internal operations but also turned out to be a very rough version of what would later become the Phoenician alphabet, which forms the basis for the way we write today. The Canaanite system, which consisted of some thirty symbols, was developed between 1700 and 1200 B.C., further simplified by the Phoenicians, and then passed on to the Greeks, who added most of the vowels—and the rest, as they say, is history (and, fortunately for scholars, written history). No other people in the history of the world had been able to create an alphabetic system; this was truly one of the greatest achievements in the history of mankind.[9]

The Canaanites were also a very religious people, and in their cultic practices must be seen the seeds of the later beliefs of Dido and her Phoenician followers. One of the earliest and most helpful sources for the study of Canaanite religion comes from the ancient north Syrian city of Ugarit. Beginning in 1928 tablets were found in large quantities by archaeologist Claude Schaeffer and his team.[10] They were written in a previously unknown Canaanite script now called Ugaritic, a Semitic language that could be dated to the fourteenth century B.C. The tablets told epic stories and songs of the gods and heroes of the region, providing a glimpse of a complex religion previously little understood but railed against by the Old Testament prophets because of its presumed appeal to the ancient Israelites.[11]

Ugarit was not some minor coastal town but a major trading

center among the peoples of Canaan, Egypt, the Greek world and the coast of what is now Turkey. It had been a melting pot since the third millennium—an international crossroads between east and west. Many other cultures besides the Egyptians vied for influence: Hurrians, who were a non-Semitic people already in Syria and Mesopotamia in the third millennium; Amorites, who were a northwest Semitic people living in Syria and Mesopotamia; and the ubiquitous Cypriotes. So it is somewhat simplistic to call Ugarit simply a Canaanite center, but the tablets enlighten us about the religious practices of the region and provide a contemporary source instead of one written five hundred or even a thousand years after the fact. Around 1200 B.C. a great fire destroyed Ugarit and sealed in the valuable tablets; it may have been the result of aggression by groups whom the Egyptians called the Sea Peoples.[12]

Of all the Canaanite religious practices the most shocking to modern eyes (and to the Greeks and Romans too, according to the sources) was human sacrifice. But there was much more to Canaanite beliefs. There were apparently three principal divinities, although they may not have been the same in each Canaanite town or city, or they may not have had the same emphasis or importance in each place. El was the great sky god, omnipotent and aloof. More colorful was Ba'al, or The Lord, who was number two in the chain of command but much more interesting. As ruler over the seasons, he died and revived annually, holding the key to death and resurrection like Egypt's Osiris and the later Roman African divinity Saturn, with whom he was intimately connected. Finally there was Ba'al's wife Astarte, whose name recalls Mesopotamia's Ishtar and who was reflected in the later Cypriote Greek Aphrodite.[13]

To attend to the rites of these gods, and numerous other major divinities such as the city god Melqart of Tyre, a well-defined religious order included high priests, lesser priests, and diviners. Sacred areas were not just temples, they were major complexes where the faithful could spend considerable time. Because of the animism that was often a part of their religion, the Canaanites were known to construct many open-air sanctuaries, where sacred trees and abundant water could be found. Sometimes these might be located on a height and would be known as high places; there animals and even humans might be sacrificed as a blood offering to the gods. Included within such a complex might be a sacred *temenos* or open-air precinct. Often stones (*matzevot*

Terra cotta statue of Ba'al-Hammon wearing a plumed crown and sitting on a throne flanked by guardian sphinxes. This is part of a group of Punic divinities found at the rural sanctuary of Thinissut, near Bir bou Rekba in the Cape Bon area. It indicates the survival of Punic religion after the Roman conquest. Neo-Punic, later first century.

in Hebrew and *baetyloi* in Greek) were used as sacred objects in place of cult statues, because it was not permitted to show the actual face of a god.

There seems to be little doubt among scholars that human sacrifice was practiced by the Canaanites. In a society where man was an equal partner with nature, such expressions of this partnership were not uncommon. Sacrifices might be carried out in times of national emergency or perhaps as part of the normal order of religious practice. This rite, along with sacred prostitution, was passed on to the Phoenicians and then found its way to Carthage, perhaps with the early Phoenician settlers.[14] (See chapter six for a discussion of human child sacrifice in Carthage.)

Canaanite civilization suffered a dramatic reversal about 1200 B.C., when many of the great centers were destroyed. Some of the marauders have not been easy to identify and have been lumped under the general and not very enlightening name Sea Peoples. Because they caused the Egyptians and other cultures so many problems, we do have at least some knowledge about them, including the names of at least some of the groups who wreaked this havoc all along the eastern Mediterranean settlements.

They probably were a mixture of peoples, diverse and not always united, including our old friends, the Libyans. But the major trouble-makers seem to have come from Greece and Crete after the Trojan War and during the time when the Greeks were themselves fleeing from invading, iron weapon–brandishing barbarians whom history has called the Dorians.

The migrants from mainland Greece were powerful and violent, and must have seemed quite tall to those who had the misfortune to come up against them. Among these Aegean peoples were the Philistines, a sophisticated group who brought with them an advanced knowledge of architecture and the remnants of the late Mycenean Greek pottery styles in vogue before their society was plunged into chaos. (The term Philistine is the biblical *peleshtim*, whence came the word Palestine.)

Wherever the Philistines and their piratic comrades went, trouble followed. It took an enormous effort by the pharaoh Rameses III in circa 1175 B.C. to confront the Sea Peoples, and he forced the Philistines to settle in the coastal communities of southern Canaan, where they produced smelted iron and olive oil for trade—demonstrated in the exciting new excavation at Ekron by an American and Israeli team. Rameses' remarkable display of bravery and skill may have changed the entire history of the Mediterranean. Many of the vanquished were put into prison camps, while the Philistines, once allowed into the Gaza strip, settled into communities which came to be known as the Philistine Pentapolis or League of Five Cities: Gaza, Ashdod, Ashkelon, Gath and Ekron. History was not finished with them; they would have future adventures against the Egyptians, the quickly developing Israelite nation and Babylonia. When King David of Israel fought the giant Goliath, he was—if the current theories advanced by some scholars are correct—coming up against a Philistine descendant of the mainland Greeks.

Here it is worth pausing to mention that nowadays archaeologists generally identify and distinguish cultures by studying their artifacts, particularly the pottery. But the artifacts of the various Sea Peoples sites do not always reveal their origin. For example, a Philistine site like Ashdod has pottery that looks Mycenean Greek and features its bird designs and panelled patterns, but much of the pottery looks Anatolian, Cypriote or native Canaanite, which suggests much intermingling of peoples. To say—as many scholars now do—that the Philistines were Achaeans, or mainland Greeks, may be an oversimplification of a highly complex problem, or even, some scholars believe, an error.[15]

About 1100 B.C., after the carnage caused by the Sea Peoples had ended and the inhabitants of the eastern Mediterranean were able to breathe a collective sigh of relief, things were very different indeed. The towns of Tyre and Sidon had been struck a grave blow by the Sea Peoples but were beginning to recover and develop. The powerful but conservative center of Byblos to the north had been an important trading site since the third millennium and would continue to prosper as a city-state and become the principal distribution center for Egyptian papyri. (The name Byblos, which seems to have attached itself to the site by the early first millennium, meant papyrus, and our own words such as bibliography and bibliophile and even Bible derive from it.)

The focus of ancient Canaan had begun to change. Byblos was eclipsed by the entrepreneurial genius of the citizens of refounded Tyre and Sidon. Improved technology was introduced into the region and a new spirit of independence took over, now that the Egyptians— suffering from sheer exhaustion as well as faulty leadership—had loosened their grip on Canaan and the Hittites had been defeated (and their magnificent Boghazköy burned) in the chaos of circa 1200 B.C.[16] Tyre and Sidon became the hubs of the new area, whose people now came to be known to the Greeks as Phoenicians, from a word probably meaning the Purple Ones. Many of them may still have considered themselves to be Canaanites, a word that may also mean Purple Ones and had its origin in the murex shells they used to make a beautiful and elegant dye (known to both Greeks and Romans as royal Tyrian purple). Again a word of caution is in order: many scholars do not accept the equating of the word Canaan or Kinahhu with the color purple, but it is such a delightful association that even if it is not true, it ought to be.[17]

Now there was a new danger waiting in the wings, that of Assyria, but the period between 1100 and about 675 B.C. was to be a golden age for the Phoenicians: drawing on the Canaanite technology, they were able to build more seaworthy ships that could take them and their merchandise back and forth across the Mediterranean. It is doubtful that the Lebanese city-states that blossomed after 1100 B.C. thought of themselves as a unified group, but they did gradually come to share a common hatred of the Assyrians, the major threat to their new power.

The Phoenician sea empire developed during this golden age accomplished everything the Canaanites had done—and much more. The Phoenicians became the master merchants of the Mediterranean, superbly organized into a wealth-gathering and distributing machine. The timber of the Lebanon was cut down and shipped to eager clients in Egypt and Israel. Gangs of workers, fine craftsmen in all materials, shipbuilders, bookkeepers, navigators, explorers—each had a role to play.

But rather than acting together as a unified nation, the Phoenicians operated in small groups, each with its own king. The king might have been the principal purveyor of commerce, but there were plenty of independent merchants plying the seas, trading and, by the early seventh century B.C., participating in the development of colonies and trading stations all over the Mediterranean.[18]

The Phoenicians were a coastal people and thus especially vulnerable to attack from the hinterland. They therefore became skilled negotiators: it was much better to buy off an enemy with tribute than to risk destruction. By 883 B.C. the Assyrian king Ashurnasirpal II threatened the very fabric of life in Phoenicia. The tribute required to keep him at bay was enormous, but it had to be paid so that the city-states could continue to function independently.

But what of Dido's native Tyre? It was the great urban center of its day, replacing Ugarit, so devastated by the Sea Peoples, and Byblos, which was growing more decrepit daily. It was a Phoenician Manhattan, with mini-skyscrapers—or at least multistoried buildings—filling the landscape. There were magnificent sanctuaries with stately temples. In the precinct of the city god Melqart the huge *stelae* (specially erected pillars made of gold and emerald) seemed to glow mysteriously in the night. As late as 700 B.C. the prophet Isaiah would still be able to describe Tyre as "the crowning city, whose merchants are princes, whose traffickers are the honorable of the earth."[19]

Presiding over the resurrection of Tyre was its most famous king, Hiram (969–936 B.C.), whose massive rebuilding scheme included expanding the city onto an island half a mile off the coast and linking it with a specially prepared causeway. Hiram also enjoyed excellent relations with his neighbors to the south, the Israelites. King David of Israel (circa 1000–960 B.C.) had his luxurious house built in Jerusalem using resources from the Lebanon—carpenters, masons and even the famed cedars—all sent by Hiram. So renowned had Tyrian work become that it was only after this event that David came fully to realize that he had "arrived" as the Lord's chosen one—as king of Israel. The excellent relations between Phoenicians and Israelites continued under King Solomon, David's youngest son and ruler between 960 and 935 B.C.

It had been David's dream to build a great temple to the Lord, but because of wars and insurrections in Israel it proved impossible. Solomon undertook the project, which, to be done right, absolutely had to have the special touch of Tyrian elegance. The project took seven years and must have impressed the king because he then built an extravagant palace for himself that took twice as long to complete. Whether or not the city of Sidon had come under Tyrian domination or supervision at this time is still the subject of much scholarly debate. In any case, we are told in the Bible that Solomon's palace was built of the famous Cedars of Lebanon and fir trees from the region and was decorated in gold using Phoenician laborers ("Hiram's servants") because "there is not among us any that can skill to hew timber like unto the Sidonians."[20]

In the Bible, Hiram even discusses how he proposed to deliver the materials for Solomon's palace: "My servants shall bring them down from Lebanon unto the sea; and I will convey them by sea in floats unto the place that thou shalt appoint me."[21] Of course we do not know exactly how much in dollars and cents a Phoenician project on this scale would cost, but we know that Hiram made a considerable profit, for he received twenty thousand measures of wheat and twenty measures of pure oil every year along with twenty cities located in Galilee. They might not have been great cities, and in fact Hiram seems not to have liked them, but the gift illustrated one important point: being a Phoenician king, and especially king of Tyre, wasn't just a political opportunity; it was big business. The close ties between Israel and Phoenicia reached a peak in the reign of Israel's King Ahab (874–852 B.C.), only a generation before the time of Dido and the supposed founding of Carthage. Ahab created a storm of controversy by marrying Jezebel, daughter of Ethbaal, king of Sidon and a former high priest of the goddess Astarte. This led to the introduction of Ba'al worship in Israel and, what was more, Jezebel's own daughter Athaliah introduced forbidden Phoenician religious practices into the southern Jewish kingdom of Judah.

In the generations to come, the Phoenicians were to become universally admired and despised throughout the Mediterranean. Greeks from as early as Homer's time had nothing but contempt (and no doubt envy) for the treacherous traders who kept bringing riches from further Spain, Assyria or the Cycladic Islands. Phoenicians would cruise into port and spread their wares out in front of their ships, hoping to get exorbitant prices. Waiting for word of mouth to advertise their bracelets, necklaces and rings, they might stay for as long as a year.

From the Greek point of view, the Phoenicians could never be trusted. They were known to kidnap children at the drop of a hat, sail off to sea and sell them into slavery at the next port of call. If given half a chance they would make off with your women (as Dido's crew seems to have done on Cyprus) and they had little regard for human life and dignity.

But how can this image be reconciled with the view of the Phoenicians as the great craftsmen of antiquity, the creators of stunningly beautiful cities like Tyre and the practitioners of a religion that demanded the ultimate sacrifice of its devotees? Perhaps even more bizarre is the fact that although they invented or at least perfected and transmitted a form of writing that has influenced dozens of cultures including our own, most of their surviving writing is of interest neither in its decorative form (it is all quite straightforward and nonornate) nor in its content. The Phoenicians primarily ask for favor from the gods on their tombstones or keep records of transactions. Was this really all the transmitters of writing had to say?

The Italian scholar Aldo Massa went so far as to say, "Having invented a marvellous instrument, the Phoenicians then proceeded to do little or nothing with it. . . . No feeling for history, and no lofty concern for posterity, only a narrow selfish attitude."[22]

In recent years this wholly negative attitude toward the Phoenicians has begun to change. This is partly because by now over six thousand inscriptions have come down to us in Phoenician or in its Carthaginian manifestations of Punic and Neo-Punic (i.e., after the Roman conquest of 146 B.C.), allowing us the chance to discover what the character of the Phoenician language was like. A study of the individual words and syntax has led scholars to the belief that there really was much more to Phoenician thought and writing than direct evidence would indicate. Some scholars now feel that the early Hebrew Bible shows an enormous amount of influence from Canaanite and Phoenician sources; W. F. Albright has gone so far as to say:

> There can be no doubt that the Bible has preserved some of the best in Phoenician literature. . . . Without the powerful influence of the Canaanite literary tradition we should lack much of the perennial appeal exerted by Hebrew poetic style and prosody, poetic imagery and the vivid description of natural phenomena. Through the Bible the entire civilized world has fallen heir to Phoenician literary art.[23]

Even if we must revise at least somewhat our traditional thinking about the literature of the Phoenicians, many questions still remain, and too few examples of Phoenician writing exist for us to get many answers. Was the Greek attitude towards the treacherous Phoenicians correct, or just the jealous rumblings of an archrival in overseas commerce? Did the Phoenician culture, which was so highly religious and technically advanced, really have shallow values and an indifference to the plight of the individual? Such a description may seem to be paradoxical, but in fact it only shows that the Phoenicians who founded Carthage—with or without Dido—were a highly complex society that scholars are only just beginning to understand.

At the time of Dido's purported expedition, Tyre and its sister cities were only just past the peak of their glory. Elegance, sophistication, advanced writing, and master artists and craftsmen had made Phoenicia renowned throughout the ancient world of the Mediterranean and Near East. In such a time of plenty, only a desperate situation could have forced a Tyrian princess to set sail on the open sea for the little-known realm of the Berbers. But Phoenician women, as we have seen from Jezebel and her brood, were not only stunning, they liked a good challenge. And Dido, granddaughter of King Mattan of Tyre, would have been Jezebel's great-niece.

The Berbers (or, more correctly, *barbaroi*) whom Dido encountered were given their name by the Greeks. This term was of course a misnomer and was used to describe any foreign, strange or even uncivilized group of people, whatever they may have looked like, believed or spoken. To many Greeks, even the Romans themselves were Berbers, barbarian bumpkins who were always up to no good. Sometimes Greeks and Romans used the term Libyans to describe the Berbers (the familiar Arabic term *Bedouin* literally means "people of the tent").

In Dido's time the Berbers of ancient Tunisia were hardy natives, who lived simply in primitive hut villages and often migrated seasonally with their flocks in search of better pastureland, food, water and shelter. Instead of building cities or even large towns, each tribe or *aguellid* placed its faith in a powerful leader called a *mas*. The various *aguellids* showed little interest in developing themselves into a supersociety or even a city-state like those of Dido's own Phoenicia or the then already age-old cultures of Egypt and Mesopotamia. Independence, not progress, was and still is the principal credo of these people.

Head of a Libyan/Berber. Modern plaster image cast from a mold found at Thysdrus and dating to the second or third quarter of the third century A.D. The mold may have been from a death mask and the man may have been killed in the rebellion of the would-be emperor Gordian I.

A great *mas* might be able to rally them for a time against a common foe, but the confederation was always to remain a loose one.[24]

The special study of the history and culture of these Berbers is known, appropriately enough, as Berberology and has been pursued for over a hundred years almost exclusively in France, largely because the French have played such an important part in the history of the coastal countries of North Africa. So many theories have been put forth to explain who the Berbers were that the whole subject remains as confusing today as it ever was.[25]

It seems clear now that there is no one race of Berbers, nothing to make them what scholars call ethnically homogeneous. Some specialists have tried to identify a particular "look" that might allow someone to recognize a Berber throughout North Africa, but it doesn't work. Berbers of the Kabylie area in northern Algeria have big long heads (and so are said to be dolichocephalic), but the Mozabites are also Berbers and have wide heads (so they are called brachycephalic). There is so much difference in head and body forms even within individual tribes that such study proves to be about as accurate as a phrenologist deciding on a criminal type by examining the bumps on a person's head. A big obstacle to any analysis based on physical typing is the inevitable mixing of peoples that has gone on for many thousands of years and still continues today. The descendants of these Berber groups still make up about one percent of the population of modern Tunisia.

It became fashionable in France thirty years ago to think of the Berbers as being made up of many different peoples who came in waves at unknown dates and were the origin of the diversity of head shapes and physical characteristics that we find today. These cultures may have been merging as early as the eighth millennium before the birth of Christ. At Gafsa in central Tunisia we can point to a culture (the Capsian) that had simple, geometrically shaped flint tools and weapons and by 6500 B.C. could boast rock sculptures, red ochre painting and bone-working. These early Tunisians, who had a great passion for escargots, were amateur artists who loved to decorate the ostrich eggs which are found in their abundant refuse pits. In Tunisia these old-timers are generally known as the Proto-Berbers.[26]

Recent research has forsaken the measuring of Berber heads for a seemingly more fruitful approach, the study of the Berber language. Although each tribe or grouping of Berbers (and thousands of different ones are known) spoke a different language and might not always be able to communicate with another group, there were assumed to be enough similarities in language that specialists could assign several major Berber language groups. The Zenatia group alone has hundreds of different subdivisions in Tunisia, Libya and part of Algeria and Morocco that may be related to one another.

Such a language group seems to be what scholars have for many years called Hamito-Semitic (or often just Hamitic), named after Noah's son Ham in the Bible, who was believed to be the ancestor of the African people. This language group, now more often discussed under the designation Afro-Asiatic, spread from an unknown center (a number of scholars have suggested the Caucasus, but this is quickly passing out of vogue) at an unknown date before the fourth millennium, developed into languages such as Akkadian, Egyptian and Hebrew, and ultimately branched into such diverse languages as Coptic and the Cushitic dialects of Ethiopia. But this whole approach to classifying the Berber language has become widely challenged because of the amazing diversity of Berber dialects and the difficulty of separating out contaminating elements that result from Berber contacts with other peoples in historical times.

It is probably safe to say that the Berbers lived outside the mainstream of cultural developments in the Near East. They were influenced in the second millennium B.C. by settlers from the eastern Mediterranean and Europe (through Spain, Sicily and Sardinia), and there were even Negroid elements assumed by many scholars to derive from the Sahara. The group that emerged by the time Dido arrived was culturally diverse, ruggedly independent and, as Herodotus has emphasized, often given to animistic religious practices, which means simply that they may have venerated natural phenomena, including mountains, stones, water sources, the sun, moon and stars, and probably also a great nurturing mother goddess. If we wish to say more than this, we will, as we have seen, get ourselves into problems of a highly complex nature. It is, in fact, usually safer to leave Berberology to the Berberologists.

In the time of the Greek poet Homer (about 700 B.C.), the term Libyan was already in use to describe Berbers in North Africa, particularly those just west of Egypt. These Libyans (or Libou, as the Egyptians call them) were already quite well documented by the later thirteenth century B.C., when they were feared as part of the invading Sea Peoples who menaced ancient Egypt. But after Homer's day the

Greeks tended to think of the entire continent of Africa (or at least as much of it as they had explored) as Libya and of all its native people as Libyans, whether they lived next to Egypt or as far away as the area of Carthage.

So in 800 B.C., if our sources can be believed, Carthage was a small coastal community settled by Tyrian Phoenicians in a countryside filled with half-friendly Libyans. But this situation would not endure for long, for Dido's successors were soon to carve out a legacy that would shake the Mediterranean world to its foundations.

❧ II ❧

Destroy Syracuse!

B ECAUSE THE ancient sources are so sketchy, it is not possible
to say exactly what happened between Dido's day (around 800 B.C.)
and 550 B.C., the approximate time of Mago, the first known king of
Carthage and the man who allegedly introduced the use of mercenaries
into the army and fleet to protect the rapidly expanding trade markets.
Mago is also credited with the major step of making the post of army
commander hereditary within his own family. This was particularly
important for just as the Canaanites and Phoenicians before them, the
Carthaginians survived on trade. By Mago's time, overseas commerce
had long since become big business.

In the seventh century B.C., Phoenician emporia or trading
stations—and no doubt colonies as well—were located all over the
Mediterranean, especially in southern Spain and France, Sicily, Sardinia and North Africa. Not all of these settlements were under the
direct control of Phoenicia. Some at least must have been the result of
independent enterprise, for the artifacts found are so disparate.

Little of the trade went very far overland. Instead, there were
regular sea routes, with numerous stopover ports along the way.[1] The
earliest Near Eastern pottery that excavators have found at Carthage
came from Phoenicia at the beginning of the seventh century B.C., or
perhaps even as early as the eighth. This has sparked a major controversy among archaeologists, some of whom feel that the traditional
founding date of Carthage in the ancient sources, 814 B.C., is quite
likely, while others argue for a founding date some time in the early
seventh or very late eighth century B.C.[2]

Did Phoenician pottery from Dido's time exist in Carthage? The answer for now is no, but it is quite possible that it simply has not yet been discovered. American investigations in the tophet (Precinct of Tanit), German excavations north of the harbor and French explorations on the Byrsa seem to have gotten down to eighth-century-B.C. layers, but more evidence is needed. Only time will tell.

For years, knowledge of the character of the international trade of Carthage was limited to excavation reports and occasional articles by scholars like C.R. Whittaker and Sabatino Moscati, who tried to put the limited and scattered evidence together.[3] Attempts (such as the work of Pierre Cintas) to create a unifying theory about the pottery often featured poor quality drawings and pottery typologies that were biased by the specific contexts in which the pottery was found, such as tophets (places of child sacrifice and subsequent burial) and tombs. Cintas had hardly anything from people's homes.[4]

But a recent, unpublished thesis by Dr. Samuel Wolff of the University of Chicago's Oriental Institute has taken advantage of the UNESCO-sponsored excavations of the past decade and a half in Carthage to study the entire range of materials that came into and went out of the Punic city.[5] Wolff's work allows for the playing of a scholar's fascinating parlor game: matching the ancient literary accounts of Carthage with the artifacts recovered. Wolff, noting that Phoenician pottery began to show up about 800 B.C. in Spain, has suggested that Spanish silver was already being exploited by cities like Tyre and Sidon at this early date, not only for trade but probably because of a pressing need to pay off huge tithes to the Assyrian landlords camped on their borders.

It was probably not until about 700 B.C. that Carthage became a major stopover on the all-important maritime trade route between Spain and the Levant. The abundance of Phoenician pottery forms in Carthage suggests that at first the settlers were reluctant to cut the umbilical cord to the increasingly weakening motherland. Later, by the time of the Magonid kings, the city-state was doing quite well breaking away on its own. The pottery styles in Magonid Carthage and other contemporary western Phoenician colonies show a trend towards uniqueness of form and decoration and a difference from contemporary wares in Tyre. In Carthaginian amphorae, for example, the typically elongated, tapered, cylindrical form began to take shape and gain in popularity.

Carthaginian transport amphora of the so-called Mañá C 1/2 type. Probably third century B.C.

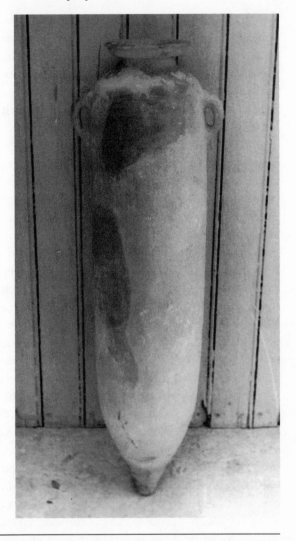

Meanwhile, in Tyre, constant pressure from Assyria in the seventh century B.C. had caused the Phoenicians to revolt twice—although both times unsuccessfully—while in 585 B.C. the newly ascendant Babylonians of King Nebuchadnezzar picked up where the Assyrians had left off, besieging the city for thirteen years before signing a treaty and leaving Tyre independent but exhausted.[6]

By the later fifth century B.C., hardly anyone living west of Greece talked about Tyre as a major power anymore. The leadership of the various Phoenician settlements of the west now fell more and more to Carthage, but there was one huge obstacle constantly blocking all hope of peaceful trade: the Sicilian Greeks. The battle for Sicily would become a consistent and tragic theme, a leitmotif of the Punic period lasting all the way down to 241 B.C. Carthage's prime adversary was the city-state of Syracuse and its allies. Syracuse had to be stopped—but how?[7]

To understand the magnitude of the problem Carthage faced, we must first understand how the Greeks got to Sicily and what happened once they arrived. In the twelfth century B.C. the mainland Greek centers such as Pylos, Mycenae and Tiryns lay in ruins. The causes of this devastation are still hotly disputed, with many scholars, as we have already seen, taking the view that the Dorians—invaders from the north armed with iron swords—swooped down into Greece causing destruction and massive displacement and migration. Economic factors and internecine feuds may also have played a part in this sudden discontinuity in what is termed Mycenean Greek civilization.

Some of the displaced Greeks sought their fortunes in the east or perhaps, like the Philistines, joined the Sea Peoples. But Greece itself was plunged into a Dark Age from which it did not emerge for centuries. Archaeologist William Biers notes that "The Dark Ages were years of poverty and recession throughout Greece, marked by depopulation . . . isolation and stagnation."[8] Gradually there was a general revival in political stability, the standard of living and the level of culture, as powerful city-states like Athens and Corinth rose to prominence and the age of overseas colonization went into high gear.

In 733 B.C. mainlanders from Corinth established a colony on the east coast of Sicily in an area occupied by Sikels (native Sicilians). The site was called Syrakousai and has come down to us as Syracuse. It was an ideal location: it had natural fortifications such as the rocky heights of Epipolae, which looked down over both a superb wide and deep natural harbor and its attractive adjacent promontory, known as Ortygia. Over the centuries Syracuse was to be a critical lookout post for observing developments in Italy, Carthage and the commercially active Straits of Messana, between Italy and Sicily. And Sicily would become a valuable, fertile center for the production of grain, olive oil and wine; its beautiful horses were renowned throughout the Mediterranean.

While Corinthians colonized the eastern area of Sicily, other enterprising Greek city-states were also founding colonies right and left. Around 700 B.C. islanders from Crete and Rhodes founded Gela on the southern coast, and the Gelans slowly expanded their sphere of influence and finally moved westward along the coast to found a trading post at Akragas in 583 B.C., taking advantage of the River Himeras to get at Sicily's rich hinterland. Megara Hyblaea, just north of Syracuse, was founded by the Greek city of Megara about 730 B.C., and the colony itself founded Selinus on the southwest coast in 628 B.C. Himera, which would become a crucial pawn in the struggle for Sicily, was founded on the north coast in 648 B.C. by Zancle, itself a colony of Cumae, one of the earliest Greek communities of South Italy.

With colonies begetting colonies which in turn begot more colonies, it was no wonder the native Sikels were growing alarmed. For these colonies were not merely cities; they were often ruled by powerful tyrants and controlled the entire surrounding region. As they grew in strength, they became increasingly independent of their mother communities and began to develop intense rivalries among themselves and with the native Sikels and, of course, Carthage. So long as these city-states remained ruggedly independent, there was little danger to the far-flung Carthaginian mercantile interests. But unfortunately for Carthage, things happened that gravely upset the balance of power.

Carthage, like the mainland Greek city-states, had strong interests in Sicily and developed powerful colonies such as Panormus, Solus and the island of Motya. Early in the sixth century B.C., a Greek alliance in Sicily tried to drive out all Carthaginian influence from the entire area and Motya in particular. A contingent of Greeks from the islands of Rhodes and Knidos tried to colonize the area of Lilybaeum on the mainland just opposite Motya.[9] Nearby, the city of Segesta on the northwest coast, founded by the native Elymian people of the region, sided with Carthage, while the Megarian Greeks of Selinus on the southwest coast, who hated the Elymians, aided the Greeks.

The Carthaginians won the mini-war, driving the few Greek survivors out to the Lipari Islands, off the northeast corner of Sicily, where for a generation they became a band of pirates living off Etruscan shipping. At the same time, Carthage was trying to maintain its foothold on the island of Sardinia, despite frequent local independence movements. By the time the fifth century B.C. began, Sicily was becoming sharply divided into rival spheres of influence: Carthaginians

in the extreme west, Greeks in the east, north and south, and Sikels and
Elymians in and around the colonial centers in the east and west
respectively.[10]

Sicily was now a melting pot that refused to melt. Besides the
principal powers, there were various mercenary groups swarming all
over the region, waiting like vultures for trouble to start. There were
also refugees from various city-states seeking their fortunes on the new
frontier. Add to this the political intrigue within and between city-
states, and it is easy to see that Sicily was ripe to implode. Nor was that
all. The problem of piracy was still unresolved, with a particular danger
coming from the island of Corsica, where Greeks from Phocis were not
only entrenched but also making a healthy living by raiding Carthaginian and Etruscan merchant ships.

In these years in Carthage flourished a distinguished king and
general called Hamilcar, a name probably derived from Ahimelqart
("Brother of Melqart"). He had watched the developments in Sicily
with growing interest. Hamilcar was doubly concerned because, although he was from a fine Carthaginian family line, the Magonids, his
mother was a Sicilian from Syracuse. Such intermarriages between
countries and/or cultures happened more than occasionally in
Carthage, even among the royal or aristocratic lines. Now Hamilcar
was being drawn into battle both for and against his own people.

The most dangerous Sicilian Greek of all at this time was a rising
star named Gelon of Gela, the powerful Greek city-state on Sicily's
south coast and the mother city of nearby Akragas.[11] Ambitious and
dynamic, he was also an anti-Punic imperialist and bristled at having
witnessed in his own lifetime Carthaginians driving out Greek colonists from western Sicily and Cyrene in what is now the modern
country of Libya.

Gelon dreamed of a unified Greek Sicily, but under his family's
rule Gela had gone as far as it could go. Its economy was bursting at
the seams, and he needed access to a major port such as his neighbor,
Syracuse, had. The big problem was how to get it. In 485 B.C., Gelon
formed an alliance with King Theron of Akragas and then bided his
time. An internal revolt in Syracuse, instigated by landed nobles and
no doubt fanned up by Gelon and his followers, led the democratic
parties to call him in as a savior for the city and a true man of the people.
But once in power, he surprised many by moving most of the people
of Gela to Syracuse, as well as bringing in citizens from other Gelan

dependencies such as Camerina. Gelon of Gela had suddenly become Gelon of Syracuse, tyrant of all of southeastern Sicily.[12]

A ripple of fear shot through the independent and pro-Carthaginian centers of Sicily. It was a dangerous moment. Like Hitler in Europe, the ruthless Gelon was making alliances of convenience, displacing peoples and gobbling up land. He had to be stopped, but who would do it? Not that Gelon didn't have his supporters and admirers. Theron of Akragas, his most important ally, was equally hungry for more land and saw the chance now to push his own frontier way to the north. Even without expanding, Akragas was already a city of incredible beauty. The Greek poet Pindar visited Theron at the leader's invitation in 490 B.C. and wrote of the city, "Lover of splendor, most beautiful of mortal cities, that lives upon the hill of fine dwellings, above the banks where the sheep graze beside the river."[13]

But Theron was never one to rest on his laurels. By capturing Himera—itself a Greek colony—on the north coast Theron could control the entire central area of Sicily coast to coast and with it the important rivers Halcyus and Himeras. The relative calm of the sixth century B.C. was now to end with a big bang.

In Himera the king, Terillos, was quickly overcome and driven out by Theron, but not before calling for help from the only major power he could: Carthage. His son-in-law Anaxilaos, the tyrant of Rhegium (located on Italy's toe) joined the battle, and the Punic fleet, long renowned as the best in the world, prepared for a major expedition to Sicily under Hamilcar. The powerful mercenary army included not only Libyans, Campanians, Sikels, Elymians and Iberians but even a good number of Gelon-hating Greeks. And even the city of Selinus, which had been anti-Punic for so long, joined the coalition.

But Gelon was a crafty and brilliant cavalry leader with wide experience, and even more important now, he was a master of dirty tricks espionage. Intercepting a secret Punic message to the cavalry of Selinus, he substituted his own men and fooled the Carthaginians by a sneak attack west of Himera. Surprised and overwhelmed, the Punic forces gave way and their ships were torched in Himera harbor. Herodotus reports,

> The tradition in Carthage—and it may well be true—is that all
> the time the battle lasted . . . Hamilcar remained in camp trying
> to obtain a favorable omen from sacrifices—whole carcasses

which he was burning in an immense fire; and at last seeing as
he poured the wine upon the sacrificial victims that his army
was routed, he leaped into the flames and was burnt to
nothing.[14]

The loss at Himera may be simply described as a megadisaster for
both Carthage and the Magonid family. Much of the Carthaginian
fleet, once so feared, lay in ashes. Huge numbers of slaves and a massive
indemnity of silver fueled a Hellenic renaissance in Sicily, which would
last for almost seventy years. As Herodotus said, "Syracuse shot up and
budded like a young tree"[15] under Gelon. A stunning new agora, or
market center, graced the region of Achradina just inland from Ortygia, and massive new docks lined the great harbor.

Sacred buildings sprang up rapidly and transformed the city,
including the magnificent Temple of Demeter and Kore, built as a
thanks-offering on the heights of Epipolae. The Temple of Athena,
today part of the cathedral, was built with war spoils and became
famous for its magnificent sculpted doors covered with ivory and gold.
Poets and philosophers flocked here now, together with playwrights
like Aeschylus, the father of Greek tragedy, who came to produce his
immortal *Prometheus Bound*. In the fifth century B.C. spectacular temples in the Greek Doric style were erected throughout Sicily from
Selinus to Segesta and from Syracuse to Himera. Often these were
more ornate and bigger than temples built on the mainland of Greece.
At Himera, to rub salt in the wounds of the defeated Carthaginians, the
tyrant Theron built the Temple of the Syracusan Victory.

Beautiful Akragas, not to be outdone, erected nine temples,
new aqueducts to supply water and an internationally renowned
fountain. But the most incredible construction of all was the
enormous Temple of Olympian Zeus built in the Valley of the
Temples south of the modern city of Agrigento.[16] This was not just
an elegant temple, it was the largest Doric temple ever attempted—
we must say attempted because it was too big a project even for
Theron. It measured 173 by 361 feet and had already been put on the
drawing board before the Battle of Himera. Innovative, dynamic
and exciting, it contained a host of architectural refinements. Lining
the exterior, placed between engaged Doric columns, were male
Atlas figures over twenty-five feet high with their arms raised as if
to support the massive architrave. The style of these fantastic figures

dates them to between 470 and 460 B.C., the decade after the Battle of Himera, and the Sicilian-Greek writer-historian Diodorus, who visited the site in the first century B.C., reported that the labor for the building of the temple was largely provided by the Carthaginian prisoners from that battle.

And so while Sicily entered upon a Hellenic golden age, Carthage found itself in an increasingly dangerous and isolated position. There were still contacts with Tyre, but the Persians were the dominant force in the Near East now and the Tyrians had been no help at all in the Sicilian expedition.

Until recently, the fifth century B.C. in Carthage was considered a period of slow recovery, although a good deal of trade certainly continued, especially with the western Punic cities. Not surprisingly, most Greek imports tailed off, although a special variety of olive that the Carthaginians loved was still imported from hated Akragas. But Carthage seems to have recovered quickly and begun a program of fortification, expansion and exploration while at the same time avoiding new confrontations with Sicily.[17]

And while Carthage was recovering, Sicily had become a major international commercial and tourist center. King Hamilcar, instead of being vilified as the man who lost at Himera, was seen as a pious victim of fate and became a figure of admiration. Herodotus noted the feeling in Carthage in his own time, the mid-fifth century B.C., ". . . he is treated with divine honors, and monuments were erected to him in all the Carthaginian colonies in addition to the one—the most splendid of all—in Carthage itself."[18]

Nonetheless the rule of the powerful Magonid dynasty was coming to a close. An aristocratic group of landowners and political activists played an increasing role in matters of state. Up until now the kings seem to have ruled by divine right, as if they themselves were the final authority on all matters. Now there would be governing bodies as well, especially a Council of One Hundred, to which the commander-in-chief had to report.

By the later fifth century B.C., war clouds were swirling yet again. The rising power of Syracuse worried another mighty city-state besides Carthage: Athens. Syracuse was supplying Athens' rival Sparta with abundant Sicilian grain, and when in 427 B.C. the city of Leontini, just north of Syracuse, tried to drive out its neighbor's overbearing influence, Athens was called in.[19] Charges and countercharges, alliances and treaties took up seven years until 415 B.C., when the Athenians, despite their critical need for manpower for their ongoing struggle with Sparta, decided to wage war. The city-state rulers, with a fleet of 134 triremes and 30,000 men, the Great Expedition, now determined to destroy Syracuse.

The Athenian fleet sailed boldly into the magnificent Syracusan harbor and set up camp by the very Temple of Olympian Zeus that had been built from the Punic spoils of Himera. Fortifications were hastily improvised by both sides all over the city, especially in the areas just north of the harbor. As the skirmishes continued, other mainland Greeks sailed to the aid of Syracuse. Corinth and Sparta joined in, making this the first truly Pan-Greek war.

In the stalemate that ensued, Nikias, the insecure Athenian commander, prepared to abandon the enterprise, but a bad omen, an eclipse of the moon, made him wait. Taking advantage of the delay, the Syracusans bottled up the Athenian fleet by closing off the harbor exit, and the result was a total disaster, what historian Thucydides at the time called "the most calamitous of defeats."[20]

All the Carthaginians eagerly followed reports of these Sicilian trials and tribulations, but none more so than Hamilcar's grandson Hannibal, who was now king of Carthage. He had a burning desire to avenge his grandfather, who by now had developed an almost mystical following. His own father, Gisco, had been exiled from Carthage for some reason lost to us now, but if Hannibal could achieve a great military victory for Carthage in Sicily, the good name of his family would surely be restored. But for the moment he had to bide his time. (Of course, this Hannibal was not the same man as Hannibal the son of Hamilcar, who later brought fame to Carthage for his campaigns against the Romans. The name, which meant "Ba'al is my favor" or "favorite of Ba'al," was as popular with Punic royalty as John or Bill is in our own culture.)

Like other Magonids, Hannibal believed deeply in the special relationship between the royal family and the great and terrible god Ba'al Hammon (the name meant either "Lord of the Perfumed Altar" or "Lord of Mount Amanus"), to whom they offered sacrifices of animals and even small children and babies. The dynasty was a proud one, and acts of violence against the family had to be avenged with the full consent and endorsement of the all-powerful gods.

Hannibal's big break finally came when he was called back to

Carthage to mastermind a new Sicilian invasion, a holy mission to reverse the fortunes of Carthage. Landing at Motya (a longtime Punic stronghold off the west coast of Sicily) in 409 B.C., he immediately besieged the city of Selinus, where his own father had been exiled. Primarily using his Libyan, South Italian, and Sikel mercenaries, Hannibal quickly overcame Selinus, but at this point a terrible tragedy and error in judgment took place, which would come back to haunt the Carthaginians for generations.

Not content with their defeat of the Sicilian city, Hannibal's mercenaries lost all control and ran wild, looting and mutilating the dead. This action, and their poorly understood religious practices, gave the Carthaginians a terrible reputation throughout the ancient world as bloodthirsty butchers. But Hannibal cannot be simply dismissed as a crazed barbarian; he was a master strategist, one of the finest and most dedicated generals Carthage would ever produce. Pretending to make for Syracuse, he diverted and confused the Greek fleet and soldiers while he went after a more emotional objective—the city of Himera, the very spot where his grandfather Hamilcar had been killed by the Greeks and the site of the Temple of the Syracusan Victory.

Hannibal surveyed his army as he prepared to attack one of Sicily's loveliest Greek cities. There were precious few pure-born Carthaginians among his men. Instead, the bulk of his troops were again the mercenaries, following Mago's Carthaginian custom. Libyans filled up much of the light infantry, while Iberians and Celts from central Iberia were also present, brandishing their characteristic short swords. There were more disgruntled Sikels now, sick of being dominated by the expansion-minded, interfering mainland Greeks and ready to throw in their lot with Carthage. There were rugged, unpredictable Campanians too, from South Italy. Of course Hannibal would no doubt have preferred to have an all-Punic army, but Carthage was too small—with a population recently estimated at fifty thousand (one hundred thousand including the immediate surrounding area), not all of whom were Phoenicians.[21] Besides, many of the able-bodied men were engaged in the international commerce that had brought the city-state such enormous wealth.

The stakes were high at Himera. For a Carthaginian general each campaign was a holy war. A loss was an impiety, and a failed leader might be expected to sacrifice himself on a pyre or starve himself to death. The general-king was expected to solicit the good favor of the gods every day through sacrifice and consultation of the omens. War was not the secular experience it has become in America since Vietnam. The phrase "for god and country" was taken literally and inseparably. Hannibal had to win.

The slaughter which now took place at Himera eclipsed that of Selinus and was not a proud moment in the history of Carthage. Perhaps it had been ordered by the Punic priests, who believed in human sacrifice both to appease the gods and to atone for sins. Whatever the reasons, the men of Himera were ceremoniously marched out to the exact spot where Hannibal's grandfather had died. There they were tortured and murdered as a blood sacrifice to his spirit. Himera itself, together with its Temple of the Syracusan Victory, was razed to the ground. The women and children, as so often happened in these years, were distributed as prizes for the troops.

Carthage was at last a true superpower, standing on the threshold of controlling the trade and manipulating the politics of the entire western Mediterranean. It was a watershed moment, one that had taken centuries to create, and Hannibal was determined to make the most of it.

The fickle city of Segesta, ever observant of which way the war winds were blowing, came over to the Punic cause, and suddenly the Carthaginians were once again masters of western Sicily. Nor did the future look bright for Syracuse. Its most talented general during the Athenian invasion, Hermokrates, had gone off to fight on behalf of Sparta against Athens. While he was away, his opponents rose up against him and declared him persona non grata. When he tried to return and set himself up as tyrant of the city, he was murdered right in the middle of Gelon's beautiful agora.

Meanwhile Hannibal had returned to Carthage and disbanded his troops. Now older and somewhat infirm, he probably thought he might spend his remaining years in an easy chair telling war stories to his host of admirers. But instead he was quickly pressed out of retirement to lead a new and even bigger expedition, this time to take control of all of Sicily. Indeed, Hannibal still had at least one old score to settle—the destruction of Akragas, the city whose king had captured Himera and caused the death of his grandfather. And so in 406 B.C.— after landing, as the Carthaginians always did, on the west coast of Sicily—he made a beeline towards his enemy to the southeast. He quickly besieged the city and desecrated its cemeteries, particularly the tomb of his grandfather's nemesis, Theron.

But when an epidemic suddenly broke out among Hannibal's troops, the leaders of the expedition began to examine possible religious reasons for all the illness. Had the gods abandoned Hannibal? Was the epidemic due to the desecration of the cemeteries? The omens continued to be unfavorable, and soon Hannibal too was sick and dying. Turning over control of the expedition to a younger relative named Himilco, Hannibal passed away just before Akragas fell in ruins.

There were no mutilations this time around. The people of Akragas were allowed to flee to Gela, but the city, once the jewel of Sicily, lay wide open and undefended. An astonishing amount of booty was pulled from the decimated site and carried off, one of the principal reasons why Sicilian-Greek artistic forms now began to influence strongly the look of Carthaginian art. To appease the gods, Himilco sacrificed a Syracusan child in a bloody rite that the Greeks had always found particularly abhorrent.

Hannibal was dead, but the struggle for Sicily was far from over. His quest for vengeance had taken Carthage back into the international arena and the bloody theater of war. But the Greeks' reaction to Hannibal's mutilations and plundering was to start their own war of revenge against Carthage. The new leader of Syracuse, Dionysius, stepped up his war preparations and his rhetoric against the vile enemy, seeing the anti-Carthage issue as the one that could unify his island. Using siege warfare, he was able to surprise and crush the vital Punic colony at Motya in 397 B.C.

The seemingly endless battles of the later fifth and early fourth centuries B.C. were not decisive and had something of the character of the recent Iran-Iraq war, with each side gaining brief advantages but neither being able to administer the death blow. When all was said and done, it was not the might of a Syracusan tyrant that kept the Carthaginians from gaining control of all Sicily. Instead, it was the plague.

Time after time, when the Punic forces had pitched their camps before Sicilian cities like Akragas or Syracuse, waves of illness would devastate the troops. Untrained in modern (or even Roman imperial) sanitation techniques, particularly the orderly disposal of waste, the Carthaginians, with their reliance on mercenaries, faced the disadvantage of having people from many different native environments and cultural levels living together in a foreign country. The opportunities for epidemics were enormous, and it is possible that diseases such as typhus and/or typhoid fever may have played a role in decimating the Punic forces.

The crowded and dirty environment of a Punic mercenary camp could have been a breeding ground for the rats that carried body lice and transmitted infectious diseases such as murine typhus, which for centuries has been commonly found on ships, in jails and in military camps. The chills, fever, pain and cramps that would have occurred just over a week after the louse bite could have severely crippled the army, and the accompanying delirium and frequent outbreaks of pneumonia could have contributed to the Carthaginians' fear that they were being punished by the gods for impiety.

Another disease which may well have affected the Punic army was typhoid fever, spread not by lice but by bacteria of the salmonella species found in food and water contaminated with feces. Typhoid fever can be transmitted by flies and especially by handlers of foods such as shellfish. The resulting dehydration, internal complications and sepsis (systemic infection) may have been a serious problem.

But Diodorus' description of the plague which struck the Carthaginian army before Syracuse in 396 B.C. does not seem to fit the symptoms of typhus or typhoid fever:

> . . . the plague began with a catarrh; then came a swelling in the throat; gradually burning sensations ensued, pains in the sinews of the back, and a heavy feeling in the limbs; then dysentery supervened and pustules upon the whole surface of the body. In most cases this was the course of the disease; but some became mad and totally lost their memory; they circulated through the camp, out of their mind, and struck at anyone they met. In general, as it turned out, even help by physicians was of no avail both because of the severity of the disease and the swiftness of the death; for death came on the fifth day or on the sixth at the latest. . . ."[22]

The noted epidemiologist Hans Zinsser believed that the plague was in fact a severe, confluent form of smallpox, although that disease is not supposed to have existed in the classical period. A new idea, proposed by Dr. Kenneth Iserson, offers another possibility, although he admits that no known disease fits the symptoms perfectly.

Iserson proposes melioidosis, a disease similar to glanders, which is quite rare today. It is caused by a bacterium transmitted to humans from stagnant streams or ponds (such as were present in Syracuse), rice paddies, or fruit and vegetables grown in such areas, but evidence suggests that it can be transmitted from person to person as well. The symptoms bear a striking resemblance to those encountered by the ancient Carthaginians in Syracuse: lung infection, disorientation, severe headache, sore throat, diarrhea, skin pustules, high fever, shortness of breath, flushed skin, muscle tenderness. The severe form of melioidosis tends to progress towards a fatal course in a very brief period of time, perhaps five or six days.

The so-called plague, perhaps a combination of epidemics, caused dramatic changes in Punic religion. A back-to-basics renewal of the old Phoenician ways pervaded the fourth century B.C., with the traditional practice of child sacrifice either increasing or at the very least continuing at full force. Yet the goddess Tanit rapidly replaced Ba'al Hammon as the principal deity to whom such sacrifices were offered. The plague at Syracuse was linked by the Punic priests to the desecration of the temple of the Greek goddesses Demeter and Persephone, and this led directly to the building of a temple to these agrarian deities in Carthage early in the fourth century B.C. A considerable market in terra-cotta Greek mother-goddess figurines wearing corn-adorned crowns sprang up almost overnight.

To be sure, these epidemics were not limited to overseas campaigns. Whenever Carthaginians were forced to live close together in times of emergency, similar problems seem to have arisen. All of this is not to say that the Carthaginians were an unsanitary, filthy lot. There is much evidence from the Punic city of Kerkouane in northeast Tunisia on Cape Bon that they were very neat people with hip baths and finely made drains in their homes. But the mercenaries were quite a different matter, and the Carthaginians seem not to have been able to manage very well in the overcrowded conditions thrust upon everyone.

By the end of the fourth century, Carthage had undergone some surprising and fundamental changes, but Syracuse, exhausted from decades of war against Greeks, Carthaginians and Sikels, collapsed utterly. Internal squabbling, political intrigues of every sort and even assassinations now became the order of the day. Once-proud Akragas lay in ruins, and Gela too was a shambles after a Punic attack in 405 B.C.

At this time of relative peace and enormous commercial prosperity, Carthage, having fully recovered from the debacle of Himera, fairly exploded with vitality. Dr. Wolff's new study documents this golden age in detail, using the materials found in the various recent UNESCO-sponsored excavations. It is at this time that Carthage truly appears as the great superpower of the west. In fact, had the army been able to avoid the plague and, perhaps, get a good sanitation engineer, we might all be speaking Punic today.

III

Beyond the Pillars of Hercules

LIKE THE CANAANITES and Phoenicians before them, the Carthaginians felt a special kinship with the open sea and a thirst for high adventure, especially when it meant opening up new markets abroad and reaping huge financial rewards. Few records are left to tell us how these hardy navigators and their crews tamed the farthest reaches of the Mediterranean and challenged the west coasts of Africa and Iberia, but one major account has come down through the centuries, even though it only survives in a controversial Greek translation. Full of excitement and wonder, the *Periplus of Hanno* offers a rare glimpse of a fantastic, all but forgotten Punic enterprise.

Hanno is, as we have seen, a common Carthaginian name, but ancient Roman sources such as Pliny the Elder let us know that this particular Hanno was a king who lived "in the time of the greatest Carthaginian prosperity."[1] Still, nobody can say with certainty when he made his celebrated voyage. The best guess is that Hanno was another son, along with the aforementioned Gisco, of the famous Hamilcar, whose loss at Himera had dealt such a blow to Punic ambitions in Sicily in 480 B.C. If this is the correct assumption, as some scholars believe, then his expedition might have taken place about 465 B.C. Nonetheless, scholarly guesses for the trip place it as far back as the mid-sixth century.[2]

In antiquity any voyage of discovery by sea was known as a *periplus*, from two Greek words *peri* (around) and *pleo* to sail or go by sea); it applied mainly to voyages of exploration that involved the circumnavigation of the coasts of a huge land mass such as Africa and Iberia. There were many such expeditions commissioned by Egypt, Phoenicia, Greek Massalia (Marseilles) and, to be sure, Carthage.

The tale of Hanno, although mentioned by several sources, comes down to us in its most complete form in one manuscript, written in Greek and probably copied from an even earlier work, which itself had been translated from Punic, so it is easy to see why the question of the accuracy of the text has caused so much consternation and confusion for scholars over the past hundred years.[3]

The idea behind the expedition may have been more practical than noble. Punic merchants were always looking for new markets, especially in the Phoenician-speaking western Mediterranean, where from the sixth century B.C., Carthage had replaced Tyre as the principal influence in such trading centers as Gadir in Spain and Lixus in Morocco.

Gadir (modern Cadiz) had been founded by the Phoenicians as early as 770 B.C. as a gateway to the silver of Tartessos as well as the mines of Huelva and the Seville area. The establishment of a temple to Melqart, the city god of Tyre, who was frequently identified later on with the Greek Herakles and the Roman Hercules, gave rise to the term Pillars of Hercules to describe the western limits of the known world and the beginning of uncharted seas.[4]

By the sixth century B.C. there were already dozens of minor Iberian coastal communities under the Punic aegis exploiting the vast resources of the region. As word of potentially greater commercial prospects came back from outside the western Mediterranean, Carthaginian leaders formulated a plan to explore the western coast of Africa, perhaps even hoping to return by way of the Arabian Gulf.

This was not the first such attempt. As early as 600 B.C. the Egyptian pharaoh Neco had pursued the same dream. A man of great ambition and a lover of daring projects, Neco had already tried (and failed) to build a predecessor of the Suez Canal between the Nile and the Arabian Gulf, a project which is said to have cost the lives of one hundred and twenty thousand Egyptians. Herodotus, writing about 445 B.C., described Neco's follow-up project, a *periplus:*

> Neco . . . sent out a fleet manned by a Phoenician crew with
> orders to sail westabout and return to Egypt and the
> Mediterranean by way of the Straits of Gibraltar. The

Phoenicians sailed from the Arabian Gulf into the southern
ocean, and every autumn put in at some convenient spot on the
Libyan coast, sowed a patch of ground, and waited for next
year's harvest. Then, having got in their grain, they put to sea
again, and after two full years rounded the Pillars of Herakles in
the course of the third and returned to Egypt. . . . This is how
Libya (i.e. Africa) was first discovered to be surrounded by
sea.[5]

We do not know if this Egyptian-Phoenician mission had any
practical result, but Herodotus tells us of another African *periplus* of
about 475 B.C., which ended in disaster.[6] A member of the Persian royal
family, Sataspes, was arrested for rape, but his mother, who was the
sister of Darius, the former king, intervened and procured an alternate
punishment: circumnavigating Libya (Africa) and returning by the
Arabian Gulf.

Sataspes arranged a vessel and crew (of Phoenicians?) and sailed
west and south of Gibraltar for many months, but he "took fright at
the length and loneliness of the voyage and turned back." He was
dismayed by the fact that no matter how far he sailed "there was always
need to sail further yet." Returning via Egypt to Persia and the court
of stern King Xerxes, he told of finding at the most southerly limit of
his expedition "small men who wore clothes made from palm leaves."
Almost certainly these were pygmies. In this region his ship could not
make any further headway in the still waters. For the failure of his
mission Sataspes was impaled anyway.

After the success of the first circumnavigation of Africa, Herodotus tells us ". . . the next people to make a similar report were the
Carthaginians."[7] Although he fails to mention Hanno by name, later
writers did. Pliny the Elder, who lived in the first century after Christ,
reported that Hanno had accomplished his *periplus* by sailing from
Carthage past Gadir and around Libya to the Arabian Gulf, the same
route that Sataspes had tried without success.[8] Furthermore, Pliny
adds, there were *commentaraii* (commentaries) by Hanno about his
ambitum or circuit of Africa. A single copy, perhaps partial, of these
commentaries apparently survived: 101 lines documenting a brave feat
of ancient daring indicative of the Carthaginian entrepreneurial spirit.

The manuscript begins by informing us that the text had been put
up in the *témenos* or sacred precinct of Kronos, the Greek name usually

assigned to Ba'al Hammon. So it may be that somewhere in the area of the Tophet of Carthage the proud sovereign posted his triumph of exploration for all to see. He had set out by Carthaginian decree to sail beyond the Pillars of Hercules for the purpose of building cities for the Liby-Phoenicians," Libyan natives who had fallen under Carthaginian control as Punic expansion caused the takeover of vast tracts of ancient Tunisia. By resettling these people on the western African coast, Carthage could foster a series of colonies that might serve as stepping-stones to the vast resources there, especially gold from the area of Guinea.

Unlike Sataspes, who certainly would have been lonely and frightened in his solitary ship, Hanno brought along plenty of company. There were said to be sixty ships, more properly called penta-conters from the Greek, with fifty oars each, along with thirty thousand men and women plus provisions. Even if this high number of people is correct, it is not likely that all of them were supposed to go the whole journey around Africa; colonies of people could be left all along the way.

Once past Gibraltar, the grand adventure began in earnest. At two more days' sail, Hanno established his first colony, called Thymiate-rion in Greek, which means incense burner. At the next stop, the promontory of Soloeis located at the modern Cape Cantin in Morocco, a shrine or *hieron* to the Punic equivalent of the god Poseidon was erected, and they put to sea again, founding five more colonies all along the coastline of what is now Morocco. One of them, known as the Wall of the Carians, might have been settled by Carian (southwest Turkish) refugees from the Athenian invasion of their lands in 468 B.C. Carian mercenaries had served the Phoenicians for many years.

Few traces of any of these Punic seacoast colonies have been found, but this is not surprising. Moroccan archaeology, particularly in the area of Punic studies, is still in its infancy and there is little excavation activity at present. Earlier Phoenician colonies such as Lixus (modern Larache) near Tangiers on the Atlantic coast of Morocco were of little use to Hanno. They may originally have been outposts for picking up the gold of Guinea but could have been destroyed by local African tribes before Hanno got there. His *periplus* gives no mention of Lixus, but some of the names of Hanno's own colonies do survive in modern settlements such as Agadir, the Akra of the *periplus*.

Hanno's next stop was at the mouth of a major river at the western

limit of Morocco. Scholars believe this to be the Wadi Dra, and here
Hanno encountered a pastoral, extremely friendly group called the
Lixitae, who may have been the remnants of an old colony established
by Lixus. Inland along the river, among foothills of the Atlas Mountains, which today may be considerably more desiccated than in Punic
times, the adventurers encountered not only considerable numbers of
wild beasts but hostile black Africans too, Ethiopians who lived in
caves and ran like the wind.

Precise identifications of the sites and sights encountered from this
point on become increasingly difficult, for here scholars disagree over
whether or not there are major gaps (lacunae) in the text, which would
affect the sequence of events and the actual topography covered. The
small island of Kerne, described in the *periplus* as being as far from
Gibraltar as the latter was from Carthage, might be Herne Island,
located just west of Western Sahara, a renowned gold-trading center
in the Middle Ages known as the Rio de Oro.

The next major coastal river that Hanno navigated was called
Chretes and seems likely to have been the Senegal River, which today
forms the border between Mauretania and Senegal. By now the desert
belt was behind him and he had crossed into a region that even today
is tropical rain forest. There, exploring well inland, Hanno encountered branches in the river, more islands and tall mountains, and a
landscape inhabited by crocodiles and hippopotami. Black savages clad
in wild beast skins burst onto the scene from the mountains, hurling
boulders and preventing the Carthaginians from disembarking.

For those on the expedition who knew Greek (and there were
some), this exotic and terrifying encounter must have seemed like
something out of Homer's *Odyssey*, with Odysseus and his men at the
ends of the earth struggling against fearsome Lastrygonian boulder
throwers. In any case, after this close encounter of the worst kind, they
all went back to Kerne and no doubt took a very deep breath before
going on. Had they overreached the limits of human endurance?

Still, Hanno continued, sailing close to the coast for twelve more
days, to lands so far south that even the Carthaginians' friendly interpreters had no idea how to communicate with the black natives. The
smells from the woodland were pleasantly fragrant, and eventually the
expedition reached a broad, handsome bay, which the interpreters
called the Horn of the West. The adventurers anchored for the night
on a large lake-bearing island. There was a strong feeling of danger

about the place: the eerie, thick forest, the sounds of flutes playing, cymbals clashing and drums pounding, and a great commotion of shouting. Such a sense of foreboding overtook the crew that, just as Hamilcar had done at Himera, Hanno had to consult the Punic mantics or soothsayers, who always accompanied a major campaign. Their reply was unquestionably a wise one: get out of here fast. Hanno was, perhaps, somewhere in the Bissagos Islands off the coast of Guinea-Bissau, just south of modern Gambia.

And even now Hanno sailed farther south, and the next stretch of coast revealed four days' worth of wondrous sights: the land was full of enormous, high fires and a towering mountain rose up, known to the interpreters as the Chariot of the Gods. Four days of slow sailing from the Bissagos Islands would have put Hanno near what is now Freetown, the coastal capital city of Sierra Leone, and the enormous mountain, readily visible from the sea, may have been lofty Mount Kakulima.

The terrific fires witnessed by the expedition could simply have been the blazes of the normal dry season, when natives even in this century often use fires to herd and trap wild animals in snares or box cages. Scholarly attempts to equate the mountain with volcanic activity seem at best unnecessary, and the same may be said of the identification of the mountain as 13,350-foot-high Mount Cameroon, located on the coast of Cameroon. Nonetheless, outside possibilities must be considered in a controversial document where so many possibilities exist.

As the *periplus* reaches its end, the most fascinating and controversial episode is saved for last. Three days' sail beyond the imposing Chariot of the Gods, Hanno reached the bay called the Horn of the South, which may have marked the limit of the area known to his interpreters. Here he discovered an island with a lake, which contained still another island filled with savages:

> The biggest number of them were females, with hairy bodies
> which our Lixite interpreters called gorillas. Chasing them we
> could not catch any of the males, because all of them escaped by
> being able to climb steep cliffs and [by] defending themselves
> with whatever was available; but we caught three females who
> bit and scratched their captors and they did not want to follow
> them. So we had to kill them and flayed them, and we brought
> their skins to Carthage.[9]

It is possible that this confrontation took place on Sherbro Sound, just off the coast of Sierra Leone below Freetown. But what did they confront? It is doubtful that the creatures could have been human, although a number of scholars have suggested that they might have been pygmies. But would the Carthaginians, even admitting their penchant for human sacrifice, skin a human being? If the creatures were not humans, could they have been gorillas?

Our term gorilla, denoting a genus of anthropoid ape native to west equatorial Africa, only goes back to the year 1847, when it was coined by the American clergyman and naturalist Thomas Staughton Savage (1804–1880), the first missionary sent to Africa by the Protestant Episcopal Church of Cromwell, Connecticut. Where did Savage get the term gorilla? He had read it in Thomas Falconer's 1797 British translation of the *Periplus of Hanno*!

There are no gorillas on Sherbro Island now, but there could have been in Hanno's time. There is no reason to suspect that Savage made a wrong identification, although guesses have included chimpanzees (smaller than a gorilla and highly intelligent), orangutans (more anthropoid-looking but also not native to the area Hanno investigated) and baboons (not humanoid enough). Whatever Hanno saw, he apparently hung the skin in the Sanctuary of Tanit back home, where the citizenry had never seen anything like it.

At this point, having perhaps reached the wide Gulf of Guinea, Hanno stopped . . . or did he? The text reads, "We did not sail further, having run out of food provisions." But are these really Hanno's words? If his were a true *periplus,* shouldn't he have actually circumnavigated Africa, as the ancient sources said he did, or was it enough that he got to Sierra Leone, which it seems was already known to his Lixite interpreters? If this so-called Gold Coast was as far as Hanno got, then he was only reestablishing old ties with former colonists and travelling with guides who led him to the limits of their own geographical expertise. True, he settled some colonies along the way, but these seem to have vanished even by Roman times.

Did Hanno go farther, as Pliny believed? Is it possible that a later scribe simply added a quick, reasonable conclusion to make the surviving fragment a complete story for his own audience? We may never know. It is, however, possible that a *periplus* did not have to be a complete circumnavigation of a continent but could simply be a circuit, a round trip: you go, turn around, come back. In a practical sense (and about commerce nobody was more practical than the Carthaginians), sailing on would have been of little value.

Hanno had arrived at the gold-trading center of Western Sahara in west Africa, opposite the Canary Islands, and he had sailed beyond to the Gold Coast of Africa itself. He had stopped to visit old colonies at the Pillars of Hercules and had established a string of new colonies beyond that. His work may have been intended as a first step, a staging operation designed to civilize a wild but fertile area, which only the Carthaginians with their sphere of influence at Gibraltar could develop.

So why should Hanno have gone on? If the Carthaginians could have made this first step work, future expeditions could have gone farther. But it didn't work. Perhaps it was just too far away from home and too wild. Or perhaps the Carthaginians became too involved in the desperate struggle for Sicily. Still, there is no reason to doubt the veracity of Hanno's account, as many scholars have. It is most certainly within the mainstream of contemporary Punic entrepreneurial thought, the proud if temporary achievement of a visionary king.

Also, Hanno may simply have overreached his capabilities. To establish a far-flung network of colonies required a powerful support system, which he couldn't deliver. Without adequate reinforcements, the rich trading centers were nothing more than tempting targets for tribes like the Pharusians, the powerful predecessors of the Moors.

But this west African expedition was apparently only one part of a two-pronged program of exploration beyond Gibraltar. At almost the same time a certain Himilco, possibly Hanno's brother and another son of Hamilcar, sailed his own group up the west coasts of Iberia and France. This trip, less easy to trace since the *periplus* did not survive directly, may have had the same objective as the African voyage: to establish major trading connections with remote centers producing valued raw materials.

Our principal source for Himilco's grand expedition is a later one, the fourth-century-A.D. Roman writer and former proconsul from Etruria, Rufius Festus Avienus. Pouring over early records of Greek and Phoenician navigation, he provided a detailed account—in an only partly preserved didactic work entitled the *Ora Maritima*—of the coasts of the Black and Caspian seas, the Sea of Azov and the Mediterranean.

The work, studied in detail by the famed historian and archaeologist Gilbert Charles-Picard, discusses Himilco's journey around Spain, along the Bay of Biscay and up to the mouth of the Loire in what is now Brittany. He may even have continued to the British Isles, and seems to have stopped for a time in the land of the Oestrymnians, an extremely industrious people adept at mining tin and lead and well known by the merchant sailors of Tartessos. The area around the Gulf of Morbihan, north of the mouth of the Loire, does contain tin mines that may have been in use as early as the sixth century B.C., so that this may have been the general region of the Oestrymnians.

From there Himilco sailed two days more, encountering "sea monsters," which no doubt were whales, and reached the "sacred island" of the Hiburnians, probably what we now call Ireland. Nearby, Avienus says, "is the island of the Albions," or England. Himilco came up against an all but impassable morass of seaweed, and the frequent shallowness of the water was no help either. "The Carthaginian Himilco who reported that he himself tried this trip affirms that it is difficult to accomplish it in four months. For no wind drives the ship and the water of this sluggish sea seems totally still."[10] His entire account, as recorded in Avienus, is full of the mystery and dangers of seafaring in little-known waters.

It seems that the Oestrymnian trade may have increased after Himilco's voyage, for the Carthaginian bronze industry flourished in the fifth and fourth centuries B.C. and required a generous supply of imported tin. But the tin seems not to have come via Himilco's overseas route but rather by land, using river systems such as the Seine and Saône in France and ports like Massalia.

That Punic traders actually got to the British Isles is suggested by occasional finds such as a Carthaginian-type stone face found at St. Johnstown, but it is harder to prove that British tin from the Cornwall area (Belerium and Ictis) was traded by the Carthaginians by sea routes. A Massalian explorer named Pytheas helped to develop British trade with his own voyage of the later fourth century B.C., but in the first century B.C., Diodorus wrote extensively of the overland transport of British tin by packhorse from western Gaul to ports like Narbo and Massalia. A tribe from Brittany known as the Veneti (not mentioned by Himilco) was actively involved as the middleman and became rather wealthy in the process.

Whatever the details of the creation of the famous tin route, the voyage of Himilco would seem to have strengthened and accelerated trade relations with lands barely known to the people of Carthage. It was an exciting new frontier waiting for the visionary, daring adventurer-merchant. While there is a persistent but unfounded tradition that Punic sailors were blown way off course and actually discovered America (or at least a great island in the ocean west of Africa), it is true that the Carthaginians, like Captain Kirk in "Star Trek," boldly went where very few Mediterranean folk had dared to go before.

But the search for markets did not stop there. For not only did the Carthaginians monopolize exploratory navigation on the far side of Gibraltar, they also had control of much of the North African coast east of Carthage, all the way up to Cyrenaica in modern Libya. As early as the sixth century B.C., trading centers such as Lepcis Magna in modern Tripolitania provided a stepping-stone to another barely tapped resource center: the interior of Africa itself.[11]

The Greeks too had designs on African riches. As early as 520 B.C., Doreius, the son of the king of Sparta, had tried to colonize the area around Lepcis, only to be driven out by an alliance of Carthaginians and native tribes such as the Macae. So we may believe that by the early fifth century B.C., Carthage was consolidating its control of the region, exploring trade possibilities and in general following an approach similar to that of Himilco and Hanno in the west.

By the late sixth century B.C., Carthage had formally served notice on foreign powers to stay out of Punic North Africa (the area between modern Libya and Morocco). Lepcis itself has yielded few traces of its early days, so elaborately and completely was it transformed into a Roman super-city.[12] Corinthian Greek pottery dating back to 500 B.C. has been recovered there, and some Punic burials under the beautiful Roman theater have come to light too, but a visit to Lepcis' western neighbor, the coastal city of Sabratha, is more instructive.[13]

Possessed of a small but adequate harbor, Sabratha may first have attracted the attention of Phoenician traders from Sidon in the eighth or seventh century B.C. In fact, excavation north of the Roman forum has revealed traces of makeshift huts whose floors were characterized by alternating layers of beaten earth and windblown sand. The implication is that the huts were used intermittently and not for continuous habitation. Was this proof that Phoenician or Carthaginian traders came here seasonally or periodically? Inside were traces of Punic *pithoi*, or storage jars, and Greek pottery of the sixth and fifth centuries B.C.

By a date well into the fifth century B.C., a small but apparently permanent village had sprung up at Sabratha. It wasn't much to look at—small mudbrick huts, beaten earth floors and a surrounding border wall located near the later forum. Unquestionably the settlement was a success, spilling out beyond its initial confines and gradually transforming a simple market area into a prominent trading center. Not far away the Italian excavator R. Bartoccini found an amphora containing sacrificed sheep bones, possibly an offering to Ba'al Hammon in the god's temple area.

Lepcis probably developed along lines similar to Sabratha, perhaps preceding it in date, and between the two colonies lay Oea, modern Tripoli.[14] On the border of the Gulf of Sidra, near Greek Cyrene, was Charax (now perhaps el-Mdeina Sultan), a town whose chief functions included providing a port for a much-prized, pirated foodstuff known as silphium, about which we shall say much more later.

The outposts in what is now Libya fulfilled several objectives for Carthage. First of all, they were the gateways to Egypt through the African hinterland, providing a way for Punic travelers to avoid hostile Greeks on the sea and in the Cyrene area. The deep-seated influence of Egyptian religion, especially on the cult of the afterlife, required that close contacts be maintained.

One of the key stops on the Libyan desert route to Egypt was the oasis sanctuary of Siwa, twelve days' distance by caravan west of the city of Memphis and 185 miles from the Mediterranean Sea.[15] Its abundant freshwater springs, green grass, lakes and stately palms must have made this fertile center seem like a mirage to the weary pilgrim. Here was the sanctuary of the ram-headed sun god Amon-Ra, who was often merged with the Greek Zeus or confused with the Punic Ba'al Hammon.

The second objective for Carthage, access to the riches of Africa, required the settlement of Tripolitania, because the region was naturally scooped out of the coastline, thus eliminating hundreds of miles of travel to get inland. Also, throughout North Africa, vast areas of desert and mountain wasteland denied access to the interior, but in what is now Libya there were numerous passes and oases, which made a bustling caravan trade possible much of the year, although it was not for the faint of heart. A British architectural historian and archaeologist, the late John Ward-Perkins, a genial veteran of many excavation campaigns in Tunisia and Libya, was fond of describing North Africa's hinterland as resembling a leopard's skin with "its inhabitants scattered like spots over a background of waterless desert."

The caravan route must have been long established by Herodotus' time (the mid-fifth century B.C.), judging from his encyclopedic knowledge of various Libyan peoples and customs and his ability to pinpoint the topography of the region. From Lepcis one could travel west towards Carthage, south to the hinterland or east to Siwa and Egypt. The eastward route led through the territory of the Nasamones, a powerful Libyan people living south and east of the Gulf of Sidra. Their principal city, Augila (Awjilah), was one of the primary oasis stops between Siwa and Phazania (the Fezzan), the vast sandy plateau peppered with valley oases that lay hundreds of miles south of Lepcis.[16]

Caravans using horses or mules could take enough supplies for nine- or ten-day treks across the barren and often intensely hot sands, but taking more than that amount of time was risky: bad weather and brigands were the chief adversaries. Fortunately the oases of the area were naturally arranged or "spotted" to allow the caravans to ply their trade.

Herodotus knew a great deal about the Nasamones and their value as guides across the desert, even though he found their polygamous practices quite strange. Several Nasamonian youths were credited with the first known expedition into deepest Africa where they, like the Persian Sataspes in his aborted *periplus*, are supposed to have encountered pygmies. A story was told by some Cyrenian Greeks on a visit to the oracle of Siwa that ". . . a group of wild young fellows, sons of chieftains in their country, had on coming to manhood planned among themselves all sorts of extravagant adventures, one of which was to draw lots for five of their number to explore the Libyan desert and try to penetrate further than had ever been done before."[17]

The young men crossed the desert "in a westerly direction" and came to an area with fruit trees where they were attacked by strange-speaking, tiny men of "less than middle height" and carried off through a swamp and a river area infested with crocodiles. They returned to tell the tale, which found its way to Herodotus. If true, the story is remarkable, because it shows the ability of the Libyans to brave hazardous conditions and cover amazing distances.

The pygmies, already mentioned by Homer in the *Iliad*, were believed by many to be mythological inventions until the French explorer Paul Belloni Du Chaillu verified their existence in equatorial Africa in 1867. Although many fantastic stories were told about the pygmies (they were one foot tall, their princess was turned into a crane, etc.), these are not stories Herodotus tells, and the tale of the Cyrenians is much more plausible today than when it was first told to a skeptical audience.

The neighbors of the Nasamones to the west, the Macae, were strong Carthaginian allies, noted for their Chief Pontiac-style hairdos. It may be a Maca who is depicted on a sculpted herm (a stone pillar with its top carved into a head) found in the Antonine Baths of Carthage, which date to the second century A.D.[18] The sculpted head is clearly Libyan and even wears a crescent pendant on its forehead, which may reflect the solar and lunar divinities worshipped by these people.

Moving south from Lepcis, Punic travelers had to pass to the east of the Great Eastern Erg of modern-day Algeria, an intimidating stretch of Sahara sandhills. Just beyond the outpost village of Cydanae (Ghadames), the trail led across the western part of a vast stony upland called the Hammada el-Hamra, bordered to the east by the scorched-looking Gebel es-Sodah, or Black Soda Mountains. Then, Herodotus says, it continued on in a westerly direction to the foothills of the Sahara and the broad desert of Idehan in the Fezzan. Finally, after about a month on the caravan, one arrived some 380 miles south of Lepcis (as the crow flies) at the valley oases of the rugged Garamantes, dominators of the central Sahara.

Noted for their struggles against the black African cave dwellers (troglodytes) of the Tibesti mountains in northwest Chad, the Libyan Garamantes raised grain and grew luscious dates in their palm-covered oases. They developed a four-horse chariot for their military campaigns and took great pride, as most Libyans did, in their hair, which might be plaited, grown in side spirals or ornamented with ostrich plumes. They often grew long pointed beards and their leaders covered themselves with tattoos.

But before they grew rich as the middlemen of the trans-Sahara trade, most Garamantes lived in simple huts, which Roman writers such as Pliny and Sallust called *mapalia,* a Punic word for a temporary nomad dwelling.[19] The Romans occasionally depicted these on their mosaics, showing hovels apparently built of wattled grass or asphodel (a stemless plant of the lily family), with the tops of the roofs swirled up like an upturned boat.

How the Punic merchants got their wares from the desert and how far south they penetrated into Africa are topics much discussed, since Herodotus' account becomes increasingly fuzzy. It was possible to travel from the Fezzan southeast to the Tibesti region or southwest into the Algerian Tassili and Ahaggar areas, the land of the ancient Atarantes. Caravans might then proceed through what is now northeastern Mali and the Tanezrouft region in a series of eight- to ten-day treks between water sources. The end of the caravan route might have been the river Niger, and it is quite possible, even likely, that Phoenician traders of the fifth century B.C. reached the vicinity of Timbuktu and Gao in Niger.

After crossing the desert, the traders reached central Niger and could continue through a less inhospitable savanna with thick forests. With the River Niger, the tropical rain forest had been reached and with it access to a wide variety of commodities for trade.[20]

It is extremely doubtful that the Carthaginians themselves were the actual traders of these goods; there were plenty of Liby-Phoenicians for that task, while the Carthaginians reaped the major profits. In fact, they tended to spread over the northern coastal areas, driving out the Libyans or keeping them virtually as indentured servants to work the small agricultural domains producing olives, grapes, almonds, pomegranates, honey and wheat or raising sheep, cattle and horses. The port cities of Tripolitania expanded so fast because merchants were charged stiff duties on exports and imports which accrued to the Punic treasury.

Survival in towns like Garama, capital city of the Garamantes, was not easy, and life on the caravan trail was also difficult, especially since camels were not yet in use.[21] Horses were fitted out with goatskin flasks filled with water and strapped under their bellies. The sun was blinding, the desert seemingly endless and subject to sudden storms, and illness remained a constant threat in the form of sunstroke and strange viral infections. The natives learned to proceed at a slow, deliberate pace. Caravans rarely galloped across the Fezzan; trade was accomplished by the slow, furrow-faced, quiet Libyans moving inexorably across the sands.

As to the booty produced by these efforts, there were beautiful stones such as carbuncle, the red garnet gemstone heavily traded by the Garamantes and called Carthaginian stone by the Romans.[22] The big money item, however, may have been ivory, which, Pliny tells us, fetched a vast sum. Ivory carvings were especially prized and chryselephantine (gold and ivory) sculptures were in demand for the cult statues used in many Greek temples, such as the Athena Parthenos in Athens and the Zeus at Olympia (whose statues were by the legendary

Phidias, a sculptor who flourished before the mid-fifth century B.C.). The vogue he created must have helped to fuel the desire for more and more "elephant teeth."

Although carbuncle and ivory led the list, other objects were brought up the trails: wild animals of all sorts valued as oddities and for their skins, ostrich plumes and eggs, African woods such as the valued *citrus*, apparently a sort of aromatic cypress enormously popular in furniture making.[23]

Caravan merchants spun their share of tall tales and exotic or heroic accounts. A Carthaginian named Mago claimed he'd crossed the Sahara three times without taking a drink. Some Libyan tribes were said to have heads that looked canine, while others purportedly had no heads at all and had their eyes in their chests. Nasamones were observed catching locusts and grinding them into a powder to sprinkle on their milk; they were among the healthiest people of the Mediterranean. In the land of the Garamantes, the cattle were supposed to graze backwards because of the design of their horns.[24]

As the fifth century ended, Carthaginians were to be found at every reachable extreme of the Mediterranean, searching for the perfect entrepreneurial scheme: the route to exclusive profits. But whether dodging gorillas at the unknown extremes of the continent or buying carbuncle from tattooed Garamantes on the caravan trail, the Carthaginians had learned a valuable lesson: try to stay out of war with Sicily and build up strength through trade.

Through the fifth, fourth and third centuries B.C., the great trading empire flourished. For over three hundred years Punic enterprises were virtually the sole link between one third of Africa and the Mediterranean. But with the advent of the Punic wars, Carthage was to be challenged and threatened by Rome. Things were most definitely not going to remain the same for long. There were great days ahead . . . and disaster.

❦ IV ❦

Glory Days

ALTHOUGH SICILY was becoming more Punic in the fourth century B.C., it is equally true that Carthage was turning more Greek. The bustling metropolis was on the brink of an age of rampant internationalism, of intensive contact with foreign ideas, including the egalitarian opportunities of democracy, the dangerous concept of rule by larger-than-life tyrants, and the fundamental change caused by the importing of new religions such as the Demeter cult, instituted in 396 B.C.[1]

With all the booty pouring into the city from Sicily, a tremendous Hellenic influence affected all the arts. Once popular Egyptian cornices yielded to Greek pediments, while Phoenician volute capitals became standard Hellenic Doric and Ionic. And the prestige and commerce that had marked Sicily's golden age of the fifth century B.C. now began to turn towards Carthage in spades.

In the late fifth and early fourth centuries B.C., Carthage had destroyed or disabled many of the greatest cities of Sicily, causing the shutoff or decline of a number of major distribution centers for international goods. For a time, Punic Motya became a major emporium, but its destruction by Syracuse in 397 B.C. and the subsequent retaliatory Carthaginian strikes left much of Sicily in chaos.

Suddenly the international trading center for the western Mediterranean was no longer Sicily. Momentum had shifted to Carthage. In the archaeological strata of Carthage's excavations, the rapid influx of beautiful black glazed ceramic wares from Athens and the appearance of Greek transport amphorae from Corinth and elsewhere demonstrate this shift of commercial power. For Carthage aggressive internationalism required the abandoning of the old trading system, which had been based simply on barter. Coins of gold and silver had to be issued, and since they were designed to capture markets that had been dominated by Sicily, or to pay soldiers fighting in Sicilian campaigns, they looked and weighed like Sicilian coins. Gold and silver were readily obtainable through the former Phoenician colonies in the Huelva region of Spain near the Guadalquivir and Tinto rivers.[2]

New port facilities were of course essential to accommodate this booming expansion and the harbor at Carthage became a true showpiece. It had to fulfill two basic functions: a commercial harbor and a place to house the famed military fleet. In 1976 separate American and British excavations were undertaken—at a site just north of El Kram and near the southern limit of modern Carthage—to see if two coastal lagoons there were actually the rectangular commercial port and the circular military harbor seen and described to Appian, a Greco-Egyptian writer of the second century A.D.:

> The harbors had communication with each other, and a
> common entrance from the sea, 70 feet wide, which could be
> closed with iron chains. The first port was for merchant vessels,
> and here were collected all kinds of ships' tackle. Within the
> second port was an island, and great quays were set at intervals
> round both the harbor and the island. These embankments were

Mosaic from Sousse showing the unloading of a ship. The mast has been lowered to rest on a metal spur, and the prow has the shape of a bird's head. Planks are being unloaded and weighed. Third century A.D.

full of shipyards which had capacity for 220 vessels. In addition
to them were magazines for their tackle and furniture. Two
Ionic columns stood in front of each dock, giving the
appearance of a continuous portico to both the harbor and the
island. On the island was built the admiral's house, from
which the trumpeter gave signals, the herald delivered orders,
and the admiral himself oversaw everything. The island lay
near the entrance to the harbor and rose to a considerable
height, so that the admiral could observe what was going on
at sea, while those who were approaching by water could not
get any clear view of what took place within. Not even
incoming merchants could see the docks at once, for a double
wall enclosed them, and there were gates by which merchant
ships could pass from the first port to the city without
traversing the dockyards. Such was the appearance of Carthage
at that time.[3]

Before the excavations, scholars had been in sharp disagreement
as to whether or not the site was really the ancient harbor area, but
archaeologists Henry Hurst of Cambridge University and Lawrence
Stager, then of the University of Chicago's Oriental Institute, quickly
removed all doubt: before the end of the fourth century B.C. there had
been no harbor here, only a channel, whose complete length could not
be traced.[4] The rectangular commercial harbor was neatly tucked
behind a man-made breakwater (such an artificial port facility is known
as a *cothon*).

Just as Appian described, there was a Punic warehouse at the
water's edge, no doubt for the storing of ships' tackle. From the earth
fills underneath this structure and behind the harbor quay wall, Stager
dug up an amazing amount of fourth-century-B.C. ceramic, much of
it imported from Greece, along with some fragments which appear to
be of a slightly later date. He now feels that the commercial harbor was
in place sometime between 300 and 250 B.C.

The recovery of this information was of the highest importance
for Punic archaeology, but the excavation of the commercial harbor
was an ongoing problem for the Stager team. Harborside fills and
structures were often found below the modern water level in what is
now a murky lagoon. Freshwater pumps, which were always temperamental, had to be unceasingly maintained to keep unwanted water
out of the trenches, and frequent bouts of bad weather filled up the

soundings almost faster than the pumps could clear them. Balks, or areas of earth left by excavators between soundings, frequently collapsed. After storms, measurements had to be taken by groping in muddy, cold water with eyes closed just to find what scant hours before had been the limits of the quay wall. Only the extreme dedication of the team members made the accomplishment of this often loathsome work possible. Would-be archaeologists learn quickly that the Indiana Jones aspects of the profession are few and far between; most of it is just plain hard work, with dull shards and lamp scraps the most frequent reward, not treasure.

Discomfort notwithstanding, the diversity of finds was extraordinary. There were examples of the long tapering cylindrical amphora (the so-called cigar-shaped form) which now became a Carthaginian trademark all over the Mediterranean from Greece to Spain. Over half of the imported amphorae found in the military harbor came from Spain, with which Carthage obviously needed to keep close contacts. Carthaginian amphorae were themselves widely imitated in Spain, where they were given Iberian-type looped handles—as opposed to the usual doughnut-shaped type. The necks of the Spanish vessels were also elongated.

What were the Carthaginians shipping all around the Mediterranean in these amphorae? We don't know for certain. The flared rim and narrow neck for a stopper suggest that the contents must have been some sort of a liquid. The lids, which were sometimes found, are simple, usually pierced, perhaps to allow the escape of a gas such as carbon dioxide, which is known to come from wine.[5]

Samuel Wolff's studies of the fine ceramic table wares pouring into Carthage at this time also give us an idea of the diversity of trade. The widely disparate clays which make up the fabric of these ceramics can be assigned to certain regions of the Mediterranean by using a process called neutron activation. This scientific analysis breaks down the composition of a given pot and, using the variations found in its chemical makeup, usually succeeds in assigning it to a particular location.

The forms or shapes of the wares can also be studied by expert art historians and typologists, such as France's Jean-Paul Morel, who has spent years compiling the forms, clay characteristics and regional variations of fine black glazed ceramics, especially those of the fourth through second centuries B.C.[6] Such studies are aided by scientific illustrators' drawings of the profiles of the pots, which allow for detailed classifications to be worked out and published. A particular type of ceramic might have a particular clay type as well as a hooked or grooved rim, for example. From these varied kinds of analyses it is possible to paint a portrait of trade connections in ancient Carthage, but the specialist synthesizing these results runs a very great risk and must be careful. Sometimes excavation gives a biased picture. A harbor may have more amphorae than a house does. Different locations or rooms within a house require different types of vessels. Perishable materials are often lost to us, while ceramics always seem to show up. Furthermore, vessels like amphorae can often have secondary uses: a wine amphora might be used to transport another type of material, or even other pots. But by and large, pottery studies, when handled in conjunction with careful archaeological evaluation of the "findspot" or context of the objects, provide us with a really good educated guess about the goings-on in a time and place.

Nonetheless, good archaeologists learn to suggest rather than firmly conclude. And the best of them will tell you of the mistakes in interpretation they have made over the years. Reaching conclusions at the end of an archaeological campaign is the most difficult and dangerous assignment for the archaeologist to face. One hundred percent accuracy almost never happens, and so the most valuable traits for a field excavator are a meticulous recording technique and a good feeling for probability and logic. Another quality of great use to the archaeologist, but rarely encountered, is the ability to admit when an error in interpretation has been made. Stubbornness and ego have impeded scientific study for generations.

By the fourth century B.C., Carthage was unquestionably one of the queen cities of the Mediterranean. Ceramics from Athens, the beautiful black glazed Attic wares so abundant and widely imitated in antiquity, showed up there in volume, reaching a peak by the middle of the century. Carthage was rapidly capturing the lion's share of the western trade of the Greeks. In the second half of the century, the Lipari Islands and western Sicily produced imitations of Attic wares so cleverly done that even today Harvard art historians cannot distinguish the real McCoy from the fake without the use of neutron activation.[7]

The Cambridge University excavations in the circular harbor next to the Oriental Institute excavations revealed the ancient home of the Punic military fleet. Although there was apparently some occupation of this area in the fourth to third centuries B.C., the director of excavations, Henry Hurst, now feels that this harbor area was not developed in the full form seen by Appian before the early second century B.C. The location looks so surprisingly small today that one wonders how the premiere fleet of the ancient Mediterranean could possibly have been lodged in such a cramped space. The central island, from which the admiral surveyed his ships and called the sailors to arms, was found to be riddled with slipways for dragging up ships into dry sheds to protect their wooden hulls from rot.

By analyzing the size of the ramps, some of them between 100 and 160 feet long with a minimum width of 16½ feet, the meticulous Hurst was able to estimate the actual size of a Punic warship, and when two small warships were found off the northwest coast of Sicily over a decade ago it was no surprise when they were determined to measure about 115 feet long by 16 feet wide. The depth of the original military harbor was estimated at only five feet, but the Punic ships had a four-foot draft. In short, the military port was custom-made for the Punic warships.

Recent excavations at the Punic settlement of Motya have revealed another harbor, this time 115 feet by 168, with a channel 18 feet wide and only 3⅓ feet deep. This space must have been too small for warships and was probably suited for nothing larger than tenders unloading cargo from ships anchored in the lagoon or in dry dock for winter storage or repairs.[8]

On the shore by the circular military harbor was a metalworking establishment of some size, one of several discovered in ancient Carthage. This is not startling, since iron could have been brought in from the great southern Spanish metal centers as well as from Sardinia and Etruria, the metal-rich area of Italy north of Rome. It may have been shipped in a presmelted form that looked like shish-kabob spits. Once brought into town, the iron was cast or beaten into shape by ironsmiths and the end product, whatever it might be, was traded around the Mediterranean. Copper and its alloy, bronze, would also have been in considerable demand for sheathing on the ships as well as for practical and artistic objects of every sort: statuary, braziers, incense burners, oil lamps and the like.

The fourth century B.C. was not only a critical period for trade and expansion in Carthage, it was also a time of substantial governmental reform, perhaps in part as a response to growing contacts with Hellenism. The Greek philosopher and statesman Aristotle, writing about 345 B.C., considered the Punic constitution to be basically democratic, a fact which surprised even Aristotle.[9] It was the only non-Greek constitution he praised. We still do not know as much as we would like about the government of Carthage, but it seems likely that the Magonid kings were ousted early in the fourth century B.C. at the latest, and although the kingship apparently continued, the Assembly of the People took more of an active role. As the city and its dominant merchant families grew richer and richer, the stakes got higher, and more people with fiscal clout wanted a part in the new order.

Apparently the kings were originally required to report to and obtain the blessings of the Council of Elders and the Assembly of the People, but they were still true kings, with broad powers in war, religion and government. We learn of rival factions and parties struggling for power early in the fourth century, resulting in trials and executions for treason. The rich and powerful King Hanno clashed with a certain Eshmuniaton, leader of the Council of Elders and strong-minded representative of the landowners. Hanno finally prevailed and became general as well as king, fighting the inevitable fight against Syracuse, but the council was gradually able to make the position of military commander-in-chief separate from the kingship, a major step in limiting royal authority.

In the year 360 B.C., Hanno is said to have attempted to kill the Council of Elders not once but several times, using the device of poisoning their food. His murderous plot, once discovered, led to a direct confrontation with the state assemblies. The seriousness of his actions were promptly matched by the severity of his punishment. He was whipped, had his eyes put out and his arms and legs broken, said one source, "as if atonement was to be exacted from every limb."[10] His mangled body was painted with stripes and nailed to a cross, and virtually his entire family was executed to avoid the possibility of the sort of revenge through generations that Carthaginians (and Greeks) were noted for. This grisly account, offered with a bit too much glee by the writer Justin, marked the end of Hanno the Great. The Council of the 104, as it may now have been called, was all powerful. Needless to say, these violent displays did little to enhance the reputation of the Carthaginians abroad, despite Aristotle's high opinion.

In the event of a dispute between the king and the council, the Assembly of the People could be used for arbitration. Vacancies on the council were chosen by a group of five aristocrats, who served without pay. How their own appointment may have been handled is not clear, but they were apparently a privy council of the highest importance and authority for setting the future course of the city-state. Aristotle found the Carthaginian constitution to be a combination of a strong executive (under the control of the monarchy), a powerful aristocratic Council of Elders and a democratic Assembly of the People. (As the noted Punic scholar Gilbert Charles-Picard has convincingly argued, the term *suffetes,* long thought to be just another name for the kings of Carthage, probably originally indicated only judges handling civil and criminal cases.)[11]

It was also in this golden age of the fourth century that Carthage may have begun a rapid expansion program designed to exploit the vast potential of the hinterland of ancient Tunisia. Without a doubt there were abundant Carthaginian "plantations" to the northeast throughout Cape Bon. Diodorus, the Sicilian-Greek historian of the first century B.C., drawing on the works of earlier historians available to him in the libraries of Rome, described this region as a land of milk and honey:

> It was divided into market gardens and orchards of all sorts of
> fruit trees, with many streams of water flowing in channels
> irrigating every part. There were country houses everywhere,
> lavishly built and covered with stucco, which testified to the
> wealth of their owners. The barns were filled with all that was
> needed to maintain a luxurious standard of living, as the
> inhabitants had been able to store up an abundance of
> everything in a long period of peace. Part of the land was
> planted with vines, part with olives and other productive trees.
> Beyond these, cattle and sheep were pastured on the plains, and
> there were meadows filled with grazing horses.[12]

One of the most fascinating and tantalizingly mysterious products, which the Carthaginians traded but could not grow themselves, was silphium.[13] Although some modern authorities believe it may have been a grass on which livestock liked to graze, most scholars think it was a plant rather similar to the wild carrot and possibly related to Queen Anne's lace. Its leaves, stalk and pulp were in such high demand that it was overcultivated in Roman times and vanished from the earth, but it was the most important and distinctive product of Cyrene, an important kingdom in what is now Libya.

Cyrene was also famous for its beautiful horses and infamous for its mysterious illnesses, but not much else, as was pointed out humorously in a mid-fourth century B.C. comedy by the Greek playwright Antiphanes, who was noted for the constant references to food in his works. One of his characters laments that "I will not sail back to the place from which we were carried away, for I want to say goodbye to all—horses, silphium, chariots, silphium stalks, steeplechasers, silphium leaves, fevers and silphium pulp."[14]

Silphium, in constant demand as a food, spice, antiseptic, medicine and aphrodisiac, was frightfully expensive, and the famous Roman chef Apicius offered a recipe to make one ounce of it last longer by keeping it in a jar of pine nuts, letting the nuts absorb the flavor, and then using the nuts in recipes which call for silphium itself. On a black-figured Lakonian (Spartan) cup of the sixth century B.C. found in Etruria (and now in Paris), the king of Cyrene, a certain Arkesilas, is shown watching the weighing of silphium and its placement in sacks in the hold of a cargo vessel. Silphium was a royal monopoly, as the vase suggests, and the plant was so important that it was portrayed on the coins of the city for centuries.

The nearest major Punic port to Cyrene in North Africa was Charax, an emporium located to the west of the area of the city-state. Here Carthaginian merchants brought wine to trade for the invaluable black-market silphium smuggled out of Cyrene. In stories like these we see the Carthaginians emulating their Phoenician predecessors as wily wholesalers short on scruples and long on the pursuit of the almighty shekel.

There were of course many other perishable products, whose traces are less easily tracked down by archaeologists but which formed a major part of the expansive Carthaginian commercial empire. Cinnabar, a powdery red mercuric sulfide, was available naturally in the silver mines of Spain; it was a highly popular commodity for making cosmetics, especially rouge, and may have had ritual importance too. One example was found in an oyster shell in a Punic tomb, where it made up part of a woman's toilette.[15] Carthage was also well known in the fourth century B.C. for its exceptional carpets and pillows as well as for perfume and flax, used for making strong fishing nets.[16]

It may also have been at this time that Punic artists, having seen pebbles being used to make elegant decorative floors in Sicily and Greece, began to cut and shape stones into mosaics. Laid upon several foundations of mortar, these simple floors have been found in Punic homes and are the earliest known examples of the true mosaic art form.[17] The Carthaginians may have passed this technology on to Sicily, where it was more fully exploited at sites like Morgantina in the third century B.C., and from this area it spread rapidly to the rest of the Greek world. Superb examples of true mosaic are known in the second century B.C. at Delos.

During the 330s B.C. a number of Phoenician imports once again began to appear in profusion in Carthage. They had tapered off to almost nothing and their sudden influx at this time may have meant that refugees from Tyre and other Phoenician centers were flooding into the city. The reason for this is not difficult to guess. Tyre, confident that it was impregnable, had resisted the forces of Alexander the Great and his invading Macedonian army in 332 B.C. The city was finally taken when Alexander constructed a causeway between the island part of Tyre and the mainland city. After this, Tyre went into a sharper decline, accelerated probably by the rise of Alexandria in Egypt as a competing commercial power in the eastern Mediterranean. It would not fully revive again until the Roman period.[18]

Also in the fourth century B.C. there was a dyeing establishment just south of the harbor area of Le Kram, where modern excavators recovered a cache of what was identified as murex shells. The murex snail, although not much to look at, was one of the major sources of revenue for Phoenician Tyre, where the color purple was painstakingly produced from the dye secreted by these marine creatures. To obtain the valued pigment, the shellfish had to be crushed, cooked in salt and sun-dried until it finally turned purple.

Clothes dyed in this way were often worn by royalty of many countries, and Tyrian purple is mentioned (frequently) in the Bible: "And Mordecai went out from the presence of the king in royal apparel of blue and white, and with a great crown of gold, and with a garment of fine linen and purple."[19] The color blue could be made by the addition of another substance in the dyeing process. One reason that murex-dyed cloth and clothing was so exotic and expensive was that it took nine thousand of these four-inch-long creatures to produce just one gram of the dye.

With all of these (and many more) commodities being traded at a brisk pace, Carthage was further aided by famine conditions throughout much of Greece, which drastically increased the need for imported food. Not surprisingly, Carthage was beginning to expand its overall city size now, as well as its ports. A suburb known as New Carthage was constructed but has never been found. It is probably still there, waiting to be discovered under the sumptuous modern villas in the northern part of the modern city.

The revolutionary fourth century B.C. must have been a time of excitement and controversy, an epoch tingling with vibrancy in business, politics and, as we shall see more fully in the next chapter, religion. But if the century rushed in on a wave of positive energy, it was to go out in a whirlwind of terror and fear.

Syracuse was on the move yet again. The Carthaginian leaders tried repeatedly to make treaties and keep the good times rolling, for few societies that have to rely on mercenary armies to defend themselves want to go to war in a time of maximum prosperity. But a brilliant and ambitious ex-potter named Agathocles was ready to test Carthage to the limit. He had risen to power amid the confusion in Sicily and consolidated his tyrannical rule with bloody reprisals against his rivals. Perceived by many contemporaries as an aggressive, exceedingly energetic man, he was to be much admired by the later Romans as someone of intellect, courage and wisdom. The people of Carthage, however, had a different opinion.[20]

By pursuing an endless policy of expansion and vengeance against all Punic influence in Sicily, Agathocles forced Carthage to respond in kind and a new war began. In 310 B.C. the Punic commander Hamilcar was able to control or obtain pledges of neutrality from much of Sicily while he exercised his main goal—setting up a blockade of Syracuse.

But the Sicilian general stunned the Carthaginians by counterattacking Carthage itself along with the rich lands and towns of the east and northeast coast of Tunisia. Never before had Carthage faced such a direct and terrifying threat and not surprisingly, the impending disaster was seen there as failure on the part of the people to pay enough attention to their gods. A decision was quickly made to do something about this, and an offering was hastily sent to the Sanctuary of Melqart in the mother city of Tyre. But this was not considered sufficient, and a massive ceremony of child sacrifices took place on the shore by the commercial harbor. At least five hundred infants and children lost their lives. Some of them were up to four years of age; a few may have been as old as ten.

The gory rites of sacrifice were far from being the only atrocities of the moment in Carthage. An internal coup d'état, Sicilian-style, saw Bomilcar, one of the city's leading generals, proclaim himself tyrant. Carthage, now sealed off by Sicilian troops outside, became an equally armed and warring camp inside. Bomilcar's forces were soon outnumbered and he, like Hanno before him, was tortured and killed. In the meantime, General Hamilcar was fighting outside the city, losing not only the principal battle but finally even his own head, which was formally presented as a gift to the Syracusan ruler.

But Agathocles had his own problems. Forced virtually to commute between threatened Syracuse and the Carthaginian front, he had to entrust his troops to lesser commanders such as his own sons, resulting in a military fiasco. With losses so heavy on both sides, a treaty was arranged, and Carthage retained its control in western Sicily. The war had actually settled very little, except that a lot of children, soldiers, innocent civilians and able leaders had died or had seen their homes destroyed, and all of the Punic world had received quite a scare.

Up until his death in 289 B.C., Agathocles, well into his seventies, hoped to gain revenge against Carthage. It was not to be, but he could at least content himself with a series of magnificent commemorative paintings of his campaigns, which he commissioned for the inner walls of the Temple of Athena at Syracuse. They showed the crusty old warrior leading a cavalry charge and were considered among the most fabulous sights for visitors to the city. So even though Agathocles never quite reached his goal of ending Punic civilization, he almost did, and at the very least, he and his exploits became quite a tourist attraction. With the death of Agathocles, Syracuse again became hopelessly embroiled in internal disputes but finally produced one final leader of great ability, the skillful, refined diplomat, Hieron II (c. 306–215 B.C.), who steered the city-state out of danger for decades.

But now, as Syracuse marched in place, no longer quite the empire it once was, a new power was exploding onto the scene with incredible swiftness—Rome!

Early in the third century B.C. the city on the Tiber was an ugly town, often the butt of disparaging jokes by the leaders of more elegant communities like Capua in South Italy or Pella in Macedonia. In the eighth century B.C., when Phoenician Tyre was one of the most beautiful cities of the Mediterranean, the Romans were still living in round huts and were barely able to begin to produce wheel-turned pottery. But once they had expelled their Etruscan overlords in or about 509 B.C. and survived a whirlwind invasion of Gallic tribes in the early fourth century, the Romans expanded from a tiny area near the west coast of central Italy, using a policy of extreme military discipline and organization and a disdain for what was considered effete luxury (especially Greek refinements like theaters).

As the Romans inexorably pushed their way north and south and bested the various tribes of the region, their generally lenient treatment of the conquered and their tolerance of native traditions and practices made them acceptable—if not always beloved—despots. In the fourth century, as Carthage plied the seas and skirmished with Sicily, Rome, which had no naval fleet at all, was using its powerful army to expand into what was known as Magna Graeca or Greater Greece, the area of South Italy that had been colonized by the Greeks.[21] The Campanians and the Samnites, fierce and militant tribes of the region, who served as mercenaries all over the Mediterranean and had overrun many of the Greek colonies, fought for decades against the relentless Romans.

By the early third century B.C. the focus was again on Sicily, but with three main players now: Carthage, Syracuse and Rome. With each vying for control of the region, it was only a matter of time until matters got out of hand. Certainly any truce between Carthage and Syracuse could hardly be expected to endure for long. The focal point of conflict now was Messana, a major city north of Syracuse that overlooked the vital straits between Sicily and Italy. The epic struggle that now began to unfold here, the First Punic War, was the first of three major conflicts between 264 and 146 B.C. between Rome and its archenemy Carthage.

Messana was one of the oldest Hellenic cities in Sicily, founded by colonists from the Greek colony of Cumae in South Italy and island Greeks from Naxos, then later resettled by mainland Greeks from Euboea.[22] Used as a pawn like its sister city Rhegium across the straits, Messana fell under the control of a rough-and-tumble group of Agathocles' former mercenaries known as the Mamertines—from the god Mamers (Mars) whom they worshipped. They were originally Oscans, one of the Campanian tribes of South Italy that had overrun many of its cities (such as Pompeii) and then had struggled tenaciously but unsuccessfully against the Romans. The original inhabitants of Messana had been murdered or simply displaced from their homes by the new tenants, and the women, children and property were divided up among the victors.

Messana was one of a number of Sicilian cities that remained loyal to Carthage and hostile to a new Greek leader named Pyrrhus, who had just arrived from Epirus, a kingdom in the northwest of Greece. Pyrrhus had the support of many Greeks; he had been invited by the city of Tarentum to stop the Roman expansion and bring general order to eastern Sicily and southern Italy. It was particularly hoped that he would take back many formerly Greek areas that had gone over to Punic control, like Segesta and Panormus. Forced to fight both Carthaginians and Romans, Pyrrhus managed to win a number of fiercely contested battles but then ran low on manpower and patience, while his mystique as a master general began to erode in the eyes of many of his allies. He soon returned to Epirus, but not before the term Pyrrhic victory entered the ancient vocabulary. It is still used today, especially in England, to describe a victory for which the price is too high.

Hieron II of Syracuse, sick and tired of the looting and raiding by the dangerous Mamertines and desirous of freeing the critical Straits of Messana from such anarchic murderers, decided to storm Messana. The Mamertines called on both Carthage and Rome for help. By answering the call, the Romans blatantly violated their long-standing treaty with Carthage of nonintervention in this region. The Romans wanted to keep Carthaginian influence out of Italy, while Carthage needed to regain its rapidly vanishing foothold in Sicily. When Rome moved in, Hieron allied himself with Carthage and the First Punic War began. But as the powerful Romans cut through the Carthaginian lines like a knife through butter and then menaced Syracuse directly, the pro-Carthaginian cities of Sicily, whose support for the war was always wavering, deserted. What was worse, even the Syracusans got cold feet and hastily defected to the Roman side.

While the Carthaginians were no match for the Romans on the battlefield even with their rugged mercenaries, they were still masters of the seas. A decision was made in Rome to rectify that situation if at all possible and to do it quickly, especially since a brilliant young general named Hamilcar (from the prominent Barca family of Carthage) was defeating the Roman forces in western Sicily.

But Hamilcar (also known as Hamilcar Barca), who was the father of the famous general Hannibal, had a rival in Carthage, a general named Hanno, who had made a name for himself expanding Punic lands westward into what is now eastern Algeria. Divided into bitter rivalries among aristocrats at home, Carthage was unable to organize effectively or rapidly enough in the field to win against the tightly organized Roman military machine.

Early in the war the Romans, who really didn't know how well they would do against a naval superpower like Carthage, received a tremendous boost to their national ego. This happened in 260 B.C., when a Carthaginian fleet was unexpectedly bested by a hastily improvised Roman force off Mylae in northeast Sicily.[23] Oddsmakers would have made this result an extreme long shot, for Rome had only had a fleet for four years, while Carthage had a maritime tradition going back to Phoenician and even Canaanite times. But the Romans, once having decided to develop a fleet, had been helped by the finding of a Punic warship, which had run aground near Messana. They immediately dispatched their best engineers and carpenters to study its method of construction and within a year began producing imitations, adding a special boarding bridge known as a *corvus* at the bow to facilitate access to enemy ships. Once they were able to storm onto the Punic crafts, they were confident of defeating the Carthaginians in hand-to-hand combat, and this proved to be the case.

Much propaganda was made of the Roman victory of Mylae, and the victor, Consul Gaius Duilius, was practically canonized. As the first Roman ever to win a naval battle over the Carthaginians, he showed that hard work, practical ingenuity, spirit and daring could triumph over adversity. In almost no time the Romans amassed a fleet of one hundred quinqueremes and twenty triremes, building some and borrowing others from allies like Tarentum in South Italy. After the Battle of Mylae, seventeen years before the First Punic War ended, Duilius became a household word, and every time he went out to dine in public a boy carrying a wax torch preceded him and a flutist played.

A column was erected in his honor in the Roman forum, and the captured beaks or prows of the Punic vessels were displayed at the *rostra* in the Roman forum. The term *rostra* (singular, *rostrum*), which we still use today, actually referred to the beaks of ships and gradually became the name given to any speakers' platform. In case anyone missed the none-too-subtle propaganda message Duilius brought to Rome with his victory, he took some of the spoils from the Sicilian campaigns and erected a Temple of Janus, the god par excellence of war and peace, and new beginnings.

Until recently little light had been shed on what a warship actually looked like during the time of the First Punic War. But a remarkably fortuitous discovery by the British archaeologist Honor Frost has changed that, although she has sparked a considerable controversy of her own making.

In 1969 a commercial sand dredger operating north of the town of Marsala accidentally uncovered traces of ships only eight feet below the surface of the water. Marsala is the modern city built over the ruins of Punic Lilybaeum, and there was the distinct possibility that the ships, if ancient, might be Punic.[24] Excavations begun in 1971 revealed traces of two sunken ships, the first of which still held the skeleton of one man (perhaps the captain or a wounded crewman who went down with the ship) and a dog.

The question of the origin of the ship was quickly resolved when Punic writing began to show up in various places on the hull, providing a labelling guide for the laborers building the craft. The scrawling of letters at key places where wood was to be joined turned the ship assembly into a colossal game of carpentry by letters, like a modern-day paint-by-numbers project. From the two vessels Frost derived a surprisingly detailed idea of what a certain type of Punic warship was like, for she believed that she had uncovered what the Romans called a *liburna,* a small warship developed by a Dalmatian (Yugoslavian) tribe noted for seafaring and piracy on the high seas.

Frost's reconstructed ship would have fit perfectly into the harbor at Carthage described earlier. There was a single bank of sixty-eight oarsmen. The stern (back) of the ship curved up gracefully to a stern-post which arched back decoratively over the deck. Below the prow and attached to the keel was a tusk-shaped timber battering ram over seven feet long, used for piercing the hulls of rival ships. The ram was, however, detachable so that it could impale a ship, break away from the mother vessel and remain lodged in the target ship while it slowly sank. Presumably, replacement rams sheathed in copper were readily available back at the docks in Carthage or Lilybaeum for successful fleet commanders. Another ancient ram has been found off Atlit in Israel.

The warships found were clearly not triremes or quinqueremes, which were the big battleships in use at this time. Triremes operated with three banks of oars and could have as many as 170 rowers, with

the group on top—rowing at the harshest angle to the water—
collecting the most pay and building up the biggest muscles. Triremes
had been used since at least 500 B.C., but quinqueremes, involving a
five-tiered, highly complicated arrangement of men and oar positions,
became fashionable in the fourth century B.C. Why were the Frost ships
so small? They may have been the advance-guard patrol for a Punic
fleet. They had seventeen oars on each side, pulled by two rowers each,
and could have been maneuvered rapidly. The Dalmatian *liburna* has
been called by underwater archaeologist George Bass "a swift single-
bank raider used by pirates."[25]

The Frost excavations also shed new light on how the Punic ships
were actually put together. Long planks fitted together with mortise
and tenon joinery made an outline of the keel, instead of a frame or
ribbed skeleton as one would expect. Afterward a skeleton or frame-
work was fitted to the already outlined keel. A similar technique was
found by George Bass in the fourteenth-century-B.C. Canaanite wreck,
suggesting that the knowledge of this shipbuilding procedure was
handed down through many generations.

Of equal interest was the cargo of the ships, which included a
goodly supply of cannabis, which Frost believes could have been made
into a tea and used to relieve tedium and uplift the spirits of the rowers.
But apart from getting slightly stoned on the Valium of the day, the
sailors could enjoy a meat-rich diet of ox, sheep and/or goat, fallow
deer, horse and pig, along with olives, hazelnuts and various fruits.

Frost believes that these ships were sunk by the Roman fleet:

> The dating, the absence of cargo, and the geographical
> position of the group of wrecks in which it [the reconstructed
> ship] lay, all point to its having been sunk in the battle of the
> Egadi Islands, which resulted in the fall of the Lilybaeum and
> the end of the First Punic War.[26]

But not everyone agrees with Frost's examination of the evidence,
particularly her idea that the ships were probably built in Etruria
because pottery found on board had such close parallels to Italy. This
conclusion does seem farfetched or at least unnecessary, for the pottery
also resembles Sicilian wares of the time, and the ship could easily have
been made in Carthage and stationed at Lilybaeum. It also could have

picked up its pottery at any port favorable to Carthage. The pottery may also date slightly earlier in the third century B.C. than Frost has suggested, so that the ships might have gone down in an earlier encounter rather than the famous Battle of the Egadi Islands.

But this kind of nitpicking may be best left for scholarly articles. It is fair to say that the Frost wrecks provide our most dramatic evidence yet for Punic life on the high seas and help to bring into tangible reality the literary accounts of the time.

Much of the crucial action of the First Punic War gradually came to focus on the fortified town of Lilybaeum on the west coast of Sicily. After the Syracusans had destroyed nearby Punic Motya in 397 B.C., Lilybaeum was founded as a replacement to look after Punic interests throughout western Sicily, coordinate trade and provide a landing station for the Carthaginian fleet. Once it fell to the Romans in 243 B.C., Carthaginian interests in Sicily were severely crippled, and Hamilcar Barca, now the principal leader of Carthage, had no option but to sue for peace on the best terms he could get.

After the First Punic War, the Carthaginian navy was shattered and would never again be the major force it once had been. The glory days in Sicily would become nothing more than memories endlessly recounted by the heads of families to their children.

Sardinia, long a major part of the Carthaginian sphere of influence, was abandoned forever, destined to become the first Roman province. To make matters worse, in the confusion and controversy back in Carthage the mercenary troops were left unpaid. The subsequent bloody insurrection, known to posterity as the Revolt of the Mercenaries and celebrated in *Salammbô* and the epic movie *Carthage in Flames* (1960), produced truly rough times for Carthage.

Now, in the second half of the third century B.C., Carthage was facing a new and even more terrifying enemy: Rome. Syracuse would remain one of the players in the future games of war, but now the Romans held the cards. A generations-old chapter in Carthaginian history had ended, and future survival depended on how well Carthage could meet the rising challenge of those tough warriors from the Tiber.

❦ V ❦

Hannibal Is at the Gates!

ASK THE MAN on the street about ancient Carthage and chances are you'll get a blank stare or, in the Midwest, someone may know it as a small town in Missouri. But if people do remember anything at all, it is usually the name of Hannibal, the archenemy of Rome, who marched thousands of men and dozens of elephants from Spain over the Alps and into Italy, where he terrorized the Romans and their allies for sixteen years.

Hannibal's adventures have become legendary. He has been the subject of numerous biographies, plays and even movies. The Algonquin wit Robert Sherwood wrote of him in *The Road to Rome* in 1927, swarthy Victor Mature played him and mushed elephants through snowy Alpine passes in the Italian epic movie *Hannibal* in 1960, and Howard Keel was a singing Hannibal in MGM's preposterous fifties' musical *Jupiter's Darling*. But despite all this attention to the man in both ancient and modern times, we really know very little about his personality and private life, nor do we have any clear idea what he looked like.

Not a single unbiased account about him has come down to us from ancient times. We have his enemies' word that he could be a cruel, violent, rash, irreligious womanizer. But even from such inimical sources comes widespread recognition of his military genius, dedication to his cause, extraordinary leadership abilities and a surprisingly wry sense of humor.

Our best source is probably the second-century-B.C. Greek historian Polybius, a wealthy Arcadian who had been a distinguished official of the Achaean League, a Hellenic group noted in Polybius' time for its pro-Macedonian and anti-Roman sentiments. After the Roman's defeat of King Perseus of Macedon in 168 B.C., Polybius became one of a thousand leading Greeks brought to Rome, detained without trial and investigated.

He was fortunate enough to become the friend and tutor of the philhellene commander Publius Cornelius Scipio Aemilianus and accompanied him on many of his military campaigns. Scipio, the grandson by adoption of that Scipio Africanus who conquered Hannibal, was able to provide Polybius with a wealth of information about the Second Punic War. In addition Polybius, famed for his interest in the truth, sought out eyewitnesses, lost treaties, letters, historical accounts and Hannibalic inscriptions. He travelled to many of the battle sites to explain, as he put it, "by what means and under what kind of constitution, almost the whole inhabited world was conquered and brought under the domination of the single city of Rome, and that, too, within a period of not quite 53 years (219–167 B.C.)."[1]

The result was his *Universal History*, covering the period of the Punic wars down to the destruction of Carthage by his friend Aemilianus in 146 B.C. There are other valued ancient sources—Livy, Plutarch, Appian, Cassius Dio, Cornelius Nepos—but Polybius was the closest to the events and when one also considers his reputation, he is the most likely to be accurate. But his is also among the dullest of ancient accounts, avoiding any analysis (or overanalysis) of the psyche of his characters and preferring a plodding narrative that was considered slow going even in antiquity.

Although Hannibal's name has become synonymous with Carthage, he actually spent very little time there. His father was none other than Hamilcar Barca, the enterprising and undefeated fleet captain of the First Punic War who had risen to the post of commander-in-chief after saving Carthage from the Revolt of the Mercenaries between 241 and 238 B.C.

Polybius informs us that Hamilcar possessed a master plan for the recovery and revitalization of Carthage as a superpower. Within him may have burned something of the proud spirit of his earlier namesake at Himera and a desire to get revenge for the loss of Sicily and Sardinia. He was angered by the damage to the good name of his city and the Roman's complicity in the mercenary revolt. We are told that he hated Romans above all else and that by focusing on the conquest of Spain he could build up trade, pay off the heavy Roman indemnity, augment his shaken army and, most importantly, set up a staging area for the invasion of Italy far from Rome's prying eyes.

Hamilcar apparently had three sons, Hannibal, Hasdrubal and Mago, who took part in the Spanish campaigns. Hannibal was the eldest but was only a child when he was packed off to the Pillars of Hercules. In a rare glimpse into Hannibal's private motivations, Polybius recounts a story he told near the end of his life at the court of Rome-hating King Antiochus of Syria:

> When my father was about to go on his Iberian expedition [238 B.C.], I was 9 years old. As he was offering the sacrifice to Zeus [Ba'al Hammon?] I stood near the altar. The sacrifice successfully performed, my father poured the libation and went through the usual ritual. He then bade all the other worshippers [to] stand a little back and, calling me to him, asked me affectionately whether I wished to go with him on his expedition. Upon my eagerly assenting and begging with boyish enthusiasm to be allowed to go, he took me by the right hand and led me up to the altar and bade me lay my hand upon the victim and swear that I would never be friends with Rome. So long, then, Antiochus, as your policy is one of hostility to Rome, you may feel quite secure of having in me a most thorough-going supporter . . . for there is nothing in my power that I would not do against her.[2]

Many scholars have disputed the accuracy of this famous Oath of Hannibal but there is no need.[3] Vengeance through generations was typically Punic, and the honest Polybius, although friendly with Hannibal's archenemies, is unlikely to have made such a point of it if it weren't essentially true.

The Iberian phase of Punic operations went well, as Hamilcar, using the Punic-speaking center of Gadir as his base, spread his control over southern and eastern Spain during the next nine years, pacifying Celtic and Iberian tribes, such as the Contestani of the fertile Gadir area.[4] The Romans were aware that something peculiar was afoot and were alarmed enough to send a fact-finding delegation to Hamilcar in 231 B.C. "We're just trying to pay off our indemnity to Rome," was the reply, but barely a year later Carthaginians, probably secret agents, showed up in Liguria across the Alps in Rome's northern frontier. When caught, they claimed they had come to help the Romans pacify the local tribes, but they were more likely recruiting mercenaries right under the Romans' noses as well as testing the waters for a trans-Alpine invasion of Italy.

Hamilcar died in battle in 229 B.C. at the siege of Helike near Alicante in southeastern Spain, and Polybius informs us that:

> . . . he died in a manner worthy of his great achievements; for he lost his life in a battle against the most warlike and powerful tribes, in which he showed a conspicuous and even reckless personal gallantry. The Carthaginians appointed his son-in-law Hasdrubal [note: apparently not his son of the same name] to succeed him, who was at the time in command of the fleet.[5]

Under Hasdrubal, Punic influence continued to spread through Iberia as much by diplomacy (he married an Iberian princess) as by violence. What little we know of him suggests that he was a man of some refinement, not averse to creature comforts, and the master plan of attacking Rome, if indeed it existed, seemed to go into a slight stall. A handsome new city called New Carthage was founded on the southeast coast, on the site of modern Cartagena. Moving up the east coast of Spain into the territory of the Torbeletai and Olkades, Hasdrubal successfully proceeded in the direction of the Ebro River, gradually increasing his territory and influence for eight years until he was assassinated in 221 B.C. by a Celtic slave with a personal grudge.

With the death of Hasdrubal, the troops immediately proclaimed as their leader the twenty-six-year-old Hannibal Barca, whose physical resemblance to his legendary father was striking and whose name apparently meant something like "Grace of Ba'al Lightning."[6] The young leader had been schooled since infancy in every aspect of military life; he had learned the tricks of the trade from the greatest Carthaginian and mercenary leaders and had years of invaluable practical experience in warfare against various Iberian tribes.

Before pursuing the master plan sworn by oath to his late father, Hannibal consolidated his power base, attacking the Olkades of the Upper Guadiana River, the Vaccei of north central Iberia and the

Capetani near the modern city of Toledo. From Hamilcar and Hasdrubal, Hannibal had learned patience—not to strike too soon or
without proper preparation. Since the time of Hasdrubal, the Romans
had insisted that Carthage stay behind the Ebro at the edge of the
Pyrenees. With Hannibal on the move at an accelerated pace, there was
much concern in Rome's ally Massalia (now Marseilles) and with good
reason—it lay between Hannibal and Rome.

A Greek colony founded in the seventh century B.C., Massalia had
sparred with Carthage before over trade rights and was by now a
Roman ally of long standing.[7] The Massaliote colony at Emporion
(Ampurias, near modern Barcelona) just northeast of the Ebro was
being threatened by the continuous Punic expansion in the area. Other
trade centers such as Akra Leuke in the area of modern Alicante south
of the Ebro had already had to be abandoned.

The Romans were extremely concerned about a powerful Punic
presence in eastern Spain. An invasion by Hannibal across the Alps
coupled with a new Gallic insurrection could lead to open revolt among
Rome's allies throughout the Italian peninsula. Forest tribes, such as the
fearless Boii, Insubres and Taurini, in what is now northern Italy were
constantly pressing Rome's new northern frontier, rushing across the
northern Apennines and striking colonies like Ariminum. They were
only defeated in 225 B.C., after having reached Telamon, halfway
between Pisa and Rome, and they still remained a major threat.

Responding to Massaliote pressure, Rome blatantly reneged on its
earlier agreement with Carthage and demanded that Hannibal keep his
hands off Saguntum, a city near modern Valencia in the territory of the
Editani. Saguntum, divided among those who favored Hannibal,
Rome or neutrality, became a hapless pawn in the superpower show-
down. Opting for Roman control, the town leaders put to death a
number of leading pro-Carthaginian citizens and threatened local tribes
under treaty with Hannibal. Professing that "it's an hereditary trait
among Carthaginians not to overlook any victim of injustice," Hannibal reduced the town after an eight-month blockade before the
Romans could figure out what to do about it. The war Hannibal had
sworn to seventeen years before was becoming a reality.

In April of 218 B.C. he began his history-making trek from New
Carthage past the Rome-designated barrier of the Ebro, beyond Emporion and the Pyrenees to the Rhône River, and across the Alps to the
area of Turin. It was not the first time the Alps had been traversed by

armed forces, but it had never before been done on such a grand scale. With perhaps as many as forty thousand men, a vast supply train and thirty-seven elephants, Hannibal faced hostile tribes and blizzard conditions as he struggled through the passes.

Probably Hannibal saw himself as the first wave of a series of Punic invasions, for his brother Hasdrubal, left behind to deal with Roman legions arriving in Spain, was supposed to join him in Italy as soon as possible. Hannibal's daring trans-Alpine foray was by no means an unqualified success. The guerilla tactics of tribes like the Volcae north of Arles in southern France and the unbearably cold conditions decimated the troops, leaving little more than half the original number of men to reach the other side of the Alps. On the plus side, Hannibal was able to gain the support of the rowdy Boii and Insubres, who drove out Roman colonists from what came to be called Gallia Cisalpina, leaving northern Italy in utter chaos.

Apparently the Romans had underestimated the stranger in their midst. After all, Punic soldiers had been no match for the Romans in the First Punic War, a scant twenty-five years earlier, and Hannibal had only recently assumed command as the result of Hasdrubal's assassination. So why should he be so effective now? The reasons, as the Romans would now find out all too quickly, were many, and his enemy had problems of its own.

The Roman army was led not by professional military men but by consuls elected for a year by the people after having been both proposed and approved beforehand by the senate. These citizen-soldiers were often veterans but seldom strategists or even true generals. Military service was normally a part of their career, important as a political credential. They were by and large rich, well-bred politicians who were usually given the *imperium*, the supreme administrative power to command in war, for one year, after which time new leaders were chosen.

Often consuls quarreled among themselves or agreed to direct troops on alternate days, a situation scarcely conducive to continuity and clarity of purpose for the army. Many leaders were self-aggrandizing political hacks or stuffy bureaucrats, but the vast majority of them were just plain mediocre, and against Hannibal mediocre wasn't good enough. For the Carthaginian leader did not simply dispatch into battle his three waves (maniples) of combat soldiers and skirmishers, followed by the cavalry. Unlike the Romans, he was a choreographer, the Busby Berkeley of military formations and a master coordinator of movement, who relied on flexibility, timing and clever signalling systems to outflank, box up and surround his less innovative opponents. And lest the comparison seem forced, it must be remembered that Busby Berkeley, like Hannibal, was steeped in military training from infancy and became an army drill sergeant before his Broadway and Hollywood years.

There were so many ways for Hannibal's unorthodox movements to confuse and unpleasantly surprise the opposition that the Roman consuls scarcely knew what would hit them next.[8] A student of the Greek military strategies of Alexander the Great and Pyrrhus of Epirus, Hannibal might send two waves of soldiers to fight while holding a third back as a surprise reserve. Or he might present a slightly curved or bowed-out front line of soldiers towards the Romans, slowly collapsing the curve inwards and giving the Romans the illusion that they were winning. Then suddenly, like a spider toying with a fly, Hannibal would be everywhere, outflanking and surrounding the Roman forces and cutting them to shreds by forcing them to defend themselves on all sides at once.

Hannibal was also a master at using the physical features of a landscape, often selecting sites for ambush that put the enemy at a disadvantage—trapped in a valley, jammed up in a confined pass or backed up against a river. He actually made the concept of a mercenary army work to his advantage by employing the disparate nationalities in ways that brought out the best talents of each. The flexible, highly skilled Numidian cavalry might be deployed to harass the Romans or provoke them to attack or they might perform complex tactical movements during a battle, while the heavily armed Celtic and Spanish horsemen served as the principal direct striking force. Celts, who often fought naked brandishing long slashing swords, might be asked to withstand a major frontal assault fighting next to Spaniards wearing elegant purple-bordered tunics, while stone slingers from the Balearic Islands might be used for mountain ambushes. Through intelligence work, Hannibal also learned when the Romans might be particularly eager to attack and likely to be lured more easily into one of his traps.

And then there were the elephants—hulking, terrifying monsters—whose charge struck fear into the Roman maniples and broke up orderly battlefield arrangements. They were probably African elephants, the small but big-eared forest variety called *loxodonta africana cyclotis*, which stood just under eight feet in height and were found at the foot of the Atlas Mountains in Morocco as well as in parts of Libya.[9]

The Hellenistic period (after the age of Alexander the Great) seems to have been the golden age of war elephants, which functioned like massive bowling balls to mow down enemy lines, whether for the Persians against Alexander or for Pyrrhus in South Italy. Their popularity waned after the Second Punic War, when it was discovered they could be rendered ineffective by leaving lanes in the maniples for them to charge down uselessly (a defense first employed by Scipio Africanus). They could also be diverted or panicked by fire.

It has been argued that Hannibal was impractical to bring the slow-moving pachyderms (and their Indian trainers) over the Alps, since so many of the thirty-seven died in the harsh October weather or fell on the battlefield at Trebia near Genoa in the first major engagement with Rome. But that would miss the point, because the creatures were there to a large degree to frighten the native tribes en route and to break up the organized formations of cavalry and foot soldiers unused to dealing with them. The harsh conditions on the road devastated not only the elephant corps. Hannibal and his men suffered greatly too, and somewhere in the marshes of the Arno River he lost the sight in one of his eyes, perhaps because of an infection.

But once he entered Roman territory everything seemed to go his way. The ill-prepared Roman forces under consuls Titus Sempronius Longus and the reluctant Publius Cornelius Scipio (who had failed to catch up with Hannibal in southern France) engaged the Punic leader at Trebia—with disastrous results for the Romans. Hannibal relied on his corps of veterans plus new recruits from the tribes of northern Italy and won a series of decisive, dramatic battles, which utterly humiliated his foe and caused widespread defections of Roman allies.

In the area of Etruria's largest lake, Trasimene, near Perugia, Hannibal laid out a typical Punic ambush for the new consul of 217 B.C., Gaius Flaminius. The latter was a popular politician among Rome's lower classes and as consul in 223 B.C. he had won crucial victories over the Gallic invaders and the hostile Insubres near the Padus River in northern Italy. His election to the consulship over the senate's candidate was a slap in the face for the senate for its handling of the war, particularly the debacle of Trebia.

On paper, Flaminius seemed the perfect choice: rugged, distinguished, free-thinking and schooled in military matters. He had built the famous Flaminian Way and an impressive circus in Rome's Campus Martius, and now he proceeded to Arretium (Arezzo) in northern Umbria, where he kept a lookout over the western Apennine mountains. But somehow Hannibal had already slipped by him into Etruria. Overeager for an engagement and hoping to stop at one blow the continuing erosion of Roman prestige resulting from Hannibal's devastation of the countryside, Flaminius marched his troops right into a trap.

Since the plain narrows northeast of the lake, the Romans found themselves forced to march in a narrow line along the edge of the lake. With his excellent scouts, Hannibal knew every move Flaminius made, while the ill-prepared Roman consul didn't have a clue as to what was going on. Surrounded and smothered in the Etrurian mist, Flaminius and his men were massacred, the losses numbering some fifteen thousand, with ten thousand men taken prisoner. Just afterwards, another surprise attack by one of Hannibal's lieutenants near the town of Assisi in Umbria left four thousand more desperately needed Roman cavalry dead.

The reaction in Rome was staggering. Furious debates between rival factions of the people's party (the pro-Flaminius group known as the Aemilians) and the old guard, called the Fabians, reached a fever pitch. It was commonly said that "things had reached the *triarii*," literally the third line of the Roman army, but the phrase actually meant that the situation called for drastic action. A *dictator*, or leader, had to be named to put into effect an overall plan to deal with Hannibal. No single Roman army, traditionally trained, was a match for him. The leaders of the senate had been too concerned with bickering and making political hay out of an opposing faction's reverses to field a properly prepared army.

The new leader was none other than Quintus Fabius Maximus Verrucosus, former consul, temple builder, conqueror of the Ligurians above Genoa, upholder of the highest moral and religious values and scion of the Fabian faction in Rome. But the bickering still did not stop, and the rival Aemilians elected Marcus Minucius Rufus as Fabius' master of horse. Fabius' new policy was a wise one: track Hannibal but do not engage him in all-out battle; there was nobody who could beat him.[10]

Fabius also realized that there were at last signs that Hannibal was having his own problems. The war in Spain against the Roman commanders Publius Cornelius Scipio and his older brother Gnaeus was going slowly, with frequent reversals preventing Hannibal's brother Hasdrubal from getting into Italy. Poor handling of the Punic fleet made resupplying Hannibal's army difficult and prevented control of crucial port areas. It seemed that the situation was the reverse of the First Punic War, with the Romans now masters of the seas and the Carthaginians suddenly unbeatable on land.

There were other problems on the Punic front, most notably inadequate support from Carthage itself, which seemed to lack the desire to offer full funding and commitment to the effort. Nor were enough allies defecting to the Punic cause in Italy; most remained loyal to Rome, and Hannibal's policy of devastating the Roman countryside only made him seem evil to many who might have been sympathetic to his message of liberation. There were even rumblings among his own Gallic supporters, who were tired of being in the front lines and taking the worst hits. Even at the crossing of the Alps they had to go last, slipping and sliding in the mud kicked up by those who had gone before them.

So Fabius, who was now becoming known as *cunctator* ("the delayer"), was merely being pragmatic. Still, Hannibal was wrecking the Italian economy by plundering and burning as he headed south to Apulia. Roman coinage had to be repeatedly devalued, and, with Fabius watching helplessly, the magnificent farmland of the Tavoliere went up in flames. When the cautious dictator missed a golden opportunity to trap Hannibal on the Volturnus River in Campania near Capua, it was too much. The senate recalled him and soon the newly elected Roman consuls, Gaius Terentius Varro and Lucius Aemilius Paullus, were pressed into service. They were members of the Aemilian faction and their orders were to attack and stop Hannibal.

East of Benevento, Hannibal craftily prepared his next move. The Romans were playing into his hands, for if he could win another big battle, he would gain defectors by the score. Hannibal prepared to fight—although outnumbered by twenty-five percent—near the village of Cannae on the south bank of the Aufidus River in Apulia. Varro, using a traditional strategy of hurling his best troops at the center of Hannibal's line, fell into a death trap. Hannibal's convex line sank back into a concave formation, sucking in the Roman heavy infantry and skirmishers, while the Roman cavalry protected the flanks and rear.

While the hard-fighting Spanish and Gallic horse outflanked and outfought the less skilled, more monolithic Romans, the allied Roman horse was put to rout by the Numidian cavalry. The Roman infantry was bottled up in a circle and annihilated. It was Hannibal at his artistic best, confining, choreographing and using masterful deployment of troops. For the Romans it was a day of infamy, as ten thousand Roman citizens lay dead on the battlefield and the bodies of ten thousand allies were strewn about the area for miles. Things had indeed "reached the *triarii*"; Paullus himself had been with the *triarii* and he too lay dead, along with eighty of Rome's aristocratic finest. Hannibal had lost six thousand and Cannae was his zenith. Over ten percent of Rome's available manpower had been killed in three short years, and the only hope on the horizon was a general who could delay Hannibal but never defeat him.

And there was more bad news. Many Apulian towns now defected to Hannibal's cause. The regions of Umbria and Etruria were ready to go, as the lower classes of many Roman-controlled communities were one step short of open revolt. At Capua the wealthy chief magistrate joined the ranks of the common people, and a number of pro-Roman aristocrats were deliberately asphyxiated in a bathing establishment. A euphoric Hannibal proclaimed that luxurious Capua, not Rome, would become the number one city of Italy, and he prepared to winter his troops in his new stronghold.

Carthage at last sent more reinforcements, even elephants, and a force of Boiis massacred the Roman troops of Lucius Postumius Albinus, the consul-elect, near Modena in northern Italy, then used his gold-mounted skull as a drinking cup in their holy of holies. These dark days after Cannae were described by Polybius.

> On their side the Romans, after the disaster, despaired of retaining their supremacy over the Italians and were in the greatest alarm, believing their own lives and the existence of their city to be in danger, and every moment expecting that Hannibal would be upon them.[11]

Fearing that the gods had abandoned them, the Romans took a page out of Carthage's book and offered human sacrifices. Two Greeks and two Gauls (a male and female) were buried alive in their ancient cattle market on the authority of the Sacred Books. According to Livy, "The burial was in a walled enclosure, which had been stained before with the blood of human sacrifice—a most un-Roman rite."[12]

But the Romans were a tough lot and were not about to give up easily. There were fresh troop levies in 215 B.C., and a near-total discrediting of the overbold policies of the Aemilian faction in the senate. It was time for more Fabian *cunctatio*. Hannibal couldn't be everywhere at once, which meant that Roman troops could keep him busy while his new allies in South Italy were systematically overcome and punished. And now began the painfully slow wearing down of Hannibal's forces. It would take thirteen years, but through skirmishes, blockades, starvation, desertion, bribery, disease and just plain boredom the Fabian policy prevailed.

There were occasional Punic successes. Tarentum joined Hannibal in 212 B.C.—more as a result of poor Roman diplomacy than anything else—but key cities like Cumae held firmly to the Roman fold. Even mighty Syracuse, which had joined Carthage, fell under siege to the Roman general Marcellus and was finally betrayed from within in 211 B.C. The gross ineptness of the Punic fleet had cost Carthage the support of Sicily, even though the mathematician Archimedes kept the Romans away from his beloved Syracuse with his sophisticated weaponry.[13]

Carthage would not raise significantly more money or provide fresh troops, while the Romans were willing to absorb defeats and make the commitment over the long haul. Their resolve bent but would not break, and even Hannibal's frightening march to the very gates of Rome failed to turn the tide and he was soon back in the south, helpless to stop Capua from returning to Roman control. A final factor in the defeat of Hannibal was the Roman appointment of the one man who was virtually Hannibal's equal as a military strategist, Publius Cornelius Scipio. Pro-Aemilian in political sentiment, he was a darling of the masses, a rugged individualist 150 years ahead of his time (he would have flourished with Pompey, Caesar and Crassus). Like Hannibal, he was brought up in the military. His father had fought Hasdrubal in Spain and Hannibal in northern Italy. Possessed of a reputation for valor under fire, he had once saved his father's life in battle and had also rallied the survivors of Cannae.

In 210 B.C., after the battlefield deaths of his father and uncle,

leaders of the Roman forces in Spain, Scipio was the people's choice to
lead the new Iberian campaign, even though at twenty-six he was
technically too young and not in a high enough office to qualify. He
became the first *privatus*, or private citizen, given the *imperium* and
unlike Fabius in Italy, he came out fighting. He had observed firsthand
Hannibal's flexible forces and carefully orchestrated battle plans, as
well as the extreme discipline of his troops. Just as the Romans had
learned to build a fleet from a Punic vessel which had run aground in
the First Punic War, so Scipio now modelled his own approach on a
Punic original, Hannibal himself. It marked a complete change in the
organization and deployment of the Roman army and . . . it worked.[14]

While the Fabian tactics kept Hannibal at bay in Italy, slowly
draining the life from his troop support systems, Scipio set out to
destroy the main Punic base in Spain at New Carthage. It was the
key center for the silver wealth of the area and the chief arsenal.
Scipio's forces, observing how during times of high wind the lagoon
area below the city walls became fordable, allegedly waded across
and surprised the inhabitants, taking the city and giving rise to "the
Scipio legend," the belief that the man was chosen by Jupiter to
work miraculous deeds.

After another defeat at Baecula, near modern Castulo in south
central Spain, Hasdrubal dashed to Italy with the remnants of his
battered, exhausted army to relieve the equally beleaguered Hannibal,
stuck down in the toe of South Italy. Perhaps if he had come years
earlier with fresher troops, he would have made a significant difference, allies would have rallied to the cause, and Rome could have been
conquered. But now, with Scipio dominating the Spanish front, and
with the Numidian hinterland in revolt as well, Carthage was running
out of options.

One by one the Roman armies had attacked the Italian towns
supporting Hannibal and, through violence or diplomacy, had won
most of them over. Hasdrubal had failed to find massive numbers of
supporters in northern Italy foolish enough to join his cause at this late
date, but he was able to field an army of thirty thousand, once again
causing great anxiety in Rome as the prospect of two united Punic
armies devastating Italy for years began to sink in.

But Hasdrubal never reached his brother, for lady luck (Fortuna),
a goddess most important to the Romans, dealt him a cruel blow. The
Roman forces had by chance intercepted his messages to Hannibal, and

he was forced into a trap by the consuls Gaius Claudius Nero and Marcus Livius Salinator. Even though the consuls were mortal enemies, they united and routed Hasdrubal's forces in the picturesque valley of Umbria's Metaurus River. Nero, with unnecessary theatricality, announced the defeat to Hannibal by flinging Hasdrubal's severed head into his camp. In the movie *Hannibal* the grim head-tossing sequence is made one of the dramatic focuses of the film, and the effect still packs a visual wallop.

Hannibal stuck it out in Italy, although barely able to survive and hanging on desperately as his support systems on land and sea crumbled. Locri, one of his centers on the toe of Italy, fell. Even Gadir in Spain, the symbol of Punic control of the far west and for centuries the premiere Phoenician colony of the region, switched to the Roman side. It was only a matter of time now before Carthage would be under siege.

Against the wishes of Fabius and amidst heated debate in the senate, Scipio was allowed to leave Spain and invade Africa in 205 B.C. He established his foothold in the area of the port of Utica, while Hannibal struggled on in Italy. Sweeping the local resistance aside, Scipio conquered Tunis, and Carthage quickly agreed to terms. Even a powerful Numidian force led by chief Syphax against his former ally Scipio failed to save the day. Syphax was forced to retreat, then tracked back to his capital city of Cirta and captured. He died in prison in Rome.

With the return of Hannibal in 202 B.C., the Carthaginians were encouraged to have one last go at Scipio and his Numidian ally, the crafty Berber Masinissa, near the Numidian town of Zama in the region of Kairouan, Tunisia.[15] A visit to the area today shows no trace of the great confrontation that took place there, and even the precise location of the town is uncertain. But here, Polybius tells us, Hannibal and Scipio, the two greatest commanders of their day, met face to face for the first and only time:

> . . . they left their escorts and met in the intervening space by
> themselves, each accompanied by an interpreter. Hannibal was
> the first to speak, after the usual salutation. He said that he
> wished that the Romans had never coveted any possession
> outside Italy, nor the Carthaginians outside Libya; for these
> were both noble empires and were, so to speak, marked out by
> nature.[16]

Scipio rejected Hannibal's appeal and the Battle of Zama, even with Hannibal in less than top shape militarily, was a donnybrook, with each master manipulator pulling out all the stops to surprise and outflank the other. Ironically, the superior Numidian cavalry turned the tide but this time, unlike the battle at Cannae, for the Romans, and it was Hannibal's army that ended up surrounded. One wonders what the result would have been with the Punic commander in his prime.

Hannibal had nearly destroyed Rome but in the process he was responsible for the revitalization and modernization of the entire Roman army, and thanks to him, a more or less united Italy had also been created. Perhaps he would have been more pleased to know that he had helped to create a near-demagogue in Scipio, the prototype for the powerful military leaders who 150 years later would bring internal chaos to the Roman Republic.

The surrender of Carthage in 201 B.C. was not unconditional, but Iberia was gone forever; it was already being colonized with Roman veterans at Italica, a site near Seville, which would later produce two Roman emperors, Trajan and Hadrian. The fabled Carthaginian navy, one of the huge disappointments of the war, was dismantled. An enormous indemnity was affixed and Carthage was barely able to defend itself from a new threat, the land-hungry Numidian leader Masinissa.

But the story of Hannibal was far from over. He was elected *suffete,* one of the two rulers of the city who functioned in the manner of Roman consuls. (The change to this form of rule in Carthage had occurred sometime after the mid-third century B.C.) Having been away from his homeland for some thirty-six years, Hannibal now stayed on as a constitutional reformer, crippling the power of the ruling aristocracy, which had refused to support him fully enough in the past eighteen years. His military accomplishments were apparently such that he felt no compulsion to kill himself after losing at Zama. In fact, when his old enemies reported to the Romans that he was hatching new plans and a delegation came from Italy to arrest him, he skipped town and finally showed up at the court of the Roman-hating King Antiochus of Syria.

Hannibal proved true to his original oath, leading a naval operation against the pro-Roman Rhodians off southern Turkey. When Antiochus' forces were crushed, he disappeared again, finally being tracked down while living in Crete. Disappearing for one last time, he escaped to mountainous Bithynia, on the south coast of the Black Sea east of Constantinople, where he became part of the court of King Prusias, another tyrant on shaky terms with Rome.

Prusias wanted to keep land taken from his rival Eumenes of Pergamum, but the Romans, now the policemen of the area, insisted it be returned. A small war resulted. Bithynia was quickly defeated and agreed to terms, one of which was the deportation of the sixty-three-year-old Hannibal. It was only then, with all hope lost, that the proud commander took his own life.

If Hannibal's story ended in tragedy, the life of his conqueror Scipio, now surnamed Africanus, was scarcely happier. He had become a living legend to the masses, many of whom believed that he was a mystical superman who communed with Jupiter himself. It was said that his mother had been impregnated by the god in the form of a snake. But to his rivals he was just a dangerous demagogue, an object of bitter jealousy, and an extreme egomaniac. He was also widely criticized for his open adoration of Hellenic art and culture, which was considered a corrupting influence on Rome's *mos maiorum* (custom of the ancestors). Nobody could take away his reputation for military genius, but he stood out too much, an individual in a bland, corporate age.

In his twelve controversial years as chief of the senate (*princeps senatus*), he was the subject of frequent attacks, often by the powerful Cato, who helped ensure that he was denied military commands and accused of misappropriating funds in the Syrian wars against Antiochus. His brother, Lucius, was formally charged on the latter count, sending Scipio into a towering rage, which culminated with his dramatic destruction of the campaign receipts on the floor of the senate. Hounded by insults from less worthy (and ungrateful) rivals, he retired from public life, sick and bitter that the republic he felt he had single-handedly saved should treat him as an enemy. He died in 184 B.C. at Liternum in northern Campania.

Scipio's entire family line went into an eclipse that would last for a generation, but over the centuries he was not forgotten.[17] Throughout the Renaissance he became the epitome of heroic excellence and high moral character. But it is Hannibal, the scourge of Rome, whom most Americans remember today, even though Scipio, a national hero, is still quite well known to the Italian people.

Carthage was severely crippled by the Second Punic War, and

Gilbert Charles-Picard has described the postwar years as "a sad time for the unhappy Republic." But the latest evidence, as the French archaeologist Serge Lancel has noted, proves quite the opposite:

> All the excavation reports published to date give the impression of an acceleration of the process of development of the city in the epoch of the Punic Wars, and of a prosperity which, paradoxically, seems to reach its apogee in the period after the Second Punic War, which was nonetheless ruinous for Carthage.[18]

Upon closer investigation, much of it undertaken again by Dr. Wolff, it becomes clear that the reasons for the revived prosperity of Carthage between 200 and 150 B.C. are hardly paradoxical. It is certainly true that a massive war indemnity had to be paid to Rome, but on the other hand no funds had to be found to support the Punic fleet and army with their mercenaries, always a huge drain on the budget.

Once Hannibal was elected *suffete,* he was able to put an end to the widespread corruption that had allowed the aristocratic Council of Thirty to raise taxes unnecessarily and to burden the lower classes unfairly. The legacy of Hannibal, far from being merely a story of defeat, was to leave Carthage with one of the most democratic governments in the entire Hellenistic world, thanks to his ability to develop the Popular Assembly (or Assembly of the People) as a powerful, irrefutable force in Punic politics. The proaristocrat, anti-Hannibal opposition party remained strong and often allied and intrigued with Rome against the prodemocratic forces, but the latter group seemed to have stayed in control in Carthage over much of the last half-century of the Punic city, long after Hannibal had been forced to flee.

By 191 B.C. Carthage had—in just ten years—bounced back enough from its troubles to pay off the entire war debt owed to Rome—had the Romans chosen to accept it. The loss of Spanish silver and gold was of course a bitter pill to swallow, but Carthaginian traders were once again back at work, peddling their beautifully crafted furniture (and probably their carpets too), embroidery, goldwork, figs, perfume, incense, sweetmeats, grain, wine and exotic animals along with the usual trinkets and geegaws. It was not a golden age, but Appian, the second-century-A.D. Alexandrian writer, wrote of the city of the second century B.C., "Carthage, blessed with unbroken peace, advanced greatly in population and power by reason of the fertility of her soil and her advantageous position on the coast."[19]

Equally surprising is the fact that Rome and Carthage clearly enjoyed a strong trading relationship, and a number of Romans, including at least one senator, spoke Punic. The comic playwright Plautus wrote *Patruos* (Uncle—also known more popularly as *Poenulus* or *The Man From Carthage*), in which an almost entirely Punic cast of characters is treated with considerable sympathy. Written about 190 B.C., at a time when the events of the Punic wars were still very much in the Roman mind, it described a young man who had been kidnapped from Carthage and sold as a slave in Kalydon (in western Greece). The man's uncle Hanno (a typical Punic name, as we have seen) is searching for his own two daughters, also victims of kidnapping and the slave trade. Of more interest to scholars than the typical mistaken-identity plot is the fact that Hanno and several other characters actually speak Punic in the play.[20]

Further evidence of contacts between Carthage and Italy in the first half of the second century B.C. is found in the tombs, where significant quantities of black glazed Italian pottery, especially Campana A (South Italian) wares, appear. Rome too was stepping up its international commerce. With the smashing of the Punic west and the failure of Sicily and South Italy to resist domination, the Romans developed the port at Puteoli (modern Pozzuoli), not far from the city of Naples, into a major colony in 194 B.C. By the end of the century, it had become one of the greatest Roman trading centers and was known by Cicero's time (the mid-first century B.C.) as *pusilla Roma* (little Rome).[21]

If it is true that Carthage had resumed at least to some extent its international role, it is also true that the tombs and funerary *stelae* of the metropolis show a decided falloff in artistic quality. In other areas, however, there is mounting evidence that Carthage was experiencing a big boom. The coinage seems to have remained relatively stable, with tetradrachms of good quality silver and occasional issues of gold. And the movement towards democracy pioneered by Hannibal and his fellow Barcids was extended to the rite of child sacrifice. Formerly only royalty could offer children to the honor of the gods; now, it seems, almost any Carthaginian could do so, and this was an important step, revealing that the once closely guarded religious rites of the ruling class were being extended to the masses.

During this fifty-year period, urban development proceeded at a fast pace.[22] Traces of housing of a sophisticated and quite elegant nature cropped up in a number of areas, especially on the Byrsa and Juno hills and in the stately porticoed dwellings found in the German excavations at the seafront. Most amazing of all was the construction of the military harbor in its final Punic form, something which had been expressly forbidden by the treaty of the Second Punic War.

But not everything was rosy for Carthage in the years before the demise of the Punic city. Much of the Carthaginian hinterland was falling under the control of Masinissa of the Massyles, whose influence by now had spread all across North Africa, even though many of his tribal subjects had converted at his instigation to the Punic religion and had set up their governments on the Punic model. (The Punic language was commonly spoken at his headquarters in Cirta; indeed, Masinissa had grown up in Carthage and his neighbor and rival *mas* Syphax had married a highly influential Carthaginian woman named Sophonisbe.)

As Masinissa pressed hard into Punic territory, the new Carthaginian leaders became increasingly alarmed. They were caught in a no-win situation. Should they give up and become subject to a hated Numidian chieftain, should they cozy up to the hated Romans and beg for help, or should they violate their treaty and prepare for war against Masinissa and, almost certainly, Rome as well?

The Romans were keeping themselves busy with their own vicious brand of internal politics, wars in Syria and Macedonia, and the bloody, seemingly endless pacification of Spain. And the Gauls revolted yet again, leading to the overrunning of northern Italian colonies such as Placentia. So the Romans were just as happy to have a leader like Masinissa keeping their traditional enemy weak and on the defensive.

Two formal delegations from Rome, one with the liberal-minded Scipio Africanus himself at the helm, tried to persuade the Berber *mas* to let things cool down. After Scipio's death his son-in-law, Publius Scipio Nasica Corculum, urged lenient treatment for Carthage, but by 153 B.C. Masinissa's threat became so great that another formal delegation had to be dispatched and this one included Cato. The eighty-one-year-old military hero, veteran of the Battle of the Metaurus, and self-proclaimed champion of public morals, was shocked and alarmed at the rapid redevelopment of the city "by no means crushed or impoverished as the Romans imagined."

The Greek biographer of Cato, Plutarch, writing in the second century A.D., noted, "He found it [Carthage] teeming with a new generation of fighting men, overflowing with wealth, amply stocked with weapons and military supplies of every kind, and full of confidence at this revival of its strength."[23] Even though some Romans feared that Masinissa would prove to be an untrustworthy ally in North Africa, Cato was more concerned that the Carthaginians would take up arms against the *mas* in violation of the treaty of 201 B.C. and then use the occasion as a "prelude to an attack on Rome."

About 155 B.C. the prodemocracy party in Carthage, led by one of its most vocal campaigners, Carthalo, succeeded in expelling many of the pro-Masinissan group from positions of influence. The new leader also made plans to resist the chieftain's repeated encroachments onto Carthaginian territory, and stirred up Libyan peasant unrest against him. By the time of the arrival of Cato's commission, Masinissa was pressing hard on Punic lands, creating a dangerous empire all across North Africa as far as Libya, and many Carthaginians were in no mood to give in to him.

Plutarch recorded Cato's famous speech in the *curia*, or senate house of Rome, in 150 B.C., in which he repeatedly warned the people that Carthage, a virtual neighbor of Rome, had no intention of honoring any treaties and was just looking for "a suitable moment" to strike up hostilities:

> As he ended this speech it is said that Cato shook out the folds
> of his toga and contrived to drop some Libyan figs on the floor
> of the Senate-house, and when the senators admired their size
> and beauty he remarked that the country which produced them
> was only three day's sail from Rome. Afterwards he adopted a
> still more forceful method of driving home his point: whenever
> his opinion was called for on any subject, he invariably
> concluded with the words, "And furthermore it is my opinion
> that Carthage must be destroyed."[24]

With Cato's warmongering intoxicating the Roman populace, a strong movement sprang up among the masses and leaders to "crush a city which had always borne them an undying hatred and had now recovered its power to an incredible extent." Such a sentiment was not unanimous. The most distinguished Roman of his generation, Nasica, who had been a war hero as well as a defender of traditional Roman values and chief of the senate, argued just as passionately against the proposed Third Punic War. Yet hardly anyone today recalls Nasica insisting "And I say Carthage must not be destroyed!"

A military hysteria, egged on by Cato, gripped the city. In 149 B.C. the Punic port of Utica at the mouth of the Medjerda River switched sides and called for Rome's help against Carthage. This manipulative measure became the excuse for war, and Utica became the base of military operations as the consuls Lucius Marcius Censorinus and Manius Manilius suddenly landed on African soil with an enormous fleet and army. With Carthage out of the way, Utica would soon become the number one city of North Africa.

Carthage surrendered immediately, giving up all its arms, and three hundred sons of leading officials were sent as hostages to the Romans. But then Censorinus revealed his additional terms: the city was to be razed to the ground and the people relocated away from the sea. They could be merchants and traders no more. They must become . . . agriculturalists. Only the temples and tombs of Carthage would be left untouched. Instead of caving in to the new demands, the courageous Carthaginian citizens decided on a last-ditch resistance movement. A city prefect and a troop commander, both named Hasdrubal, were appointed. Short of ropes to launch hastily improvised catapults, the Punic leaders used the long hair of their women, which could be braided into an effective substitute.

It was true that Carthage was defended by some twenty-two miles of walls and ditches but things seemed black nonetheless. However, Nasica had long warned of the lack of proper discipline and training in the Roman army and of the arrogance and insolence occasioned by prosperity. As had been the case before Scipio Africanus' time, the Roman troops were once again poorly disciplined and led by well-fed consuls who were political hacks. Surprisingly, the Roman forces were kept at bay, unable to break through the walls of Carthage, while the Punic cavalry, hastily pressed into service, devastated Censorinus' troops. A series of mediocre leaders did no better, and for an instant the Carthaginians dared to hope for a miraculous victory.

But it was only a flicker of hope. Internal bickering in Carthage led to a coup and the removal of the city prefect. In Rome the popular feeling was that only a Scipio could take Carthage, and young Publius Scipio Aemilianus, although technically underage just as his grandfather Africanus had been, assumed the *imperium*.[25] Cato was to die before seeing his dream of a burning Carthage come true but even he, a devout hater of the entire Scipio family, observed of Aemilianus, "He alone has the breath of wisdom in him. The rest are but flitting phantoms."

The disciplining of the troops into an effective fighting machine, the sealing-off of the city from outside access, and the systematic reduction of Carthage took several years. And just as Africanus had probed to find the weakness in the defenses of New Carthage in Spain in order to break the back of the Punic forces, so the same approach led eventually to the storming of the walls of Carthage at their weakest points by a new darling of the masses.

As the fighting in 146 B.C. raged through the streets, the Romans set fire to building after building until, with most of the enemy forces killed, captured or begging for mercy, only a few were left standing. On the Byrsa hill, where Dido had laid out Punic Carthage, the final resisters made their last stand at the temple of the god Eshmoun. Here Hasdrubal, the potbellied, swaggering last commander of Punic Carthage, shamed his nation's glorious past by begging at Scipio's knees. This became a favorite image of pro-Roman writers.

The final group of citizens and Roman deserters, seeing the end at hand, prepared a traditional funeral pyre. Dressed in her finest robes, Hasdrubal's wife cursed her husband, stood boldly before the doors of the temple holding her two children and immediately jumped into the flames. Her example of heroism lingered long in the Roman consciousness and may have influenced Virgil's description of Dido in *The Aeneid*.

The Romans had exacted a cruel and many felt unnecessary penalty for Carthage's transgressions. With a sense of vengeance going back many generations, many of the treasures plundered from Sicily in the fifth century B.C. were taken back. Although Scipio's own grandfather, Lucius Aemilius Paullus, had fallen to Hannibal at Cannae, he felt little sense of satisfaction at seeing Carthage in flames. With the historian Polybius, his tutor, at his side, he quoted Homer: "The day shall be when holy Troy shall fall, And Priam lord of spears, and Priam's folk." When asked what he meant, he replied, "O Polybius . . . I feel a terror and dread, lest someone someday should give the same order about my own native city."[26]

As Scipio waxed melancholy on the "mutability of Fortune," a century of struggle between Rome and Carthage came to a crashing finale. A curse was placed on any who might settle on the site, and the creation of any new colony was strictly forbidden. Carthage and its dependencies became the new Roman province of Africa.

And that would have been the end of Carthage, except that gradually the Romans came to realize that this was simply too great a location to leave unused. Veterans might be settled here, and of course Cato had let those figs slip out of his toga and shown the Romans that Africa was a conveniently located land of enormous economic potential. Curse or no curse, in centuries to come the practical and enterprising Romans would exploit and develop the entire area into something bigger and more opulent than ever before. Carthage, which had to be destroyed forever, would rise again into a super-city under the banner of Rome.

❦ VI ❦

The Precinct of Death

NO ASPECT of Carthaginian culture has so horrified the modern mind as the sacrifice of babies and small children in ritual fashion in the sacred open-air precinct known as the tophet. It is impossible to excavate here in this broad, half-overgrown area pressed up tight against the Punic ports at the southern limit of the city without becoming filled with an overwhelming feeling of sadness and dread. That may be why the area is played down as a tourist attraction and frequently cut out of many travel itineraries. "It is not the image of Carthage we wish to give to visitors," said one local guide, "and yet it is important that people know about this, and that they understand it really did happen."

Many scholars have simply refused to believe that the horrors the enemies of Carthage reported actually occurred here, but as the archaeological diggings go on, the emerging picture is one of a highly civilized culture that performed rites which still shock, and defy rational understanding. For now it appears that thousands upon thousands of infants were slaughtered to appease the gods Ba'al Hammon and Tanit. The charred ashes of the victims were swept up into ceramic urns and buried in pits capped with funerary markers (*stelae*).

Until recently the tophet appeared to be clearly understood by scholars, and in 1974 Samuel Matthews could write confidently in *National Geographic:*

> Firstborn sons and daughters were offered by Carthaginian
> parents as living sacrifices in times of great calamities—war,

Votive stele *from the Tophet of Carthage showing "priest" preparing to sacrifice a child. Punic, third century* B.C.

famine, drought, and plague. On a moonlit night, ancient writers say, a priest placed a child, mercifully killed moments earlier, on the outstretched arms of a statue of Ba'al. As the infant's body rolled into a flaming pit—entering the company of the gods—flutes, tambourines, and lyres drowned out the parents' cries. Later the ashes and bones were collected in a small urn and placed with thousands of others in the sacrificial precinct, or tophet of the goddess Tanit at Carthage.[1]

However, as the ancient literary and archaeological evidence has continued to be examined over the past decade, the role of the tophet in

Punic culture has been increasingly called into question. Matthews' statement, which reflected the prevalent scholarly beliefs of his time, now seems at least partially suspect, and one has to wonder if we ever will fully understand in detail what secret rites actually transpired.

Even the discovery of the site of the tophet in 1921 was shrouded in romantic mystery, as becomes immediately evident when one reads the account of the dapper adventurer-archaeologist Count Byron Khun de Prorok. "The germ of digging has laid hold on me," he confessed in his highly entertaining account of his work in Tunisia, *Digging for Lost African Gods,* written in 1926. The Count began his narrative of the discovery of the tophet, sometimes known as the Precinct or Sanctuary of Tanit or the Temple with a flair for the dramatic and mysterious worthy of Conan Doyle: "How we discovered the temple is a story not far removed from the exploits of Sherlock Holmes."[2]

The Count, who was one of few archaeologists ever to be photographed at work while wearing both a pith helmet and necktie, learned about the site through a local public official named P. Geilly. A part-time antiquarian, Geilly had become aware of the sale of funerary *stelae* on the black market by a resourceful Arab. By tracking the man down to his home in a Roman cistern or water storage area in Carthage and plying him with alcohol, Geilly, de Prorok, and the local police chief, François Icard, were able to get the looter to admit his deed and tell them where he was finding his artifacts.

But the Arab's story proved to be a falsehood, and the trio was led "into the mountains" somewhere around Tunis on a wild-goose chase. Thinking he had outsmarted the police, the looter continued plying his trade, and de Prorok, Geilly and Icard resolved to track him down under cover of night. By the light of the moon, the thief was observed digging in the area of what would later be identified as the tophet of Carthage. The Count described the moment: "He was caught red-handed, and nearby lay ten votive stones. The site he was working on warranted full excavation, so the land was acquired, and we set to work. The sanctuary of Tanit is the result."[3]

The Count's team included some of the top Punic scholars of the time, true pioneers in the field of Carthaginian archaeology and cultural history: Francis W. Kelsey, tophet project director from the University of Michigan; the Abbé J.-B. Chabot, president of the Académie des inscriptions et belles-lettres and editor of the *Corpus of Semitic*

Inscriptions; Professor Stéphane Gsell, the indefatigable epigrapher, historian and archaeologist; Alfred Merlin of the Louvre, an archaeologist who excavated a first-century-B.C. shipwreck off the east coast of Tunisia containing the famed Mahdia bronzes, now on traveling exhibition throughout Europe; Instructor Donald B. Harden of Aberdeen University, whose keen eye for stratigraphy would help enormously in the understanding of the area; and finally George R. Swain, outstanding photographer for the University of Michigan, whose clear photographs provided exceptionally fine documentation of the methodology and early discoveries at the tophet.

To the Count's credit, he was clearly as enamored of the scientific possibilities of archaeology as he was of the romantic, and Kelsey remained enormously grateful to him for not simply plunging ahead and ripping everything out after he had bought up the land:

> To Byron Khun de Prorok belongs the credit of having inspired
> in a group of Americans an interest in the problem of
> excavating ancient Carthage. By lectures, conferences and
> publications he urged the importance of salvaging something of
> value from the ancient site before it is completely overspread
> with new buildings, and he sought assistance on the scientific
> as well as the pecuniary side in carrying on the work.[4]

But de Prorok's narratives, unlike Kelsey's, are constantly drawn back to the sensational and bizarre. When a *stele* was found to contain a warning that "whoever overthrows this stone shall be shattered by Baal," its curse was seen to strike down a local museum curator, and the stone itself is credited with gashing his forehead and making him fall into an excavation pit. The Count had no doubt heard of the famous King Tut curse, popularized some few years earlier, and succumbed to the temptation to have his own version.

He peppered his text with racist quips ("Your true Arab dearly loves a strike. It saves him working. . . ."), and seems never to have been bothered that Arabs had found the site in the first place and were currently doing all of the hard labor of excavation for him. In fact, they were receiving minimal pay, while he posed for Swain's pictures and basked in the fame of the discoveries.

The early excavators of the tophet knew that the term was commonly found in the Bible (Jer. 7:30–32 and 32:35; 2 Kings 17:16–17 and 23:10) and appeared to mean a high place in the Valley of Hinnom near Jerusalem, where children were sacrificed by being made to pass through fire. Such cult places, well known to the Phoenicians, were widespread in the Punic world, where thus far ten different tophets have been noted in Tunisia, Algeria, Sicily and Sardinia. But just exactly what went on in this strange and secret area is the subject of considerable scholarly debate.

Numerous ancient accounts, sometimes confusing, tantalizingly insufficient or even contradictory, give us at least some ideas, but we must remember that these summaries were all written by anti-Carthaginian authors.[5] Perhaps the most famous description comes from the Sicilian Greek historian of the first century B.C., Diodorus. He was familiar with tophets, which had existed almost up to the time of his birth in his own country, while in nearby Sardinia tophets were still functioning although human sacrifice had stopped. In a well-known passage he describes how the Carthaginians reacted at the end of the fourth century B.C., when the Sicilian tyrant Agathocles of Syracuse was pressing at their gates:

> They were filled with superstitious dread, for they believed that
> they had neglected the honors of the gods that had been
> established by their fathers. In their zeal to make amends for
> their omission, they selected 200 of the noblest children and
> sacrificed them publicly; and others who were under suspicion
> sacrificed themselves voluntarily, in number not less than 300.
> There was in their city a bronze image of Cronus, extending its
> hands, palms up and sloping toward the ground, so that each of
> the children when placed thereon rolled down and fell into a
> sort of gaping pit filled with fire.[6]

Diodorus' account underscores a seeming hesitancy on the part of the Carthaginian people in the fourth century B.C. to observe the traditional rites, and apparently it took a national calamity to force a return to the old ways. The account is particularly valuable for its description of the actual procedure of the sacrifice. Diodorus also recorded elsewhere that Himilco, the Carthaginian general, had sacrificed a child before the siege of Akragas took place in Sicily in the year 406 B.C.

For a more personal view of this bloody rite, one must turn to the Greek essayist and biographer, Plutarch, and his early-second-century-A.D. account of ancient superstitions:

> . . . those [families] with no children would buy little ones from poor people and cut their throats as if they were so many lambs or young birds; meanwhile the mother stood by without a tear or moan but should she utter a single moan or let fall a single tear, she had to forfeit the money, and her child was sacrificed nevertheless and the whole area before the statue was filled with a loud noise of flutes and drums so that the cries of wailing should not reach the ears of the people.[7]

Again, in this account, the reluctance of mothers to give up their offspring touches us deeply, and the feeling is that the Carthaginians were forced by their religious convictions to enact a ritual that even they found difficult to sustain and endure, even resorting to paying others to fulfill their vows.

Another source, Kleitarchos, a flamboyant Alexandrian-Greek writer of the third century B.C., who was much read by the later Romans, was quoted as saying that the Carthaginians sacrificed a child to Cronus (the term given by the Romans to Ba'al Hammon) whenever they needed a truly big favor or vow fulfilled by the god. Again, the bronze Cronus/Ba'al is mentioned, with its arms extended to hold up the burning baby before allowing it to collapse into a flaming brazier beneath the statue.

In a particularly hideous passage not atypical of Kleitarchos, he describes how the flames from the brazier caused the baby's limbs to contract and its mouth to open in a grimace known as "sardonic laughter" because the child appeared to die laughing. The term sardonic refers to a poisonous plant from Sardinia that caused convulsions resembling laughter whenever it was eaten.[8]

One of the most important sources for the rite of Carthaginian child sacrifice is the early-second-century-A.D. author Philon of Byblos. His *Phoenician History* was reportedly culled from original and early Phoenician sources such as Sanchuniathon, whose works on religion and the origins of civilization were considered to be of the highest importance.[9] Unfortunately, Philon's account only survives in fragmentary form in an even later source, so that the original information comes to us thirdhand. Accepting this caveat, it is worth noting that Philon again mentions that the infants had their throats cut and that the Phoenicians offered the best-loved child of all their children as a sacrifice in times of civic crisis.

A surprising number of other ancient sources reinforce the idea that the Carthaginians slaughtered their children, at least on special occasions of danger and stress. The famous Greek playwright Sophocles had already written in the fifth century B.C. about foreigners (he doesn't mention the Carthaginians by name) who sacrificed to Cronus (Ba'al Hammon). On the Roman side, the poet and historian Quintus Ennius is a valued source from a period when the practice was still allegedly in vogue. As a Hellenized native of northeastern Sicily, probably educated in Tarentum in southern Italy about 220 B.C., he would have known Punic people personally. He even served with the Roman army in Sardinia during the Second Punic War, distinguishing himself so much that he was brought to Rome and introduced to the important families by none other than Cato himself. Ennius also became friends with the Scipios, even dedicating an important poem to Scipio Africanus. His statement, made early in the second century B.C., that the Carthaginians sacrificed their sons to the gods must be given considerable weight.

Several sources less close in time to the actual events still manage to provide some useful information. The Roman historian Quintus Curtius Rufus, who flourished about the middle of the first century A.D. during the reign of the emperor Claudius, has become known more for his readability than his overall accuracy. Still, he drew on many now lost early sources, including Kleitarchos, for his biography of the fourth-century-B.C. Macedonian ruler and legendary commander, Alexander the Great. He noted that when Alexander threatened to storm Tyre in 331 B.C., the people of that Phoenician mother city briefly considered reinstituting their old practice of sacrificing a freeborn boy to Saturn. In such a statement, Curtius Rufus is revealing the apparently Eastern origins of the Carthaginian rite.

The normally reliable first-century-B.C. Roman statesman, Cicero, numbered the Carthaginians among those peoples who considered human sacrifice a pious act. Justin, the third-century-A.D. writer who drew on earlier sources such as Pompeius Trogus, discusses Darius, the Achaemenid Persian king who issued an edict forbidding the Carthaginians to sacrifice humans or eat dog meat. Justin added that sacrifices had been performed in Carthage in order to stop the spread of plague. Finally, a curious passage from the *Natural History* of Pliny, written in the later first century A.D., mentions a statue of Hercules (Melqart?) now in Rome but which once stood in Carthage, where it was the object of annual child sacrifices.

The term annual used by Pliny is of particular interest, for the writers who use it are usually rather far removed in time from the actual events. It is extremely hard to know if they are telling the truth. Silius Italicus was a Roman poet of the first century A.D. who grew up in the former Barcid stronghold of southern Spain, perhaps even at Italica, the veterans' colony established by Scipio Africanus at the end of the Second Punic War. One of Silius Italicus' claims to fame was a poem on that very war written in seventeen books and known as the *Punica*. In it he notes that the rite of sacrificing young children was annual and the selection made by lot. He even recounts a rather questionable story about Hannibal's rival Hanno, who arranged an official order that the renowned general and his wife sacrifice their own son to Ba'al.

The image that might be drawn from these and other ancient accounts is that the tophet was a vast open area where babies or small children were brought and then killed on special occasions—if not annually—to the accompaniment of flutes and drums (or perhaps tambourines?). They may indeed have had their throats cut first, and the freshly killed body may have then been placed in the outstretched arms of the image of Ba'al Hammon and exposed to the flames until the sardonic effect took place and the child plunged into a flaming pit or large brazier below the cult image.

The reasons for these bizarre and distasteful ceremonies may be as varied as the number of people making the offerings, for the sources are in no particular agreement on the subject. The rite may have been the result of an annual religious sacrifice chosen by lot; a national emergency requiring immediate divine intervention, such as a war or an epidemic; a simple belief in the need to carry on Phoenician and possibly also Canaanite traditions; a hope for personal success; a desire to preserve the health of another child or a family member; and/or a feeling that by making the ultimate sacrifice, one achieved a greater union with the divinity.

A new and intriguing theory suggests that child sacrifice may have been intended to provide a way of regulating excessive population growth.[10] The social elite of Carthage may have had to limit the number of children allowed to live so there would not be so many claimants to family wealth and land. With no other effective means of birth control, the wealthy parents would have to either abandon or expose children to avoid dividing up the wealth into too many individual parcels.

The problem with this theory is that there seems to be no literary evidence to confirm or deny it, and there is no way to tell whether the reduction of population was a reason for or by-product of the sacrifices.

One last theory may also be mentioned: the Carthaginians may have feared the consequences of *not* sacrificing. Along with their frequent allies, the Etruscans, they are among antiquity's most religious and superstitious peoples. The need to maintain the traditional rites may thus have been prompted by concern that all would be lost if they did not do so. Curses and evil spells were rampant in Carthage, and every family, whether royal or not, needed to find that special edge needed to survive. Soothsayers and diviners found steady employment, and the ritual of *defixio* (nailing or even burying a curse or hex scrawled onto a sheet of lead) became popular and remained so through Roman times. One such inscription of the third century B.C., found in a tomb in a Carthaginian necropolis, describes a goddess named Hawwat (but otherwise unknown) who is called upon to use powerful black magic to help a woman, named Maslih, resolve a bitter financial dispute with another, named Emashtart.[11]

Whatever the reasons were for sacrificing children, the rite seems to have been reserved originally for royal families and may have been a way for royalty to sacrifice royalty to the most royal divine Lord; in short, it might have been a device to link the earthly king with the heavenly Ba'al. As the city of Carthage became less monarchic and more oligarchic and democratic between the fourth and second centuries B.C., the rite of child sacrifice became similarly democratized, so that, oddly enough, increased freedom in Carthage meant that eventually just about everyone got the right to slaughter their children for god.

But how does all of the literary information square with the archaeological evidence? Since 1921 the excavation of the tophet has proceeded sporadically, with some of the best work having been done by the Franco-American team in the 1920s. The Kelsey and Count de Prorok group began the analysis of the ceramic urns which contained the infant remains and they also examined the *stelae* and other blocky, L-shaped, early funerary markers known as *cippi* (the singular is *cippus*), which were often stuccoed after they had been roughly carved. From these investigations it appeared that the child's bones and ashes were gathered up right after the sacrifice and placed in an urn.[12]

It is still not clear if the multiple sacrifices occasionally found all in one urn were made at one time by one family, although there is at least one case where twins seem to have been offered at the same time. Animals, particularly young sheep or goats, were sometimes offered as well. Into the cremation urn, which was less than a foot high, were placed tiny grave offerings such as bracelets and protective amulets, and the vessel was sunk down into a pit in the earth after being closed with a stopper, a flat stone or a plate. Sometimes several urns might occupy the same pit. A *cippus* or *stele* was then placed above the urn or urns, but it was clear that not every urn had a commemorative marker. In short order the tophet became extremely congested and clogged with offerings, so that periodic clean-outs were necessary.

No trace of the great bronze statue of Ba'al or of the precise area where the slaughters took place has ever been recovered. Occasionally, images of an altar appear on the *stele,* but they are difficult to interpret clearly; some look like a piece of meat between two big hamburger buns, prompting archaeologist Shelby Brown to give them the code designation BIGMAC in her dissertation.

Archaeologist Donald Harden, the young Aberdeen instructor with the original tophet team, classified the pottery types and divided the soil strata of the tophet into three major periods, which he named after the goddess Tanit and called Tanit I, II, and III. Although these divisions were broad, they at least allowed for a general understanding of how *stelae,* urns and the character of tophet sacrifice itself changed through time.[13]

After limited excavation in the 1940s the tophet was only summarily investigated in the decades that followed. In the 1970s, with Carthage growing rapidly as a resort, the tophet was becoming hemmed in on all sides by villas, a problem that Count de Prorok had already foreseen in the 1920s. A team from Chicago, again headed by Lawrence Stager, attacked the site with a number of specific objectives: straightening out the different periods and phases of the tophet; analyzing the human and nonhuman contents of the urns; classifying the funerary markers; and studying their inscriptions. Two outstanding dissertations emerged from these campaigns. The first is Shelby Brown's soon-to-be published *Late Carthaginian Child Sacrifice and Sacrificial Monuments in their Mediterranean Context* and the other Paul Mosca's *Child Sacrifice in Canaanite and Israelite Religion*.

The Stager excavations, once again carried out in swampy, difficult conditions caused by the water table, confirmed Harden's three major divisions of the stratigraphy of the tophet, but subdivided them into nine smaller phases.[14] Tanit I was seen to span the years from 725 B.C. (or possibly even slightly earlier) to 600 B.C., a period characterized by *cippi* that featured many Egyptian decorative elements and images of chapels and thrones. In Tanit II (600–200 B.C.), the *cippi* remained popular at first, frequently with images of a female deity in an Egyptian shrine, but were gradually replaced by *stelae* resembling modern tombstones. Decorative elements of the period were often pillars, one, two or three in number, sometimes rounded or shaped like a bowling pin or Coca Cola bottle. Such images were *baetyloi* or holy stone symbols for the Ba'al.

From the fifth century B.C. on, the sign of Tanit, a sort of apex-up triangle with a circle over it and a horizontal bar between circle and triangle, became popular, suggesting a fundamental adjustment in Carthaginian religion. Kelsey believed that he could explain the rising popularity of the goddess:

> But who was this potent goddess Tanit, that in the joint
> dedications has precedence over the god Ba'al-Hammon? . . .
> Tanit is distinctively Carthaginian, and may represent a
> primitive Libyan divinity, whose cult, blended with Phoenician
> elements, was taken over by the Phoenician colony.[15]

The actual idea of the Libyan origin of the worship of Tanit had been circulating for decades before Kelsey picked up on it and remained popular until a decade ago; now, as we have seen, there is evidence that Tanit herself and her sign were already known (if not well known) to the ancient Canaanites and Phoenicians centuries before she appeared in the tophet. In fact, at Hazor in northern Israel the sign appears in a context perhaps one thousand years earlier than the creation of the tophet. Also, several examples are known from the area of Phoenician Sidon. An ivory plaque from the seventh

Neo-Punic stele featuring the sign of Tanit, from Teboursouk. First century B.C.–first century A.D.

century B.C., found at nearby Sarepta, mentions Tanit Ashtart, to whom a statue was apparently dedicated. Still, the sudden popularity of Tanit in Carthage may indicate that some kind of major priestly decree or religious reformation occurred to put her in vogue, and her relationship with the Libyan divinities still remains a big question mark. The crescent moon and solar disk, common symbols on the *stelae* of Tanit II and III, are the emblems of Tanit and Ba'al Hammon respectively.[16]

By the middle of the Tanit II period, gabled *stelae* often show marked Greek influence, attesting to the strong Carthaginian connections with the classical world and illustrating the dramatic change brought about when the spoils were taken in such abundance from Greek Sicily. By Tanit III (between 200 B.C. and the Roman destruction of Carthage in 146 B.C.) the *stelae* have become thinner, taller and less carefully produced, but they are still Greek in inspiration. Hellenic decorations known as *acroteria,* already frequent in Tanit II, consistently adorn the gable ends in Tanit III.

The cremation urns varied only slightly in shape and decoration over the centuries, but their most striking characteristic is their sheer numbers. The latest examples are tiny and extremely plain, and look as though they were hastily mass-produced. Generally, the decoration of the urns over the centuries is of little help in enlightening us about the character of the tophet: red slip or burnished horizontal bands, occasional vertical line patterns or no decoration at all. One estimate suggests that as many as twenty thousand urns, most with one or more children's bodies (only about ten percent of them had animal offerings), were interred between 400 B.C. and 200 B.C. alone. This is guesswork, but many thousands have already been unearthed in earlier excavations and by looting.

Carefully studying the contents of each urn, Stager found beads, which once formed necklaces of silver, amber, glass and carnelian, and numerous faience amulets of Egyptian style. Also popular were representations of Ptah, the protector of the working man, shown as a naked dwarf with an oversized head, protruding belly, short arms and severely bowed legs. He had a strongly apotropaic aspect (as the warder-off of evil spirits) and as such, his image was commonly used as a figurehead on Phoenician ships. Another frequent companion in the urns was the *oudja,* an amulet featuring the eye of the Egyptian god Horus, possessor of extraordinary magic powers especially beneficial to the dead, for the eye can help the dead ascend to the heavenly solar disk. In such images as these the strong Egyptian connections of the Punic people, which reached back to Phoenician and Canaanite times, can clearly be seen.

But what of the babies? How widespread was the practice of child sacrifice in ancient Carthage? Jeffrey Schwartz, physical anthropologist at the University of Pittsburgh, has studied the human and animal remains from the urns for the Oriental Institute excavations—with important and even startling results.

Examining a representative sample of four hundred urns excavated, Schwartz had abundant material from both the seventh and fourth centuries B.C., but he also had a big problem on his hands. Baby bones are soft and cartilaginous and rarely preserve well over time so the question of whether only males or children of both sexes were sacrificed can never be answered archaeologically. But by analyzing traces of the skulls, the arm and leg bones and especially the teeth, Schwartz determined (according to excavator Stager) that in the early days of the tophet most of the offered babies were either newborn or stillborn, and about one out of every three offerings was a sheep or a goat (sheep can almost never be distinguished from goat on excavations except in cases of excellent preservation of the teeth). A more detailed study of this tophet material is expected soon, and it will be important to note if the conclusions presented thus far hold up, or whether new interpretations or revisions of the original data will be offered.

The role of animal sacrifice at Carthage has also come under recent scholarly scrutiny, using tariff lists from the fourth or third centuries B.C. which give detailed information about how to conduct animal sacrifices in ancient Carthage. Such lists were no doubt posted at entrances to temples or sacred precincts by priests or cult officials. They offered an accounting of charges assessed for the proper offering of oxen, calves, rams, lambs, birds, poultry and game. There were rules about dividing the meat among divinity, priest and dedicant and, if the dedicant did all of the sacrificing, the priest got less. Such a system provided work, food and income for the priests and sanctuary magistrates, and kept the congregation actively involved in the cult.[17]

Although most scholars have suggested that over the centuries animal sacrifice increasingly replaced child sacrifice in Carthage, the fourth-century-B.C. levels analyzed suggest that at that time only one offering in ten was an animal, while most of the offerings were children between one and three years of age. Fully a third of the children sacrificed were between two and three. Schwartz even found a few urns with the remains of as many as three children inside, and these may illustrate an important concept, although it remains only a hypothesis.

Once a vow to sacrifice had been made, it may have had to be fulfilled. The birth of a stillborn child or one who died before the sacrificial rite may not have been acceptable to the gods of the tophet and an older child—either from the same family or acquired from another—may have had to be substituted. Perhaps the already dead child, or twins, were cremated and then thrown into the urn for good measure but did not count enough to offset the vow. According to Stager, the sacrificed children were probably dead and certainly were completely still at the time they were burned, suggesting that their throats were indeed cut prior to cremation.

From the finds in the urns as well as the ancient literature, it is clear that it may not have always been the firstborn child who was offered up. That idea came from the Bible (Exod. 22:28–29, for example), where it was applied to the Jerusalem Tophet, and the notion then was summarily transferred and applied to Carthage in a report filed by tophet excavators Louis Poinssot and Raymond Lantier in 1923. Since then it has often been repeated, usually unchallenged, and it has remained in popular literature such as *National Geographic,* where it is simply stated as a fact. The jury is still out on how many of the children offered were firstborn and whether or not the policy was the same at all times, for all events and in other tophets.[18]

The sources suggest that a child might be vowed at any time, with the requirement apparently being that the offering must be the youngest living or best-loved child. Stager has suggested that children at least up to four years of age were sacrificed. Schwartz in his study of the skeletal remains could give no indication of whether the children were noble babies or commoners.

That task became the special study of Punic epigrapher Paul Mosca, now of the University of British Columbia, who examined all the inscribed *stelae.*[19] Mosca's work, although rarely noted in Punic scholarship, is of profound importance, for he surveys and integrates the biblical, classical and archaeological traditions at Carthage into a coherent story for the first time.

Mosca began by upholding a view which had first been proposed in the 1930s, namely that the term Moloch so often associated with the tophets of Carthage and Jerusalem had a very precise meaning, and not the one that has been commonly accepted by many religious groups. For generations, biblical scholars had thought that the children of Israel worshipped a foreign god named Moloch instead of the one true god Yahweh and appeased him with human sacrifice. Even Charles Dickens wrote, of a terribly noisy, demanding and manipulative infant in *The Haunted Man,* "He was a very Moloch of a baby on whose insatiate altar the whole existence of this particular younger brother was offered up as a daily sacrifice."

But Mosca insists that *moloch,* or MLK in Punic, is the rite of sacrifice itself, not a god, and that the Israelites were actually sacrificing to their own god in this way, a practice they may have learned from

Canaanite religion. Furthermore, he asserts, MLK is a royal word, suggesting the sacrifice of royal offspring by a royal dedicant. Mosca may not be the first to put forth these ideas, but he has taken the study further than any of his predecessors.

According to Mosca, there may even have been different classes of Carthaginian sacrifices. For example, MLK'MR appears to have been the offering of a lamb to fulfill a vow. The use of a young lamb to substitute for a human child (*agnum pro vicario*) has given rise to our own term scapegoat. (We also speak of a vicarious experience when we refer to an event where someone has substituted for us or is experiencing something we cannot.) MLK'BA'AL was the sacrifice of a noble, the offering of a baby from an aristocratic family. But MLK ADAM, a term not found at Carthage but rather in a tophet in Constantinople, Algeria, indicates the sacrifice of a commoner. Were such sharp class distinctions practiced at Carthage? Mosca believes so.

But whatever the details of the sacrifice, the tophet was a busy place, so busy that funerary markers had to be periodically removed, boundaries extended and layers relevelled. Shelby Brown notes: "At least twice before the destruction of the site by the Romans, either a large area or the entire tophet was roughly leveled and covered with a layer of sand, earth or clay to provide fresh ground for burial."[20] Literally thousands of *stelae* were found intentionally broken up and buried outside the tophet area. The rite of child sacrifice seems to have gone on with considerable frequency right down to the Roman conquest.

In the early days of the tophet, Mosca goes on to point out, sacrifice was limited to the few and the aristocratic. That some tried to avoid their obligation is strongly suggested by the literary sources, but for many, indeed probably most, citizens the religious vows were regarded with deep fervor and commitment. Names like *shufet* (judge), *rab* (great one, like a Jewish rabbi), priest, high priest, and awakener of the gods appear on the earlier *stelae*, and family trees are commonly listed. Just as in ancient Rome, who you were was often a factor of who your family was, and access to the rites of the tophet may have been kept as the ultimate mystery distinguishing the elite from the commoner.

In the third and second centuries B.C. and probably even earlier, a rapid process of democratization, an opening-up of the tophet for all, took place on a grand scale. The list of dedicants reads like a guidebook to everyday life in the Hellenistic city. For now we see children offered by doctors, teachers, scribes, weavers, embroiderers, goldsmiths, iron casters, craftsmen, master craftsmen, salt workers, sailors, surveyors, weighers, perfumers and incense sellers. Not surprisingly, these Johnnies-come-lately to the tophet often had a less distinguished family lineage and could seldom trace their pedigrees back as far as the nobles could. However, the doctors, teachers, and civil and cult officials may have been held in higher esteem than their comrades, since they had more elaborate genealogies than the artisans or scribes; one traced his roots back sixteen generations.

But the average *stele* is hardly verbose, usually giving the name of the dedicant, the genealogy and the name of the god to whom the vow was made. A typical example from the fourth century B.C. reads "To the lady Tanit Face of Ba'al, and to the Lord Ba'al Hammon to whom had dedicated H." Another says "To the lady Tanit Face of Ba'al and to the lord Ba'al Hammon that which was vowed by PN, son of PN because he (the deity) heard his (the dedicant's) voice and blessed him."[21] As the tophet reached its maximum area, with all levels of society making offerings, it may have taken up as much as 64,000 square feet.

Despite the evidence unearthed in the recent and earlier excavations, a considerable number of scholars refuse to believe that child sacrifice played a regular role in Punic life, stating that the Tophet of Carthage is really just a children's cemetery, where actual child sacrifice only happened during the gravest of emergencies. Biblical scholars such as Moshe Weinfeld have written that the rite was never ritually institutionalized and was simply the result of biblical hyperbole and anti-Phoenician slander.[22]

Lending further support to this recent revisionist movement, the Italian scholar Sergio Ribichini has argued, "In fact this ritual was probably reserved for exceptional circumstances, when the seriousness of the situation demanded more powerful religious intervention."[23]

To such scholars, most of the burials at the tophet were simply children who died prematurely and were then dedicated or sacrificed to the god. The presumed evidence for this is that few childrens' graves have been found in the other, normal cemeteries of ancient Carthage. And an extensive Roman children's cemetery where sacrifices did not take place has been located at El Jem in eastern Tunisia, placed under the protection of a mother goddess (Romanized Tanit?), whose tiny enthroned images survive.

The MLK inscriptions, for many of these scholars, are not at all indicative of sacrifices but simply of offerings, for the most part, of already dead children. The quantity of apparent sacrifices found by Stager in the fourth-century-B.C. levels, if indeed they are really sacrifices, must then be the emergency offerings cited by Diodorus to ward off Agathocles. In short, many scholars now say that sacrifices were highly unusual and did not indicate a growing trend toward human sacrifice in Carthage over the centuries of Punic rule. And the ancient sources, enemies of Carthage, are said to have distorted and exaggerated the evidence and given the Carthaginians an undeserved bad name as regular, or annual, sacrificers of humans.

In the revisionist view, the offering of a prematurely deceased child in the rite of MLK may have been a way to provide relief for the grieving parents, whose child would receive the blessings of the benevolent Ba'al Hammon and Tanit, protectors of children. This scenario provides for the principal Carthaginian deities to be genial and nurturing instead of bloodthirsty, and the family ends up feeling good in knowing that its offspring, despite being lost too early in life, will have a happy afterlife.

This idea represents, of course, a 180-degree shift in scholarly thinking about the tophet and its gods, and the Carthaginians can now be seen as a sophisticated culture that was too metropolitan—or at least urbane—to allow a major portion of its citizens to become ritual murderers on a regular basis. Since a precinct of sacrifice requires no temples and little more than an open space and some perishable materials, it is very difficult to ascertain archaeologically exactly what happened there.

The tophet question may never be settled to everyone's satisfaction. Nonetheless, the antitophet arguments, which are currently enjoying a major vogue in France and especially Italy, do not seem convincing. It seems that sacrifices occurred at the tophet, and in considerable numbers. MLK seems more likely to mean a sacrifice and not just a dead offering, and child sacrifice seems definitely to have occurred at special times, so why not regularly as well? It is possible that the custom did not abate but might have actually increased over time, no doubt due to constantly pressing problems in Carthage and the democratization of the rite. Although the ancient Greek and Roman authors were no friends of Carthage, it seems highly unlikely that they would all make up such similar allegations, and while their accounts do differ in some details, there is a homogeneity about them which cannot be ignored.

Shelby Brown sums up the antirevisionist stance neatly:

> Many scholars, although forced to accept the fact that the
> Phoenicians sacrificed some of their children, are unwilling to
> believe that a tophet contained only sacrificial victims. While it
> may be true that some infants who died naturally were buried
> in a tophet, the only written evidence we possess (both literary
> and inscriptional) indicates that the tophet was intended only for
> victims. Many authors seem overly eager to exonerate the
> Phoenicians from a "crime" (in our eyes) that, by Phoenician
> standards, was simply not an offense.[24]

The Tophet of Carthage was not the first to be discovered. Two years before Count de Prorok began his scientific investigations, archaeologist Joseph Whitaker had already discovered another one and published the results of his work in *Motya: A Phoenician Colony in Sicily*.[25] And long before that, in 1884, 145 miles southeast of Tunis and just at the edge of the ancient coastline, the Punic Tophet of Sousse (the ancient Hadrumetum) was stumbled upon. Damaged yet also partly brought to light by bombings during World War II, the area was studied by Pierre Cintas, who had also dug at Carthage. But Cintas, although a true scholar and a man of catholic interests, never realized the importance of hiring a good photographer or architect-mapper on any of his projects, and his digging technique was always suspect. However, the Sousse tophet appears to have contained six major periods.[26] It began in the sixth or fifth century B.C., well after the debut of the Carthage sanctuary and it continued well into the first century after Christ, by which time the Romans had been in at least nominal control of the region for a hundred years. By the first century B.C., however, human sacrifice seems to have stopped completely.

The Motya tophet, rather more carefully studied, lasted only from the sixth through fourth centuries B.C. The surprising range of offerings included not just children, kids, lambs and calves, but also dogs (which, as we have seen, Carthaginians ate), cats and even a monkey. After the destruction of the city in 397 B.C. by Syracuse, a tophet sprang up in the new port city of Lilybaeum and continued there well into the third century B.C., when Carthaginian influence was systematically driven out of Sicily.

The most important Punic tophet outside Carthage, at least from the point of view of archaeologists, was found at Tharros in western Sardinia. Recently dug and carefully studied by one of the outstanding scholars in the field of Punic and Phoenician archaeology, Professor Enrico Acquaro of the University of Bologna, it bears evidence of thousands of ceramic urns with the charred remains of children up to six months old.[27] Almost forty percent of the time, lambs or goats were deliberately mixed in with the child burials.

Despite the large numbers of burials, only hundreds of *stelae* were found, placed over pits in which multiple urn burials were frequently found. This raises all sorts of questions, for the same situation was found at Carthage. Did several dedicants join forces and erect one *stele* or did one dedicant make or organize multiple offerings at one time? And Acquaro made an amazing discovery adjacent to the burials: traces of what appear to be an actual funeral pyre of wild grasses and olive wood.

The blaze had been lit on the ground in the open air at the end of summer and generated a fluctuating heat, perhaps because it was a rather windy day. According to the excavator, the dead babies had been sacrificed with their flesh still on them and they were motionless when burned, which is to say that they were probably already dead. Sabatino Moscati, organizer of the recent spectacular exhibition in Venice, "I Fenici" ("The Phoenicians"), believes that the Tharros tophet was a mix of children who had died naturally and actual child sacrifices, the latter being the only ones commemorated with a *stele*. It may be that the same situation took place in Carthage, or that some families chose to let one *stele* stand for a group of sacrifices.

Of course not every Punic burial was a human sacrifice. There were plenty of other cemeteries dotting the hills of Carthage. These necropolises, or cities of the dead, contained full-blown tombs of various forms: shafts cut down into the living rock with chambers opening off either side, simple pit tombs and monumental subterranean rooms reached by a long, carefully cut flight of steps. They spread rather haphazardly around the fringes of the old city, with those of the fourth century B.C. and after generally farthest away from the center of town. Cremation, the rite used in the tophet, became very common in these later tombs.[28]

But none of the normal graveyards has sparked the morbid fascination or controversy of the Tophet of Carthage. The formal, ritualized execution of children is so repulsive to us that it frequently prevents us from trying to understand that it was not ever intended as an act of cruelty but rather quite the opposite. And tophet excavator Stager has a sharp word of advice for those too quick to criticize:

> From a comparative cultural perspective, child sacrifice or ritual infanticide, is simply a special form of infanticide. The "noninstitutionalized" form has appeared in Graeco-Roman society and in the Christian West with more regularity than we usually are comfortable in admitting. Unwanted or abandoned children have been subjected to exposure, drowning, starvation, strangulation, smothering, and poisoning, but the most common and lethal way of disposing of unwanted children has been simply neglect.[29]

In the ancient Mediterranean, although human sacrifice never became institutionalized outside of the Canaanite-Phoenician-Punic orbit, it is still true that the Mycenean-Greek king Agamemnon was supposed to have offered his own daughter to speed up the Trojan War campaign, and in the Bible Abraham was certainly willing to sacrifice Isaac, until a ram was substituted at the last minute. The Romans too were more than eager to bury impious vestal virgins alive to appease the gods and actually practiced human sacrifice—a most un-Roman rite—on a number of occasions to ward off Hannibal during the Second Punic War! Did they do this to emulate the Punic practice, fearing that their own gods and practices were not able to save the situation for them? The Carthaginians may be judged guilty by modern society but it must only be because of their apparent frequent use of the rite and their institutionalizing of it, not because they were the only ones doing it.

The rite of child sacrifice died hard in ancient Tunisia. Christian author Tertullian, a Libyan who had spent most of his life in Carthage, reported around A.D. 200 that "to this day that holy crime persists in secret" and that, despite Roman efforts to stamp it out, it continued "quite openly, down to the proconsulship of Tiberius, who took the priests themselves and on the very trees of their temple, under whose shadow their crimes had been committed, hung them alive like votive offerings on crosses."[30]

Neo-Punic votive stele from the 1980 excavations at Maktar, featuring a man holding a twisted caduceus and a fruit (?). It is inscribed: "Offering from Ba'al Sama, son of MKGM to Ba'al Hammon; he has blessed him and heard his voice."

As late as the fourth century A.D., ritual sacrifice (which had changed from MLK to *molchomor* in Latin) of animals to Ba'al Hammon (now called Saturn) still continued in the Tunisian hinterland at a time when Christianity had overtaken Rome's gods in importance. On a *stele* from Beja in northwestern Tunisia, a stylized and bearded Ba'al Hammon/Saturn still holds his sickle, symbol of power over the harvest, and his solar disk appears at his right shoulder.[31] Beneath the god's feet a worshiper leads a ram to an altar laden with fruit. On November 8, A.D. 323, the dedicating priest "with heartfelt joy, has fulfilled the vow that he had promised to execute." But that is the last gasp for Ba'al Hammon /Saturn, whose Carthaginian home had long since given way to a Roman cistern.

Henceforward the tophet of Carthage and its rite of MLK or *moloch* would become the stuff of half-remembered romantic fantasy, a dream sequence in Fritz Lang's *Metropolis* or an epic re-creation in a quasi-historical novel by Gustave Flaubert. But the true story may never be fully known.

❦ VII ❦

International Metropolis

ISTORY HAS NOT been kind to the Carthaginians. The esteemed Senior Lecturer in Classics and Ancient History at the University of London, Brian Caven, wrote as recently as 1980:

> The Carthaginians were hardly an attractive people. They did not have it in them to be the standard bearers of a higher civilization. Selfish, parasitic, money-grubbing, corrupt, and when it cost them nothing, oppressive, they could never have provided the means by which all that was best in Hellenic culture, supplemented and reinforced by what was best in their own, could be disseminated over so much of Europe, Asia and Africa itself, providing the foundation for the far loftier moral edifice of Christendom.[1]

While statements like this are legion and nobody can argue from the surviving remains that Carthage surpassed Athens in elegance, the evidence continues to mount that the Punic metropolis was quite a civilized, cosmopolitan and possibly even aesthetically pleasant place to live. The agora, or forum area, was just northwest of the ports in the fourth century B.C., but we have no record of what it looked like except that it was surrounded by high buildings. In fact, the center of Carthage up to the slopes of the Byrsa Hill seems to have been densely packed with high rises, some of them allegedly reaching six stories during the Hellenistic period.[2]

Carthage included an area of over seven square miles which was protected to the north, east and southeast by the sea and a defensive wall. Some traces of the wall, built perhaps in the early fifth century B.C., have actually been found one kilometer north of the ports in the exemplary German excavations of Professor Rakob of the German Archaeological Institute in Rome.[3] It stretched about five kilometers and featured sandstone boulders and rectangular towers.

The vulnerable westward side of Carthage was turned into a virtually impenetrable series of ditches, parapets and walls, stretching from the northern seafront to the southern. The major wall was said to have been some forty-five feet high, with towers every two hundred feet and lofty battlements as well. There were stables inside for keeping hundreds of battle elephants and thousands of horses, while barracks lodged Punic and mercenary soldiers. It has been calculated that altogether more than twenty-one miles of walls protected Carthage, but to the southwest the city's defenses posed a serious problem.

Although most of that area was surrounded by water, there was a three-hundred-foot-wide sandbar (called the *taenia* by the Greeks) in front of the city wall near the tophet and commercial harbor. For some reason the Carthaginian defenders didn't feel this area was particularly vulnerable, and here only a single wall separated the city from the Roman menace in the Third Punic War.

It was exactly at this area that several Roman commanders hammered away. Scipio Aemilianus blockaded the city, building his own ditch and wall against the westward defenses, and then moving in massive amounts of sand to construct a mole on the troubled southwest side. He pursued his attack on this weak link relentlessly, until his sixteen-year-old cousin, Tiberius Sempronius Gracchus, became the first of a sea of Romans over the wall and into the city. Once inside the Romans, with the ever-observant historian Polybius present, headed towards the Byrsa, allowing us a chance to learn something of the layout of the city they encountered on their fiery way.[4]

Between the wall and the commercial docks there was a residential area with bustling narrow streets that was torched by the Punic commander defending the city; in the ensuing chaos the fighting was slowed down, and the Romans could not reach the agora until nightfall. The zone well north of the harbor and agora may have been what was called the New City. We do not know just where the old city was located, although recent discoveries by German and Tunisian archaeologists show that the settlement of the seventh century B.C. should lie about one kilometer northeast of the ports between the coast and the Byrsa. No doubt there was originally some kind of simple port facility arranged for this region. Perhaps the settlement of the ninth and eighth centuries was limited to the Byrsa itself.

In any case, when the Roman soldiers of 146 B.C. continued on their march to the Byrsa, they saw the magnificent temple of Apollo (probably the Punic Reshef) and its gold treasures, and they were seized by a desire to loot and destroy. But northwest of the agora the going got slow where three streets crammed with tall apartment houses lined the slopes of the Byrsa. Facing stiff resistance, the Romans were forced to storm one building after another, set countless fires and go from house to house by laying planks from roof to roof. It took six days to clear enough of an area to bring in siege engines to batter down the Byrsa's ring wall.

The city became a burned-out shell of its former self, and among the buildings on the Byrsa forever lost to us was the fabulous Temple of Eshmoun, with its sixty steps leading to the summit. It was destroyed not only by Scipio's torch but also by massive Roman terracing walls installed 150 years later, when the Byrsa was shaved down and reused as the center of the Roman city.

With the heart of Punic Carthage destroyed, excavators have generally found only slim pickings, but the French archaeologist Serge Lancel, studying and continuing earlier French excavations on the southern slope of the Byrsa, found major new evidence of a thriving residential and commercial district of the time of Hannibal, after the Second Punic War. Although their drainage system leaves a lot to be desired, the early-second-century-B.C. houses are sturdily made, certainly contained multiple stories and were placed in a carefully and regularly planned series of city blocks called *insulae* by the Romans.[5] Shops included what seemed to be a goldsmith's establishment and a Pompeii-style bakery complex complete with a large hourglass-shaped turning mill to produce fresh bread for the district.

Many of the houses were of a type which can also be seen at the better-preserved Punic city of Kerkouane on Cape Bon, established in the sixth century B.C. but destroyed by a Roman foray of the First Punic War.[6] There was an entrance corridor with an open drain running down it to the street. A courtyard was quickly reached, while three or four small rooms opened out from the court. The large cisterns under the courtyards of the Carthage houses suggest that these buildings were multistory dwellings designed to house lots of people, an impression one does not get at Kerkouane.

At both sites one sees the famous *pavimenta punica* for house floors, a mortar foundation sprinkled with potsherds, cut squares of ceramic and/or small cubes (*tesserae*) of marble. Floor fragments found in a fourth-century-B.C. house near the theater of Carthage by the Tunisian archaeologist Fethi Chelbi show cut *tesserae* of ceramic and marble, apparently the earliest examples known of true mosaic technique (as opposed to floors made with pebbles) in the history of the Mediterranean.[7] The German team found more examples at their site and this poses a difficult question: did the Carthaginians, those so-called parasites with no creative aesthetic sense, actually invent the mosaic art form? It may indeed be so, although one can argue that they did not do much with it. Instead of covering their floors with beautiful figures like the Greeks did, they barely managed to produce a sign of Tanit in mosaic on a floor in a Semitic-style temple at Kerkouane.

But Kerkouane has a few surprises of its own. The excavator, former I.N.A.A. director Mhamed Fantar, found that in many houses the courtyards were fitted out with charming little sinks and bathtubs. These hipbaths contain both a seat and a lower area in which to put your feet. They seem too small to accommodate most modern adults, but one must recall that ancient Carthaginian men probably were not much taller than five feet and the women less than that.

In the German excavation Professor Rakob also found housing and considerable evidence of gridded city blocks going back to the fifth century, as well as some rather elegant houses with porticoed court-yards from the second century B.C. These latter recall Greek houses on the island of Delos but are not quite so fancy. The early second century was supposedly a time when a defeated Carthage was in decline, but we know that this was not the case. No wonder Cato was so shocked to visit Carthage then and find that it wasn't at all in eclipse.

Back on the southeast slopes of the Byrsa, Lancel found abundant evidence of a metalworking district that feverishly produced materials in iron and copper alloy during the Punic wars. On the southwest slopes, French archaeologists have uncovered large numbers of burials and tombs. By far the most fascinating discovery was a series of simple burials found over an area of one hundred square meters. Hundreds of skeletons laid out side by side were found by the archaeologist R.P. Delattre shortly before the turn of the century. These were not normal interments, and one thinks immediately of the epidemics that continually ravaged the Carthaginian ranks at home or abroad. These and other finds suggested that this particular disaster occurred early in the second century B.C.

The cemeteries of Carthage have been the focus of enormous archaeological interest for over a century, but the excavations have often been unscientific, haphazard and uncoordinated. In 1982 the French scholar Hélène Benichou-Safar bravely collected all the scattered evidence and published a detailed guide to tomb types, locations of each necropolis, when possible, and types of objects found, all of which yielded important conclusions.

First of all, it seemed a likely assumption that the Carthaginians, like the Romans, preferred to bury their dead just outside of town, and Benichou-Safar's guide produced evidence of a ring of graveyards encircling the Punic city in the seventh and sixth centuries B.C. Starting from the tophet itself, early tombs were found well southwest of the Byrsa as well as along the southwest and east slopes of the hill.

Continuing northeast, more early tombs occupied the southwest flank of the Hill of Juno, then continued east from there across what is now the electric tramway, occupying the flatter areas of Douimès, Dermech and Ard Et-Touibi, and stopping at the ancient coastline. The ring thus formed neatly enveloped the supposed site of the new city forum and also embraced the seventh- and sixth-century vestiges still to be probed north of the ports, east of the Byrsa and south of Ard Et-Touibi.

Later, in the fifth and fourth centuries B.C., the cemeteries expanded northward to the hill on which the much later Roman theater sits and east to the area known today as Ancona. In the fourth through second centuries B.C., more cemeteries appeared to the northeast on the hill by the Roman odeon, and east to Dahar El Morali, Bou-Mnigel and Bordj-Djedid, while even farther away, on the hill of Sainte Monique, some tombs from the fifth through second centuries B.C. are among the most aristocratic yet found.

Although child sacrifice was practiced in the tophet, cremation with burial in ceramic urns or stone ossuaries (small containers for bones) was always a minor rite at Carthage and in Phoenicia; the citizens preferred to bury their dead intact (inhumation), often in

well-like shafts with chambers at the bottom or sides. While the tombs
were occasionally stately and reached by a stepped entry passage
(*dromos*), they were never extraordinarily ornate or overelaborate.

However, in the hinterland at sites like Dougga, lofty tower
tombs celebrated Libyan rulers on a grand scale, often using Punic
architects.[8] There a Liby-Phoenician mausoleum dates from the time
of the hegemony of the Berber leader Masinissa and his sons (the first
half of the second century B.C. or just after). The architect signed his
name as Ateban, son of Iepmatath, in Libyco-Punic script, but the
three-story monument features Egyptian cornices and Greco-Roman
Ionic columns, with a regal lion on top, suggesting connections with
the royal family. It is with this sort of syncretization, this fusing
together of the beliefs and cultures with which the Carthaginians were
in contact, that Punic artistic capabilities occasionally break through
and create a form with its own unique identity. At its worst, Carthaginian art could be a pale imitation of the works of other Mediterranean cultures on their trading routes.

From the seventh- and sixth-century-B.C. tombs came a wealth of
artifacts of considerable interest, but by anyone's standards, including
the archaeologists who work the sites, Punic pottery is pretty awful.
David Soren, who worked Roman sites in Tunisia for years without
incident, was seriously affected by the touch of the coarse, sandy, Punic
clay fabric. During the tophet excavations of the 1970s, whenever
project director Lawrence Stager sought verification that a questionable shard was truly Punic, one almost fail-safe technique was to rub
it vigorously on Soren's arm and wait to see if a rash appeared. At a time
when the Etruscans were producing the sublime bucchero wares, the
Corinthians issuing ceramic with orientalizing ornament and exotic
animals, and the Athenians developing black-figured vases, the Punic
potters ground out irritating, coarse ware.[9]

In the early tombs of Carthage, the funerary offerings were generally modest and included everyday objects that had brought the
deceased pleasure in life and would help guide the spirit after death.
There were pouring vessels called *oenochoes,* sometimes with a triple
spout and sometimes with flat rims and/or bulging flat neck disks too.
There were little plates and cups, small casserole-type containers
known as *marmites,* and simple jars and amphorae with reddish and
sometimes black painted horizontal bands and occasional vertical
slashes. Incense burners and open-bodied lamps with two spouts sat
on small stands.

There were also imports, as one might expect, especially in the early period, when much that was of note was brought in. The Etruscan bucchero was well known, along with Corinthian cups called *kotyles* and perfume jars. And Egyptian influence was particularly strong, with scarabs cut from stones like jasper and frequently used as amulets.[10]

Due to a widespread belief in the power of magic and the need to protect the dead from harm, much attention was paid to the use of such apotropaics (devices to ward off evil spirits). Among the most dynamic examples are a series of unforgettable grimacing male masks of what many scholars think are demons, functioning like sardonically grinning gorgons to keep away would-be desecrators.[11]

These masks are among the most characteristic manifestations of Phoenician and Punic art around the Mediterranean. The fact that they have apertures where the eyes and sometimes the mouth should be suggests that they might actually be worn either during religious ceremonies relating to the dead or, perhaps, symbolically by the deceased to frighten away evil.

Apotropaic grimacing mask from Dermech Necropolis of Carthage. The facial grooves may represent entrails and are found on Mesopotamian images of the monster herdsman Humbaba as well as on certain Greek images of the Gorgon. Punic, circa 500 B.C.

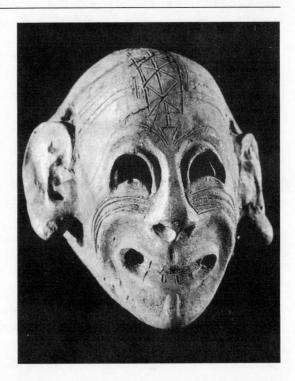

Often the early masks exhibit a process known as scarification, where parts of the face, usually the forehead and cheeks, are scored or grooved in a frightening manner reminiscent of the furrowed imagery of the Mesopotamian demon Humbaba celebrated in the *Epic of Gilgamesh*. According to Pierre Cintas, who catalogued many examples, the masks sometimes have Negroid features and can also have holes left for the inlay of glass or precious stones. The bald top of the head and the forehead are sometimes used for elaborate signs in raised relief such as the solar disk and crescent moon.

The masks became less popular in the later sixth century B.C., but heads, which were more sculptural in form and without apertures, became popular. Known as *protomes,* they could be male or female and were seldom grotesque demons. Instead, they often showed the burgeoning influence of Archaic Greek art and could be images of Dionysus' companion Silenus (Seilenos) or a big-eared, sweetly smiling woman.

Faces were also frequently painted onto ostrich eggs, a Phoenician practice popular before it reached Carthage.[12] It is widely believed that the eggs may have been intended to have a twofold purpose—as an apotropaic and as a symbol of rebirth into a new life. The eggshells with painted faces were common offerings throughout the lifespan of Punic Carthage; the early examples were characterized by large, red-brown, almond-shaped eyes. The shells were occasionally cut to use as receptacles in the tomb.

In addition, a broad range of rod-formed glass head pendants used as amulets appear frequently as offerings from the seventh century B.C.[13] They were made from blobs of hot glass placed on the tip of metal rods with separately added blobs for the details.

But the most fascinating of tomb objects are the so-called sacred razors, made of copper alloy and sometimes thought to be hatchets.[14] They first become frequent in the sixth century B.C., but by the time Carthage hit its stride in the fourth century they had become distinctive, impressive works of art. In the finest examples the form is that of a flaring sharp blade with an almost rectangular body and a handle or finial elegantly fashioned into the neck and head of a swan or ibis, sometimes with glass beads for the eyes. This shape is among the most pleasing made in the numerous Carthaginian metalwork shops, and the flat body is adorned with a rich variety of incised scenes, which range from the apparently decorative to the mystical and religious.

The swan's feathers and/or wings are usually shown and there is a projecting hanging ring. On one poignant example a seated woman is shown with distaff and spindle, just as in life she might have passed much of her day, and facing her are the traditional Punic protective symbols of the disk and crescent. In the register below her is a half-empty throne or funeral bed, an altar and a candelabrum. Has she left the bed and been resurrected into another world or is this an empty throne symbolizing the presence of the unseen divinity? We cannot know for sure, but we are not unmoved.

The sense of solemn piety continues on the reverse with another disk and crescent and beneath them an altar, on which rests an *oenochoe* such as is found frequently in the tombs. Beneath the altar is a *hydria,* or water-carrying vessel.

Normally found in the tombs of Carthage and other Punic sites, these implements are now widely believed to have been used as razors to shave the deceased, perhaps in preparation for the world to come, but this interpretation is not universally accepted. They may exemplify a cult which was not Phoenician at all, but rather one that developed specifically in Carthage. It is also possible that the objects themselves took on a magical value as *sacra punica,* useful as a symbol of piety or as an apotropaic.

Again, the scenes represent a typical intermingling of Greek, Phoenician and Egyptian themes. The frequent use of animals may be decorative, or the animals themselves may have magical meanings, which would account for their great popularity. With these sacred razors the artists of Carthage show a desire to produce varied and sometimes unusual scenes, which are influenced by but often break away from prototypes in Egypt, Greece or the Near East. They are among the most original examples of Punic art.

Another area where Punic art can make a strong claim for excellence is metalworking, and the famous mini-room of Punic jewelry in the Bardo Museum is a consistent crowd-pleaser. Magnificent necklaces of many different elements and materials have been found at Kerkouane and Carthage. Superb tiny circular and rectangular gold boxes decorated in filigree and granulation were worn as elements of the necklace. Popular decorations included rosettes and the eye of Horus, known traditionally as the *oudja.*

This symbol, Egyptian in origin, was one of the most common and enduring in the tombs and Tophet of Carthage, doing yeoman's service as the amulet par excellence of the Punic people.[15] It features an eye and eyebrow with a linear feature and a sort of volute below. The eye possessed magic properties, and each part of it was intended to be made according to a particular mathematical formula that would ultimately help the dead achieve a desirable afterlife.

Necklaces included other protective elements such as scarabs of faience, jade or jasper, and *oudja* images in bone or faience. There were often also beads of carnelian, gold, faience, lapis, silver and glass, and these could assume various forms ranging from geometric cones to fir cones. While the gold and yellow boxes remained a staple of the finer necklaces for several centuries, elegant stones such as hyacinth and turquoise in a gold setting were occasionally used to create a stunning disk and crescent motif.

Exceptionally fine jewelry was typical of the seventh through fourth century B.C., although it is only recently that excavations at Carthage have been able to provide substantial information about the fifth century.[16] The apparent falloff in imports after the disaster of Himera had made fifth-century levels hard to distinguish, until the German excavations of Rakob established the period as one of surprising expansion and concentrated building. Rakob's new finds fit well with the notion that the Carthaginian explorers Hanno and Himilco did indeed accomplish their missions at this time.

The detail work on many gold earrings and pendants is frequently of the highest quality, showing a technique often associated with Etruria but also with a fondness for Egyptian subject matter, including the *uraeus* or divine cobra, which could spit fire in order to protect its wearer. Another popular image was the winged solar disk, emblem of Horus and one of many protective winged images. Gold rings from the sixth century B.C. show strong Archaic Greek influence as well. Dozens of the handsome gilt copper earrings have been found at Kerkouane alone. The large numbers of examples of goldwork of high quality and individuality attest that this was a major industry in Carthage, revealing a strong sensitivity to the need for attractive art and good craftsmanship, which critics of Punic art have been strongly reluctant to acknowledge.

Not all the goldwork is top-notch, but it is usually interesting. Take, for example, a gold amulet carrier of the fifth or fourth century B.C. from the necropolis of Kerkouane. It is an image of a standing Sekhmet, the lion-headed Egyptian solar goddess and ally of the

popular protective deity Ptah. The goddess, who was noted for ward-
ing off disease and illness, has the *uraeus* on her head.[17]

What makes this work unusual is that it shows the entire goddess,
which no other amulet carrier does. Furthermore, she is allowed to
hold ivy leaves, which have actually been inlaid in green glass, but these
are symbols of the Greek god Dionysus, whose cult was just beginning
to influence Carthage. Her normal attribute, the sceptre, is absent.
While the workmanship is decidedly not first-rate, the piece rates an
A-plus for inventiveness, fusing Greek and Egyptian ideas into something attractive and unique.

Throughout the tombs of Carthage many ritual objects of limited
artistic value occur in profusion. There are mirrors of copper alloy with
bone handles for the deceased to have close at hand while preparing for
the afterlife. Traces of ancient lyres and cymbals survive, which might
have provided music for the dead and/or made noise to frighten off
evil. The tiny bells often found probably served this same function.
Women's tombs abounded in hairpins, makeup boxes, perfume containers and cosmetic applicators.

In the tombs are also countless tiny faience amulets, primarily with
Egyptian protective divinities or signs.[18] They were simply made, but
their presence was obviously considered extremely important. Ptah, as
the master craftsman who brought forth everything, was especially
popular and he is frequently shown as a chunky dwarf standing on
crocodiles while falcons perch on his shoulder. The falcon occurs as the
symbol of the sky god Horus, with or without a double crown, while
Bastet, the cat goddess, also puts in cameo appearances to ward off evil.
Another curious dwarf god is Bes, usually shown with a big bearded
head and a protruding tongue, which the Greeks later borrowed for
their own gorgon. Sometimes shown in an excited, ithyphallic state,
Bes was a frequent good-luck charm.

In ceramics there were charming, almost comical baby feeding
bottles known as *biberons,* which often bore the protective sign of
Tanit. They were made into faces with the sucking nipple turned into
a nose flanked by two big painted eyes. It has been a point of contention
among scholars whether or not Carthaginians who could make works
like the *biberons*[19] had any sense of humor when they weren't busy
being parasitic and money-grubbing. Hannibal was supposedly quite
amusing at times. When a lieutenant named Gisco complained before
a battle of the large numbers of Romans to be fought, Hannibal is said

to have replied: "And not a one of them is named Gisco." It may not be sparkling comedy but it is something, as is a delightful imported clay-pouring vessel from South Italy or Sicily in the form of a mouse or shrew, which looks like a modern piggy bank.

Another import, perhaps from Alexandria, is a molded clay lamp of a bearded human head, which suddenly turns into a frog when inverted.[20] Its findspot in a tomb suggests it may have a religious significance, but tourists who buy ceramic copies of it today simply find it a funny conversation piece. Of course the tombs are hardly the place to discover abundant evidence of Carthaginian humor, so it is surprising to find a number of examples of such grace and wit, even though admittedly many were imports.

Much has been made of the lack of quality sculpture in ancient Carthage, but a look at the Sainte Monique hill necropolis, where elegant chamber tombs of the later Classical and Hellenistic periods can be seen, reveals sarcophagi and ossuaries of considerable artistic sophistication.[21] Many of them have gabled lids of the so-called anthropoid type, depicting human figures in the supple, sensitive forms of Greek art, complete with Hellenic ancillary decoration for the moldings. Some preserve their bright painted colors, and on one we see a Scylla, the terrible sea monster and wrecker of ships, shown with old-fashioned (archaistic) sickle-shaped wings. A number of scholars have raised the possibility that these sculptures were made by Greek artists living in Carthage. Yet there is a decidedly non-Greek, international style about some of them. For example, a female figure lies on her back on the lid of a handsome gabled sarcophagus. Her solemn, dispassionate face and the treatment of the folds of her robe, or *peplos,* linking the breasts with catenaries or chains of drapery, appear Greek, but the coiffure and the large vulture wings which enclose her body belong to the Egyptian sphere, reminding us of Isis or Nephthys, divinities known in Carthage on rings and seals.

The woman, whoever she is, is actually lying on a bird, whose countenance appears above her head and whose wings wrap her in a protective grip. Susan Levy of the New Orleans Museum has pointed out that protective bird gods are well documented in Egypt, the image of the falcon of Horus often appearing as a protector standing behind the sculpture of a pharaoh such as Rameses. Our mysterious lady (is she Isis, Nephthys, a priestess or even Tanit?) holds a cup as an offering in her left hand and a dove in her right. The midriff and upper body are

Punic "Priestess" Sarcophagus from the cemetery of the Rabs, Sainte-Monique Hill, Carthage. Probably Punic or Sicilian, third century B.C.

treated with a simplification and stylization of the folds that has strong parallels in Syracusan art of the later fourth century B.C. The emphasis on the classical head and the treatment of the upper body make one think of similar Etruscan reclining figure sarcophagi from Tarquinia and Cerveteri.

Writer Mabel Moore was present when Delattre was working the necropolis at the turn of the century, and she made an observation about the priestess sarcophagus, which was then put on exhibit in the Carthage Museum. Her comments, recorded in the book *Carthage of the Phoenicians,* still ring true today:

It is easy to understand how so many visitors, on leaving the
hall of the Museum where she has been placed, after having
gazed at this sweet priestess for a long time, cannot refrain from
turning one last admiring glance towards her before they pass
through the door.[22]

The body in the sarcophagus had been disturbed, but careful study at
the time showed it was embalmed with terebinth resin and placed in
state with the traditional bronze coins on her body. It was a woman,
apparently an old one, possibly with Negroid features. Was this the
priestess shown on the lid? No one can say for sure.

Other anthropoid sarcophagi and ossuaries of fine white marble
from the same cemetery exhibit similar artistic ambiguities. Some are
so closely modelled on Hellenic formulae that they seem to be of
Sicilian-Greek manufacture, but many, like the priestess, are unset-
tling, unique mixtures of Hellenistic Greek, Egyptian, Etruscan and/
or Phoenician influences. It is a sort of koine style, a fascinating
mishmash produced by competent artisans—but from where?

The marble has been variously identified as Sicilian and Greek
Island, but did Punic patrons, perhaps from an official cult, specify
what was needed and have the carvings done abroad, or was it a Greek
or Greek-trained Punic artist working at an atelier in Carthage? With
a hybrid society like this it is often hard to know.

Punic coinage developed surprisingly late, for the Phoenician
people were more accustomed to the barter system described by
Herodotus.[23] Still, coins offered another trading option, and by the
later fifth century B.C., Carthage, as well as the Punic cities of Panormus and Motya on Sicily, was issuing coins. Of course the Lydian
people of Anatolia had been issuing coins since early in the seventh
century B.C., as had Greek centers like Athens and Aegina.

Carthage borrowed the look of its coins—a female head on the
obverse and a galloping or standing horse on the reverse—from Greek-
Sicilian examples, most notably those of Syracuse. The early silver
issues were even done on the Syracusan (or Euboean-Attic) weight
standard. But the gold issues, which became increasingly popular in the
fourth century B.C., used the Phoenician standard, which was quite
different. It now seems that most of the coinage of Carthage followed
this standard; coins were ultimately issued in gold, silver, electrum (a
light yellow alloy of gold and silver) and copper alloy (commonly

referred to as bronze). The coins show a remarkable unity of type with only occasional radical departures from the Greek-styled norm.

The identity of the female head on the coin remains controversial. She may be Kore or Persephone, the daughter of the vegetation goddess Demeter, whose cult had been introduced into Carthage about 396 B.C. (On some coins sprigs of wheat, her symbol, appear as a crown.) This unprecedented official admission to Carthage of a Hellenic divinity occurred, as we have seen, when the Punic army, about to bring Syracuse to its knees in 397 B.C., was devastated by a disease that was assumed to have resulted from the desecration of the Sicilian temples of the goddesses. A new temple to Demeter, renowned for its statues and gold and silver work, was hastily built in Carthage. Ceramic incense burners in the form of a Demeter head with a *polos* or high projecting crown, sometimes adorned with ears of corn, became a popular item in the Hellenistic tombs.

An especially attractive series designed for the Sicilian market shows the female head surrounded by swimming dolphins with a horse head on the reverse. The dolphin and female head are blatant borrowings from the famous tetradrachms of Carthage's great rival Syracuse, where the female is Arethusa, the legendary nymph of the island of Ortygia, whose lovely fountain was the pride of the city. But who then is supposed to be represented on the Carthaginian coin? It can hardly be Arethusa, who meant nothing to the Punic people.

Could it be intended as a new image of Demeter? But why should Demeter or Kore be so popular and pervasive on the coins? Had they taken over the Carthaginian pantheon completely? A wiser guess may be that the goddess was Tanit, known from the tophet to have emerged as a super-goddess. Since there was no tradition of depicting her, a beautiful Hellenic image might have been thought to serve nicely. The Punic people could see it as their own goddess personified, while Sicilians or foreign clients would note the similarity in look, weight and design to the coins of Syracuse and would think that the coin itself was equal in value to the well-known and valuable Syracusan Arethusa tetradrachm. This interpretation is not without its own problems, and some scholars have seen the female head as intended to represent queen Dido herself. Illegal coin-hawkers in Carthage today still confront tourists with that opinion.

Even from this brief survey of some of the artistic production associated with Carthage, it can be argued that in architecture, jewelry, metalworking, terra-cotta ware and possibly stone sculpture, Carthage generated an attractive and hybrid art. It is a little difficult to see why scholars have made such a point of attacking the aesthetic sensibilities of the Punic people.

A typical comment is the one made by the French art historian Max-Pol Fouchet in his *L'Art à Carthage*: "As regards artistic creation, the historians refuse to grant Carthage any true genius or to see a personal talent. They are unanimous. Punic art belongs to archaeology, not aesthetics."[24]

But such a statement fails to take into consideration the cosmopolitan, international nature of the Punic metropolis or the religious convictions of its people. Carthage was a port city bustling with deeply felt influences. First there was the Phoenician motherland, itself a mélange of partially digested Near Eastern styles and noted for superb craftsmanship in architecture, minor art and shipbuilding. Tyre was, as we have seen, a jewel of the Near East, and it would almost certainly be wrong to believe that Carthage, with its own temples and spectacular port, ignored its heritage in an overwhelming desire to become a grubby backwater.

The influence of Egypt went back to the Phoenician and even Canaanite periods, and those contacts were never lost. The major and magical Egyptian divinities were as well known in Carthage as the Phoenician gods. Add to this the Punic propensity for allowing intermarriage with other peoples in the Punic orbit, such as the Iberians, and the overwhelming use of foreign-born or native African mercenaries for the Punic military, and one can appreciate the degree of cross-fertilization that took place in Carthaginian life from early times. From the Libyans came the dyeing of bodies, extensive tattooing, the popularity of a great mother goddess and fascinating styles of hair and dress. Liby-Phoenicians became colonists, worked the farms and plied the trade routes, spreading the syncretized culture to the ends of the known world.

Carthage was also seduced by Hellenic art, both from mainland Greece (with centers like Corinth and Athens) and from the Greek colonies of Sicily. There were strong Etruscan connections too, at least for a while, which brought in fine pottery, sculpted sarcophagi and jewelry-making techniques. So it is not surprising that this trading society produced an art that reflected all the places on its trade routes. What other kind of art could it have produced? Unlike Egypt with its strong sense of place, Carthage was a compendium of everywhere it had been.

It may be argued that if Carthage did have a great art, then why are its tombs so drab? But, with few exceptions, it was not in the necropolis that great religious art would be found. The Carthaginians seldom showed their gods; instead they were an aniconic society, preferring to symbolize their divinities with crescents, disks, triangles, circles, pillars and the like. For the most part, lively Etruscan or stately Greek-style tomb paintings were not their style. The seriousness of their piety even seems to have led them to the sacrifice of their own young long after the practice had been discontinued in the motherland. The tomb was, in general, a place of austerity.

But even from the tombs it is possible to realize that these were people who took pride in beauty. Women used abundant makeup and perfumes. Jewelry could be exceptionally lovely, with distinctive, exquisite necklaces, bracelets, rings and amulet carriers. Regrettably, the famous carpets of Carthage all lost to us, and the extraordinary temples with their sculptures and gold were utterly demolished by the Romans.

Carthage, as we have seen, may have used mosaics for the first time too and had substantial wall mortars well in advance of the

Glass mask amulets from the necropolises of Carthage. Circa 350 to 300 B.C.

Romans, who were supposed to have developed them. They also delighted in agricultural techniques such as grafting seemingly long before it was common practice. The Roman writer Pliny noted that a special substance know as Punic wax, known for its purity and its ability to mix with nitre (potassium nitrate, a crystalline salt preservative) and oil, was extremely popular in Rome for the process known as *ganosis,* by which painted statues or walls could be lacquered and preserved. The fortifications of Carthage, only now starting to emerge, are among the most sophisticated of any contemporary city in the Mediterranean.

It therefore seems odd that so many scholars seek to criticize a totally international-minded culture for not being more single-minded about its art. People with a strong sense of their own place tend to produce art that has distinctive style as well as important content. An eclectic society produces hybrid art, but it is a modern value judgment to call it bad art and to criticize it because it did not directly influence other art in other places. The Carthaginians influenced art in other places by directly transmitting the artistic styles of the Mediterranean from one place to another. What could be more influential?

The reputation of the Carthaginians has suffered severely at the hands of the Roman writers. Not only was their city razed into oblivion and thoroughly looted, but their memory was blasted to bits as well. They became, according to Herodotus and Livy, "treaty breakers," "rabble," "cruel and ferocious by nature and custom."

Their practice of human sacrifice, the result of supreme religious piety, so horrified ancient and modern minds that it has made a reassessment of their character and art difficult. The image of the Carthaginians as disreputable, scruffy peddlers needs revision. It is hard to excavate their soil or read of their technical accomplishments and conclude that they were heartless and artless. There is no doubt that many a Punic trader put a fast one over on a less quick-thinking foreigner, but Carthaginian art, or at least that which is left to us in Carthage or survives in other Punic communities in Tunisia and abroad, does at its best most certainly reveal a sophisticated aesthetic sensibility.

VIII

Roman Dawn

THE DRAMATIC FALL of Carthage in 146 B.C. put an end to one of the most glorious episodes in the ancient history of Tunisia. From the time when the Phoenicians had fixed their sights on the banks of which Virgil had sung, Carthage had blossomed into a major power disputing with the Greeks and Romans the hegemony of the Mediterranean. But the three Punic wars had destroyed the heart of the Punic empire, and Carthage was now no more than a vast, dismal field of ruins.

However, the great city was not to remain dead forever; it still had a major role to play in Tunisian history and in the political, cultural and economic life of the ancient world. Now Rome had become the most powerful state in the world, and Carthage, along with its dependencies, was nothing more than a simple province, integrated into a vast and little-understood foreign empire. The uniting of these two great civilizations, even though it was obtained by force, could not help but produce a fascinating hybrid culture in which old and new ideas came together in fascinating ways.

The Punic territory which Rome annexed in 146 B.C. was, despite all the fighting, not very extensive, covering only about sixteen thousand square miles. This was because the original land holdings of Carthage had been steadily shrunk as a result of the relentless attacks of the king of the Numidian Massyles, the feared Masinissa. This Berber *mas*, molding his nomads and farmers into a powerful coalition and striking force, terrorized and then overran the major part of Punic territory and left the Carthaginians with only the northeastern area of what is now Tunisia, along with a thin coastal band running from the Gulf of Tunis to the Gulf of Gabes (about one sixth of the area of the modern country).[1]

After the Roman takeover, Scipio Aemilianus, the hero of the Third Punic War, supervised the digging of an enormous protective border area known as the *fossa regia* (royal ditch), which was to mark out the precise limits of the new province of Africa. The ditch served as a notice to the successors of Masinissa that this area was a domain belonging exclusively to the people of Rome (*ager publicus populi romani*).[2]

The Romans, who found themselves lords of all the properties within the *fossa,* whether Punic or Berber, had the wisdom in most cases to allow the original owners, whether they were individuals or members of tribal collectives, to continue to work their own land. In exchange they exacted a rent or tax, known as a *stipendium,* and levied a personal tax on all natives of the area (the *capitatio,* or head tax).

To make sure that all of this money was rounded up and that the confiscated lands would be awarded to new Roman or friendly native settlers, the entire territory was carefully surveyed by architects and divided up into square lots measuring about twenty-five hundred feet on each side. Each of these contained about fifty hectares (a hectare is equal to about two and one half acres) and was known as a century, or *centuria.*[3]

The time-consuming process of physically marking the available farm and settlement lands of the province of Africa illustrated the determination and thoroughness of the Romans in putting a vast area in order; the chessboard patterns of furrows made in the earth can still be seen in many areas of the country from low-flying aircraft. Tax gathering was administered efficiently by special groups made up largely of middle-class Romans of the equestrian order (*equites*).

The new province was governed by a proconsul, a high magistrate of noble family and a member of the Roman senate, and he was assisted by a number of high functionaries. There were various legates with special assignments, a *quaestor,* or paymaster, to look after financial problems, and numerous minor magistrates and assistants, who were for the most part young men of the best families just starting out in politics and in need of something to put on their respective resumes. Native communities were still regularly governed by *suffetes,* following the system established in Carthage in the Hellenistic period.[4]

It would be a mistake to think that the new Roman administration was interested primarily in the welfare of the conquered people of the province. Instead, it was designed to cast a benign and watchful eye over the exploitation of the resources of the various regions; often deals were cut with men of affairs to ensure that agricultural produce or real estate stayed under the control of a limited number of families. Three hundred powerful merchants and bankers made up the special council to the proconsul at Utica, recently promoted to capital of the fledgling province after the destruction of Carthage.

The first attempt at official Roman colonization of Carthage took place in 123 B.C., just twenty-three years after the conquest, in the middle of a social and political struggle that had racked Rome since the middle of the century, putting at odds the conservative Roman aristocracy and a partisan group of reformers, who were trying to distribute some of the conquered lands to the poor. The leader of the latter movement was the tribune and member of the agrarian commission Caius Gracchus, whose older brother had been murdered for espousing similar ideas.[5]

Caius was able to push through a number of laws securing the distribution of food to the impoverished and providing for the setting aside of lands for six thousand needy Roman and Latin settlers. But this enterprise, which was to center on Carthage, was stopped dead in its tracks by the conservative views and avarice of the aristocrats, who trumped up all sorts of fantastic charges against the tribune.

First, he was accused of committing sacrilege for attempting to establish a colony on cursed land. Next, it was said that the gods were showing their displeasure through mysterious portents. A standard relating to the new colony had been snatched up by the wind and torn apart. The entrails of victims prepared for sacrifice had been dispersed by a tempest and scattered outside the limits of the proposed new city. Milestones of the new community had been snatched up and deposited far away, supposedly by wolves. Even though these occurrences were probably the result of either patrician cunning or angry, dispossessed locals, the enterprise was successfully sabotaged.

Those lots of land already assigned were for the most part sold by the would-be settlers, who, not being legally sophisticated, were often swindled; the lots which had never been distributed were sold by auction and acquired by speculators, some of whom were either Romans or wealthy locals, usually of Punic ancestry. Within a few years the race for the accumulation of African land had begun to put a good number of non-Romans as well as Romans into positions of local power.

Although the Romans were slow to take advantage of the potential of the province and were often content to stay in the cities and let the locals do much of the dirty work of actually gathering taxes, managing estates and collecting produce, a gradual influx of entrepreneurs led to increasing Romanization of the province. One reason the Romans waited so long to move in was that the hinterland was still so wild and dangerous—Libyan tribes were always threatening to do something horrible.

One native chieftain who saw himself as the new Masinissa (and why not? he was Masinissa's grandson) was the Numidian *mas* Jugurtha.[6] Like his grandfather, he had been well trained in the Roman army, with no less a mentor than Scipio Aemilianus himself. While engaged in a life-and-death struggle with his brother for the throne, he attacked a Roman *conventus* (a trading organization of Italian businessmen) that was helping to defend the city of Cirta (now Constantine, in Algeria) against him. Such events sent shock waves through all the Roman trading communities of North Africa.

Although Jugurtha actually went to Rome under a safe conduct summons and pleaded his case in Latin with some eloquence, he was not favorably received; upon his return to Numidia war began in earnest. The Roman army, which had once again lapsed into a period of mediocre leadership and poor discipline, was taken by surprise in a number of engagements with the crafty leader, allowing him to carry out ferocious attacks against the Roman legions for years (112–107 B.C.). Finally the consul, Marius, was forced to resort to intrigue to bring him to justice in 105 B.C., and he was executed within a year.

Marius, the new leader of the common people (*populares*), looked for lands on which to settle his veterans of the North African campaigns, finally deciding on richly fertile spots along the Medjerda River valley, which could also serve as a front line to watch over the *fossa regia* of Scipio. Marius' beneficiaries also included Libyans, who had aided the Roman troops and were now rewarded with the privilege of Roman citizenship. Now, for the first time, Roman troops were drawn from the lowest levels of society, and the promise of a brighter future tended to make them more loyal to their general than to the state, a dangerous precedent that led to the rise of Roman demagogues in the next century.

Since racism did not, apparently, play as much of a role in Roman society then as it has (and sometimes still does) in America, intermarriage between a Libyan and a poor Roman was not uncommon. By 100 B.C. the province was beginning to people itself with poor Romans and Italians, hostile and Romanized Libyans, disenfranchised Carthaginians and enterprising Punic survivors, Roman merchants and speculators of the middle classes, and aristocratic high magistrates and land developers. It was quite a group, living in an area that was like an ancient version of the American Wild West, where the Libyans, like the Indians, often kept their distance and tried to cling to their ancestral traditions, rebelling and resisting when their life-style was disrupted.

The Romans had not yet figured out how to develop fully this fertile new prize. It was alien and dangerous, and yet potentially important. Members of the senate in Rome, unsure how to deal with it, at least knew it had to be kept out of the hands of enemies like, perhaps, the followers of Hannibal or Masinissa. As the historian Theodor Mommsen has said,

> The Romans held fast the territory which Carthage had
> possessed at its fall, but less in order to develop it for their
> own benefit than to prevent its benefiting others, not to
> awaken new life there, but to watch the dead body; it was fear
> and envy, rather than ambition and covetousness, that created
> the province of Africa.[7]

The province became a prime area of concern in the mid-first century B.C., during the bloody struggles which ravaged the entire Roman Republic. The followers of Pompey the Great and Julius Caesar clashed openly, and Cato the Younger, great-grandson of that Cato who had hastened the downfall of Carthage, rallied the Numidian chieftain Juba I at Africa's capital Utica to help the supporters of Pompey. Arrogant and still harboring a grudge against Caesar for a snub received while he was a youth, Juba entertained hopes of uniting the Mahgreb as Masinissa and Jugurtha had done before.

Despite initial setbacks, Caesar's personal intervention in the African campaigns in 47 B.C. led to a series of spectacular triumphs.[8] The

Pompeians were soundly defeated at Thapsus, even though Juba managed to escape. With all hope lost, Cato held out at Utica, but the citizens begged him to surrender and not let their city be destroyed. Utica opened its doors, and Cato committed suicide, becoming known to posterity as Cato Uticensis. The grateful (if cowardly) citizens did the least they could have done—they put up a monument to him on the seashore. Despite a concentrated site survey made at Utica in 1970, that monument has never been found, although aerial photography has revealed through changes in vegetation the densely overgrown area where the port must have been located. A thorough weeding job in the vicinity might yet yield positive results.[9]

In the meantime Juba persevered until he ran out of time and options, finally committing suicide near the town of Zama, where Hannibal had unsuccessfully risked the fortunes of Carthage 155 years earlier. Juba's territories were swiftly added to the lands of the Roman Republic so that right along side of the province of Africa, now called Vetus or Old Africa, was the new province, Africa Nova. Caesar levied heavy fines on all the towns and cities which had been the bedfellows of his adversaries, and he sold at public auction the wealthy estates of Juba and other Roman collaborators living in his capital.

This became the occasion for senators, equestrians and general speculators to carve out vast empires for themselves in the new land. And as a result of Caesar's triumph and the destruction of much of the dangerous Libyan opposition, Rome now found itself able to annex a completely new province, to provide vast revenues for the state, and to demand (and get) an astronomically large annual tribute of 3,000,000 pounds of olive oil and 1,200,000 bushels of wheat.

At last a Roman, Caesar, had finally begun to realize the incredible economic potential of Africa and set in motion a new plan that contrasted sharply with the laissez-faire policies of his predecessors in the Roman government. Placing himself squarely in the tradition of other proplebeian reformers like Marius and the Gracchi, he conceived a vast and comprehensive program of economic, social, political and administrative reform. At the top of the list was the decision to colonize Carthage, a site so strategically located that it would give Rome a toehold on both the north and south sides of the Mediterranean. But Caesar's dreams were still unachieved at the time of his assassination in 44 B.C., and it fell to his successor and great nephew Octavian (Augustus) to implement them.

Still, Caesar's accomplishments were considerable.[10] Following the Carthaginian model, other settlements were established, particularly in the northeast of Tunisia, along Cape Bon: Clupea (modern Kelibia), Curubis (Korba), Carpis (Mraissa) and maybe Neapolis (now the pottery-making center of Nabeul). But these colonies too only really came fully into existence under Augustus. The choice of Cape Bon as a target area for development was hardly a matter of chance. Its fertility was, as we have seen earlier, well known even to the Sicilian Greeks of Agathocles' time, and it was in one of the safest regions of the country, insulated against native attacks and hardly more than several days distance by sea to Rome.

The vision of Caesar and, later, of Octavian was clever indeed. It installed loyal, needy veterans on rich lands and created an instant claque of political supporters in the new province. The settlers could help to maintain order and keep the flow of agricultural produce heading towards Rome, and, with their own life-style and beliefs, they would help to Romanize the province.

Between the death of Julius Caesar in 44 B.C. and Octavian's victory in 31 B.C., the province suffered a period of neglect as Mark Antony, Octavian and Lepidus emerged as new champions of the people, and civil war disrupted the harmony of the Republic all over again. But as early as 40 B.C., Octavian may have decided to unite the disparate African provinces into one that now became known as Africa Proconsularis, with its capital not at Utica but at Carthage itself. Once this was finally accomplished, it became evident that Carthage, which Cato had said had to be destroyed, had in fact been resurrected by the enemies of Cato's own great-grandson.

With this development began a long period of material progress, during which time the new province and the new capital city attained a prosperity and cultural sophistication never even dreamed of earlier. To help ensure the peace, Roman legions began to push out farther into the province and establish centers of control. At Haidra, the ancient Ammaedara, in western Tunisia near the Algerian border, the first permanent camp of the Third Augustan Legion was established in a region formerly under Libyan and Punic control.[11]

Certainly all was not sweetness and light throughout the province. Troubles, of which we know only the most famous episodes, struck the hinterland from time to time and disrupted the peace. As the Roman merchants and armies expanded their interests to the south, they ran into hostile Libyans. In effect the Romans really provoked the native resistance movement by failing to take into account that many Libyans needed to migrate seasonally as part of their nomadic or seminomadic life-style. When a number of their basic routes and pasturelands were seized, they believed their entire way of life was being threatened and they struck back, led by a skillful commander named Tacfarinas, who, again like Masinissa and Jugurtha, had served in the auxiliary corps of the Roman army and was prepared to show the Romans all that he had learned in their employ, while adding some guerilla tactics of his own.[12]

For seven years the Romans under three different consuls struggled against him, often winning victories but never the war. Augustus had died in A.D. 14, and Tiberius, a not very popular member of the same ruling dynasty, known by its family name of Julio-Claudians, was now emperor. He lacked the vision to realize that the Roman policy in southern Africa Proconsularis was a mistake. The Roman historian Tacitus, writing about Tacfarinas more than half a century later, observed, "No personal or national slur, it is said, ever provoked the emperor more than the sight of this deserter and brigand behaving like a hostile sovereign."[13]

Refusing to give back the lands Tacfarinas had demanded for himself and his followers, Tiberius redoubled his efforts to force a brutal end to this seemingly interminable war. Finally, the defiant chieftain's camp was infiltrated by Roman agents and he was surprised while his army was resting. Although he had a chance to escape, he chose to die with his men rather than face the horrors and degradation of Roman captivity. In this way, although a Romanized native, he died like a true Roman—or ancient Carthaginian.

The Tacfarinas affair was the most important of a series of revolts, which continued sporadically all through the first century A.D., but the Libyans were never able to shake loose the Roman menace from their territories, and the resistance confined itself to small-scale guerilla tactics at the borders of the occupied lands.

Between the later first century and the middle of the third, the province of Africa Proconsularis enjoyed a peaceful, golden age, the *pax romana* (Roman peace), and with the lack of major problems the economy was able to blossom as never before. Ammaedara, which had been a beachhead area in the fight to pacify the province in Augustan times, was completely tranquil by the time of the emperor Nero, just sixty years later. The garrison, no longer needed, moved on to less secure areas like Tebessa in Algeria in A.D. 75, and when that area calmed down, to Lambaesis by the turn of the second century.[14] Haidra became a colony under the Flavian emperors, largely filled with military campaign veterans, many of whom had been part of auxiliary troops and had come from other areas of North Africa or Europe now under Roman control, like Gaul.

The agricultural knowledge of the past was put to good use throughout the newly pacified province. Labor was cheap and plentiful, and the trade network, which had already been developed in the Punic period, was expanded. Everything was done to exploit the abundant resources of the land rather than to settle it with people.[15]

In the Roman scheme for maximum utilization of the region, the vineyards and olive groves that had played such an important part in the Punic agricultural program were abandoned. They had been devastated anyway during the Punic wars and were not revived. The reason for this was simple: Italy already dominated the international market for wine and olive oil with homegrown production, and the introduction of African goods of a similar nature would have completely fouled up their economy. The removal of this competition was one of the main reasons for taking over the land of Africa.

Instead, a monoculture was imposed on the province. Only one crop could be grown in quantity: wheat. In his *Natural History,* the Roman writer Pliny the Elder noted that by the middle of the first century A.D., "The soil of Africa has been given over by nature entirely to Ceres [goddess of agriculture and especially grains]; the oil and the vine have almost been refused; all the glory of the country is in its harvest."[16]

This forced monoculture of wheat was made necessary by the fact that at Rome there were some two hundred thousand needy citizens on the dole receiving free distribution of wheat at the precise moment when Italian production of the crop was experiencing serious shortages. Africa Proconsularis had to furnish 1,260,000 quintals (each quintal measures 100 kilograms) of wheat, which would take care of the needs of two thirds of the plebeians, or put another way, the hungry could be fed for eight months of the year by Africa Proconsularis, while the other four months became the responsibility of Egypt. In this way Rome saved itself from famine, and many merchants, farmers and real-estate developers in Africa got rich—very rich.

The province thus developed a reputation for unlimited prosperity. The Jewish priest and author of the first century A.D., Flavius Josephus, wrote that Africa was the breadbasket of Rome, and numerous Latin authors waxed poetic about the fecundity of the area. Pliny claimed that a single grain could produce a shoot bearing 150 new grains. In fact, such productivity was not just an exaggeration; in certain favorable conditions it was entirely possible and probably did happen. However, the claim of the Greek writer Strabo, writing around the time of Christ, that the Libyans had two harvests per year seems to be nothing more than an exaggeration of the famed agricultural prowess of the African natives. African wheat was also praised for its extraordinary quality.

As the first century continued, however, certain changes had to be made in the production system. With the conquest and pacification of more of western North Africa (Numidia and Mauretania), the Romans developed other areas to grow wheat for them. Furthermore, in Italy itself, and especially in the wine-growing areas such as Umbria, there seems to have been a crisis in the production of agricultural products, including wine and, particularly, olive oil. This led to diversification of the African economy. And, as the second century began, the advent of non-Italian emperors such as Trajan and Hadrian (Spaniards of Italian families) led to more liberal treatment for the provinces.

It now became possible to try to use all the available land in the most profitable way. Wheat, olives and wine began to be produced, just as they had in Punic times, but in much greater quantities. The olive in particular adapted well to the mountain and steppe areas of Tunisia, where the water supply was severely limited, and proved to be a crop in heavy demand in Rome. It was distributed to the poor along with wheat and, as well as being a principal food source, could be used as fuel for oil lamps and the most popular base for the making of perfumes.

The ubiquitous Pliny, who seemed to have had a comment on everything, noted that "Olive oil has the property to warm up the body, to protect it from cold, and to calm a fever in the head. The Greeks, inventors of all vices, made of it a deluxe product pouring it out in all their gymnasia."[17]

In the later fourth century A.D., Saint Augustine, who lived, studied and taught in Carthage for many years, was well acquainted with the popularity and abundance of olive oil. People in Africa

Proconsularis consumed it like water and left their clay and bronze oil lamps burning all night.[18] But when Augustine went to Milan, he found that things were different, and olive oil was quite scarce, leaving the nights very black indeed: "We found ourselves in the dark, which is almost a necessity here even for the very rich."

Augustine's comment is a far cry from the words of Juvenal, the Roman satirist who lived in the later first and early second century A.D. and who had a healthy distrust of foreign influences and a considerable bias in favor of native products. African oil for him was vastly inferior to the famous oil of Venafrum in Campania, southern Italy. "The wealthy patron," he said in his famous fifth satire,

> sprinkles his fish with the abundant olive oil of Venafrum, while the wretched cabbage brought to you [the humble client] reeks of oil fit for use only in a lamp. And that's because the oil they put in your saucers is that which the descendants of Micipsa [the Libyan king who may have had his headquarters at Dougga] bring to Rome in their sharp-prowed reed boats [i.e., flimsy craft that could never have crossed the Mediterranean]. It's the sort of stuff that when Boccar the African uses it at Rome no one wants to bathe at the same time he does, and, moreover, it even protects you against the bite of black snakes.[19]

From Juvenal, full of prejudice as he is, one could deduce that at least at first, African oil may not have been purified properly, but it may just be that he is exaggerating in order to promote his native product to the detriment of a provincial rival. In any case, the product that Juvenal hated so went on to become one of the staples of the Italian diet and was exported all over the Mediterranean. Today, archaeologists find the vestiges of this prosperity all over Tunisia. The remains of olive presses are common in towns like Thuburbo Maius, and clay oil lamps are found in excavations almost as often as fine pottery ware.

One of the industries which developed alongside the agricultural products was pottery making.[20] At first, of course, large numbers of locally made pots were needed to transport the grain abroad, while most of the better pottery and oil lamps had to be imported from Italy, Gaul or even the Near East. But by the later first century A.D., the province was producing an enormous amount of transport amphorae

Behind the Capitolium *of* Thuburbo Maius *which appears at the top right, the ruins of an olive press and olive oil storage vats appear in the foreground. This olive oil production center dates to the second half of the second century* A.D.

and fine ware to supplement the common and cooking wares. Oil lamps of all sorts became a particular specialty, but unlike the Punic models, which were largely open at the center, the Roman lamps were closed.[21] This was a practical improvement, for it stopped mice from licking out the oil at night and kept insects, attracted by the light, from falling into the oil.

The most successful pottery production was the fine ware of red-orange color, which the pottery specialist John Hayes of the Royal Ontario Museum has dubbed African red slip ware. Almost (but not quite) as attractive as the Italian wares produced at Arezzo and other centers and the Gallic wares of La Graufesenque, it was no doubt a good value, and its area of distribution increased to the point where it was driving the Italian and Gallic products away. It was produced in quantity until the time of the Islamic invasions, with numerous centers of fabrication, particularly the steppe area of central Tunisia around the regions of modern Kairouan, El Ayoun, El Aouja and possibly El Jem (the ancient Thysdrus). A study of these centers is being prepared by Professor David Peacock at the University of Southampton, which has become an international center for all sorts of ancient pottery analysis.

The pottery-producing centers were areas less fertile for agriculture and richer in the clay deposits so essential to pottery production. In addition to imitations of Italian and Gallic products and certain basic shapes, specialty forms proved popular as well. In the early third century A.D., attractive thin-walled vases with appliqué decorations in relief featured motifs often inspired by the games of the amphitheater, while in the fourth century little round cups featured decoration with impressed crosses. There were large rectangular plates in the fifth century, made in molds but inspired by silver originals.

Besides the hundreds of forms of ceramics, the potters also made all sorts of statuettes of animals, humans, grotesques and divinities (especially Venus), which are found in huge quantities in the necropolises of Thysdrus and Hadrumetum (Sousse). In the fifth and sixth centuries, square plaques made of terra-cotta and often showing scenes from the Bible were used as ceiling and wall decorations in Christian basilicas.[22]

One of the most fascinating and popular of the ancient industries produced a condiment called *garum*.[23] It consisted of a fish sauce made by reducing dried fish and shellfish to a powder and/or marinating them in a salty solution mixed with aromatic herbs. This was done in large vats, with the result that a sauce or liqueur could eventually be extracted and used as the ketchup of antiquity or even as an aperitif or digestif. *Garum* was made in a number of areas in the Roman world, including Spain and Portugal, but along the Tunisian coast traces of *garum* or fish-conserving establishments have been noted at Sullectum (Sallacta), Neapolis (Nabeul) and Clupea (Kelibia).

To satisfy the taste for opulence of the new ruling class of Africa, a number of luxury industries began to crop up, of which the most important products were mosaics, rugs and wool clothing, along with all sorts of leather goods. Dyeing and felt-making establishments, such as the one recently found at Thuburbo Maius, were also popular, following in the long tradition of Punic dyeing using murex shells.

As the economy diversified in the second century A.D., the province became increasingly powerful politically, more independent from the control of Rome, and increasingly elegant, especially on the large estates and in the cities. Port towns did a staggering business. Carthage, full of vast warehouses, and Utica shipped off the produce of the Medjerda valley. Thabraca (Tabarka) was the shipping point for the much-sought-after marbles of Chemtou (the ancient Simittu). Hippo Diarhytus (now Bizerte) delivered produce from fertile Cape Bon's Caesarian settlements, including fish and *garum,* as did Clupea, Missua and Neapolis. Hadrumetum, Sullectum, Thaenae, Tacape and Gightis (Gighti) were the ports for the hinterland, and the numerous ships constantly plying the sea routes around the Mediterranean were able to carry as much as 250 tons of cargo each. A mosaic from the hinterland community of Althiburos has left us a visual catalogue of these sailing vessels. The grain transport ships, known as *naves frumentariae,* usually featured a square mainsail set on a mast permanently fixed amidship. They had a high flaring sternpost (*aplustre*), rounded rear hull and a pointed cutwater in front. Their shallow draft allowed them to beach in shallow water and they were fitted out with oars.[24]

Besides the maritime commerce, the trans-Saharan route, which had been established in Punic times, continued to link the province to the heart of Africa through the Fezzan and the Hoggar, but the camel, a more dour if temperamental beast much better adapted to arid conditions, replaced the horse as the ship of the desert. Back came gold, ivory, slaves and precious stones, not to mention wild beasts, which were in constant demand and fetched a high price. To these remote regions the Romans bartered manufactured goods like glass, pottery and textiles, and of course wine. There was still trade with the Near East, seen as an exotic paradise for merchants, who could bring back spices, incense, myrrh and rare gems.

The quality of life in Africa Proconsularis in the second century A.D. was in many ways as good or better than life in Italy or other centers with a longer tradition of civilized living.[25] A steadily increasing network of roads surrounded the big cities and made every place in the province accessible without great difficulty. In order to let the weary traveler know he was on the right road, markers were installed every fifteen hundred meters, featuring first the name of the emperor and underneath that the name of the next town. The bigger towns were the centers or hubs of large areas or commercial districts and were often ringed with roads. Excellent bridges spanned each major waterway or waddy (known as *oued* in Tunisia today), such as that of Vaga, which crossed the Medjerda with three arches and measured 224 feet long and 22 feet wide. A massive causeway cut off the sea and joined the island of Jerba to the adjacent Kerkenna Islands.

In small towns and villages, weekly markets and occasional fairs allowed the locals to purchase goods from travelling merchants, and the Berbers could sell their crops and animals or trade them for manufactured goods. Even modest towns had large market areas around the forum, or town square, frequently fitted out with shady porticoes and flanked by temples, which were often dedicated to Mercury, the patron divinity of commerce. The circulation of all these goods was helped along by very light taxation.

All of this economic growth and increasing prosperity led to some fascinating social developments. To be sure, ancient Roman society had aristocrats at the top and slaves at the bottom, but the social structure of Tunisia was a lot more complicated than that. First of all, there was the old Punic society, which, although of Phoenician origin, was firmly rooted in the province it had been the first to civilize. These Punic survivors consisted of aristocrats (many of whom were still well-off as a result of collaboration with the Romans, which had led them into effective land deals), a middle class (which was partly Punic and partly educated and Punicized Libyans), an anomalous urban proletariat, rural masses (mostly of Berber origin and living almost as slaves or as migrant workers) and actual slaves.

One must add that in this pre-Roman social structure, already complex enough, there were many different life-styles.[26] There were, besides the city and town dwellers and the farmers, Libyans who were nomads and seminomads. And there were already numerous legal systems operating: regional tribal laws and Punic law.

Now came the Romans to make things even more complex as they imposed their own laws, a third language (to go with the Libyan dialects and Punic) and their own customs, so that a triple-layered society was created. First were Romans living in their own settlements or in small trading groups. Second was the Punic group, which clung to its traditions, and third were the Libyans in the rural areas. But from all this complexity of social organization two broad groups emerged: those with the money and those without.

The Romans who were either born to wealth or who had amassed great wealth through trade and land deals were a very small group.

They lived like kings on feudal estates called *latifundia* or built *villae urbanae* in the cities.[27] At the top of this social ladder was the emperor himself, and only six wealthy proprietors had control of half of the land of the entire province by the time of the emperor Nero (A.D. 54–68). However, this unstable emperor, through persecution of his enemies and irrational behavior, confiscated a great deal of land, forced numerous executions and effected sweeping changes in the aristocracy. Nonetheless, the very wealthy continued to control much of the province and many of them were Roman senators.

Besides this crème de la crème of society, there was a wealthy group of senatorial rank (there were already numerous provincial senators in Rome by Nero's time) consisting of about one hundred families, who were either Romans from distinguished families or Romanized natives who had managed to attain senatorial rank. The minimum qualification necessary for this was the holding of property worth one million *sesterces* (perhaps about $50,000, although the equivalencies are difficult to make). Most senators were considerably richer. At this time, poverty level was considered to be property holdings worth about five thousand *sesterces* (or $250).

Next in the social pecking order came the upper middle class, consisting of about one thousand families belonging to the equestrian order. They were often high officials, or just Roman or Romanized businessmen who had done well, for their property qualification was between four hundred thousand and one million *sesterces*. When one qualified for the equestrian order, it was often the start of a high-paying career in imperial administration. Not quite so well-off but still comfortable was the municipal middle class, perhaps thirty thousand Roman or Romanized families. These minor but respected officials lived their lives in local senates and were lesser magistrates with property of one hundred thousand *sesterces*.

Moving down the list to those with less money and property for living the good life, we come to the middle class of laborers, farmers and small-scale merchants, who were living rather successfully or at least working steadily at a profession. They are the last group to make up what we might call the privileged classes.

It is common for beginning students of Roman provincial life to believe that this hierarchy of wealth remained completely fixed throughout antiquity, but that is just not true. Due to the sharply changing political scene during the first century A.D., there was a great deal of change among the powerful groups and a good deal of upward mobility from the lesser groups. But it is also true that the best families usually perpetuated their influence, and a person's ancestry was considered extremely important. That fact notwithstanding, fully one tenth of the senators in the second century came from families which had not been of senatorial rank before. This still meant that ninety percent of the senate didn't really change, but at least outsiders with talent and resources could nourish hope for a better life.

The society that now formed in Africa viewed itself as hierarchic, even though the castes were not always fixed. The limited oligarchy often looked down its collective nose at its inferiors, but its members so often fought among themselves and with the emperor that considerable upward mobility seemed to many to exist just beyond the horizon. But before we think that everyone got a piece of the pie, it is necessary to remember that this entire upper class made up barely one sixth of the entire population of the province, and the other five sixths lived in a poverty that was at times terribly hard to bear and almost impossible to escape. Survival, or at least the simple pleasures of life, were often dependent upon the whims of the very rich, who sponsored banquets, symposia, sacrifices accompanied by food distributions, and architectural complexes such as baths, theaters and amphitheaters. Usually the rich then inscribed their names all over the structures so that the poor would never forget to whom they owed their enjoyment.

The thermal or bath complexes in particular were like adult Disneylands with hot rooms, promenade areas, art galleries, shops of all sorts, areas for philosophical discussion, Greek and Roman libraries, classrooms, cult centers, exercise grounds, swimming pools, running tracks, rubdown centers, steam rooms and brothels.[28] For a pittance, a poor man could surround himself with splendid marble halls, the finest art and the most pleasant of atmospheres.

Within this otherwise generally wretched proletariat it is possible to distinguish two major categories: free men and slaves. The free men were largely of Libyan or Punic ancestry, but a good number of Romans were included as well. They included common laborers in low-paying jobs, shopkeepers and handymen, all living often from day to day with no pension or social security. In the boondocks they might live in tiny, dank *gourbis,* or shacks, which were often called *mapalia* in the countryside. In the cities they were crowded into walk-up garrets in the worst part of town.

In the agricultural areas this group included farmers working areas of land too small to allow them to live comfortably. These people were often forced to hire themselves out to others to survive, while leaving their offspring to work the land at home. In times of drought these lower-class proprietors were extremely hard hit; they were also at the mercy of wealthy Roman land barons in the area, who were ever eager to gobble up small farms.

But even in this social group the possibility for improvement was not completely blocked. Inscriptions preserve a number of examples of poor farmers, indeed migrant workers, who succeeded in life due to their own hard work, careful planning and ingenuity. This was the case of the famous harvester of the rural city of Maktar, located about one hundred miles southwest of Tunis, who erected a pillar with this inscription:

> I was born to a poor family; my father had neither money nor a roof over his head. Since the day of my birth I have always cultivated my field. Neither my earth nor I myself took any repose. When the time of the year came when the crops were ready for harvest I was the first to cut my field; when there appeared in the countryside groups of migrant workers who were going to hire themselves out to work around Cirta, the capital of the Numidians, or in the plains which dominate the mountain of Jupiter, I was the first to reap my field. Then, leaving my country, I have for 12 years harvested elsewhere under a burning sun; for 11 years I directed a team of harvesters and I have cut the wheat in the Numidian fields. Because of my work, having been able to content myself with very little, I finally became the proprietor of a house and land. Today, I live a life of ease. I have even managed to attain honors for I was called to sit on the senate of my city, and from simple farm-worker I became censor. I have witnessed the birth and growing up around me of my children and grandchildren; my life has passed peacefully and honored by all.[29]

The date of this document is still debated, but the pillar seems to have been erected between A.D. 260 and 270, so our harvester would have achieved his rise to fame and happiness in the course of the first half of the century. This invaluable inscription gives us a rare glimpse into the hard life of migrant workers, who moved about renting their talents wherever needed, even outside their own regions, leaving their families to tend their own plots.

After twenty-three years of exile and hard labor, this harvester was able, through energy and self-deprivation, to make a career in his own city and to amass property valued at fifty thousand *sesterces,* the minimum requirement for admission to the local senate. A second, less modest citizen of Maktar, who died at the age of seventy-five, was content that he had "lived rather a long time, raised a happy family, and achieved a respectable fortune, having made a little profit without ever committing fraud. Exalted by my honors and those of my sons, I leave behind in death an eternal and brilliant renown."[30]

If the goddess Fortuna occasionally smiled on a few hardworking farmers who owned tiny lots, she seems to have completely turned her back on the *coloni,* the hapless cultivators of fruits or harvesters of grain or olives. They had to turn the bulk of their yield over to greedy *conductores,* who acquired for a period of five years the right to exploit the lands or domains on which the *coloni* worked and/or were allowed to live. The *coloni* had virtually no possibility of success, since the imperial procurators, who were supposed to look out for their rights and see that they were not forced to give up all their crops, were often in league with the *conductores.*

The *coloni* of a mountainous pastureland in the northwest of Tunisia known as the saltus Burunitanus formally complained to the emperor of being exploited:

> (This situation) . . . forces us unhappy men to seek your
> divine aid. We ask, therefore, most sacred Imperator
> [*commodus*], that in accordance with the clause of the *lex
> Hadriana* we owe not more than two days' work per year; two
> of cultivating, two of harvesting . . . so that through the
> kindliness of your majesty we, your rural workers . . . may
> no longer be harassed by the lessors.[31]

Conscious of their responsibility to protect the poor against overexacting of debt or produce, emperors such as Hadrian left careful instructions for the governor of the province to look out for "those people of modest condition so they might not be deprived of their only lamp or their poor furnishings or be unjustly molested under the pretext of the arrival of officials or soldiers." Those who were powerful were ordered "not to injure the humble unjustly."

The wretched plight of the *coloni* in Africa Proconsularis has become known thanks to the discovery of a series of inscriptions concerning social unrest between landlords, farmers and *coloni* in the area of Souk El Khemis, and from legislation regulating land use called the *Lex Manciana* or Mancian Law, cited in inscriptions from Ain Mettich and Ain Djemala.[32] The plight of the *coloni*, who often worked on imperial estates, was the more lamentable because it was due to their backbreaking labor that the province had become so rich. This unrest was to grow in the later empire and would become one of the major causes of the empire-wide breakdown of civilization that began in the third century A.D.

Besides the *coloni,* there were numerous poor souls who were actually slaves, working in the city or the country and treated well or ill depending on the whims of their masters.[33] Quite surprisingly, one historian has estimated that as much as eighty percent of the population of Africa Proconsularis may have been families that were in a servile condition. By the second century slavery was on the decrease, primarily because there were fewer sources for recruitment, fewer wars and therefore fewer prisoners of war and increased freeing of slaves (*manumissiones*).

Petronius, the first-century-A.D. satirist, once said that there were so many slaves working in the fields of Numidia that they could take over Carthage. The wife of the later-second-century-A.D. writer Apuleius, herself owned four hundred rural slaves but had only fifteen in her household, considered a rather small number for such a rich family. Pliny himself had given freedom to one hundred of his slaves in his will, the law not allowing him to free any more. With the limited number of *latifundia* after the first century A.D., there were usually only large numbers of slaves working in the fields owned by the wealthy proprietors, who often lived in the city. In the second century there seem to have been fewer slaves and more of a work force of free men of modest means.

A person could end up a slave in a variety of ways. Domestic slaves were especially sought after and were sold by specialists, who actually saw to their education before selling them in the large slave markets of the Near East or in the south of Italy. By contrast, migrant workers were readily available locally, as well as prisoners of war or members of dissident tribes who were being taught a lesson. The trans-Sahara trade also furnished large numbers of black slaves. The cost of a slave was very little, only about one hundred dollars; an excellent horse might fetch much more.

As one might expect, the slaves' conditions were often quite dreadful, although domestic slaves frequently lived right in the home, in a part of the house which might have beaten earth floors and small rooms. In later antiquity the decreasing numbers of slaves led to a general amelioration of their condition. At Bulla Regia in northwest Tunisia, a female skeleton was found, buried in the forum. The woman was about forty and had still affixed to her neck a lead collar which bore the following inscription: "Adultera Meretrix, tene quia fugitivi de Bulla Regia." This may be translated: "I am an adulteress, courtesan; hold on to me, I am a runaway slave from Bulla Regia."[34]

This collar, datable perhaps to the end of the fourth century A.D., shows how runaways were dealt with and how the rebellious nature of slaves could be curbed. (Amputation of fingers or feet was another deterrent.) It may be that this woman was the property of the city itself, since no master was named; perhaps she was employed at a municipal *lupanar* (brothel). The unfortunate woman may have tried to escape her sad lot by flight and once recaptured, was forced to wear this humiliating collar. Other interpretations are also possible, including the idea that she was a matron who had committed adultery and tried to run away at a time when Christianity prevailed in Tunisia and adultery was a sin.

The sadism of certain slave masters has become legendary. Apuleius in his celebrated second-century work, *Metamorphoses,* describes slaves employed on mills, their bodies racked from beatings, their heads shaved and branded with red-hot irons.[35] There was also the case of a slave attached to a tree and coated with honey so that he could be devoured by ants. Another slave chose to hang himself rather than endure the abuse of his master, who was angry because he had failed to stop a dog from stealing a bit of venison.

Such acts, strictly forbidden by law, were nonetheless not at all uncommon in the rural domains, so far from outside control, and they form a sharp contrast to the kind treatment of slaves by more rational masters. To be fair, it must be noted that slaves occasionally turned on their masters as well, and such incidents as household servants holding down their master until he was scorched on the floor in a very hot room of a bath facility are not unknown.

The slaves and other have-nots had a lot to gripe about, for if only one sixth of the population lived a life of relative comfort, then fully five sixths lived virtually at the poverty level. Promotions, like that experienced by the harvester of Maktar, were the exception, not the rule. The great society which the Romans created was clearly not for everybody.

❦ IX ❦

Creating the Age of Gold

AFRICA PROCONSULARIS, in the words of the late British archaeologist Mortimer Wheeler, was a land ". . . rich in corn, and, later, in olives, rich also in the Saharan trade which brought gold and ivory, slaves and show animals to the Mediterranean ports, and proportionally rich in its urban life."[1]

The modern visitor to the Roman ruins of Tunisia is astounded at the organization that obviously went into these exemplary communities, although it is not quite true that these centers were the result of Roman creativity alone. In many cases the Romans took advantage of the skills of Punic and Berber craftsmen and laborers, and built up sites that Punic leaders had carefully chosen and laid out centuries before.

Nonetheless, never before had the Tunisian landscape seen such continuous and sudden development. Roads were laid in all directions and communities were linked by elaborate bridges, dams and aqueducts. For the Romans as for the Greeks, the city, or *urbs,* was the only place where man could live the cultured and complete life. And although satirists like Juvenal could complain about crowded conditions and the influx of lower-class foreigners, and Horace could extol the virtues of a Sabine farm, the imperial civic leaders and planners thought in terms of large scale, rigidly controlled urban spaces, designed in the Baroque manner to dazzle and delight the senses.

The city became a great magnet for the entire population for everyday and special shopping, special events or festivals; it was also the great center of government and administration. All of the political, economic and social organization of the province had been conceived in relation to cities. The ancient urban centers were quickly built over, and even the new cities overran their original prescribed limits and burst out into suburbs. Lest this seem an exaggeration, it must be remembered that Tunisia contains the ruins of more than two hundred major Roman cities, situated surprisingly close to one another. Around the former Libyan center of Dougga, no fewer than ten towns form a ring within just six square miles. Aerial photography has revealed an amazing density of occupation.

Each city adopted a life-style copied from Rome itself, leading to the creation of numerous buildings designed specifically for leisure-time use—playlands for the masses. Each city had one or two colossal bath complexes and, every few blocks, smaller local *thermae*. No community of any size would lack at least one amphitheater or theater, and many cities also had circuses for chariot racing. Recent estimates suggest that perhaps one fourth to one third of all of the people of Roman Tunisia lived in cities, a surprising figure for an area which had been rural by tradition.

The extraordinary number of cities in Africa Proconsularis sets that province apart from others such as Gaul, which was also wealthy but essentially rural. With people becoming increasingly exposed to the delights of city living, a demand suddenly arose for large quantities of water. People who had used it only for basic needs before now absolutely had to have it not only for drinking, washing clothes and bathing, but also for fountains with dancing water displays in their homes, featuring noisy cascades or waterfalls that spilled over shimmering fish mosaics and delighted dinner guests. Water was also in demand for private baths (*balneae*) and public swimming pools (*piscinae*).[2]

The providing of water in the cities was the responsibility of urban planners, while water maintenance was the job of the *aediles,* the important public officers in charge of streets, traffic, markets and public games. Romans in Gaul, Spain and Italy had developed an economy and life-style centered on water, which was extremely abundant in those areas. But the transferring of that life-style to Tunisia took some doing, since water was (and is) most certainly not always plentiful there. Even though the country is touched by the Mediterranean Sea over an area of some eight hundred miles, it is also true that the southern part of the country is bordered by the Sahara, one of the greatest and most desolate deserts of the world. In fact, as every tourist discovers, Tunisia gets progressively more arid as one goes from north to south.

The northern chain of the Atlas mountains frequently serves as a screen from the humid winds coming from Numidia (Algeria) to the northwest, so that only the northern and northeastern parts of the country truly benefit from the influence of the Mediterranean. The remaining three quarters of the country are either semiarid or arid land, where water and waterways are less than common. Furthermore, during the rainy season following the long summer dryness, devastating rains do more harm than good, carrying away everything in their path as they create torrents leading to the sea, rivers or salt lakes. Bridges are particularly subject to the destructive effects of these violent outbursts.

In the Roman period an all-out attempt was made to saturate the province with water. Tiny dams were built all over the country to try to limit the devastating effects of flooding, and retaining terraces were constructed to help keep the arable earth on hillsides from washing away (a technique still commonly employed). Reservoirs—some of enormous size—were constructed to retain water during the dry season, while a network of canals also fed these structures with rainwater. The countryside around the rivers, particularly along the Medjerda, was honeycombed with irrigation canals.

In selecting sites for their cities, the Romans tended to choose places near water sources, especially rivers and springs. This was the case with communities such as Bulla Regia, Dougga, Sbeitla and Haidra. The water source could then be supplemented by the digging of numerous wells and extra-large cisterns for the capture of rainwater from the roofs of buildings. These efforts would have been adequate to satisfy a community that used water in a moderate way.

But they were insufficient for cities which had developed the insatiable Roman taste for water. So Dougga, a small city of under one thousand inhabitants, installed enormous public cisterns in order to bring in water for its huge bath building, smaller baths, public fountains, impressive latrines and private baths. The citizens were obliged to construct an aqueduct at considerable cost; it was seven miles long and traversed a ravine on a single-arched bridge, then crossed the Oued Melah on a beautiful structure consisting of two superposed arches. And the example of Dougga is not an isolated one.[3]

Most cities were willing to pay a great sum to have an aqueduct bringing good quality water from a desirable source over an aqueduct. A water channel, or *specus,* which carried water at about a two percent gradient, ran along the top of these lengthy structures as they bridged valleys and waterways to bring the mountain springs to the cities. Once built, they had to be maintained, and the *specus* was fitted with manholes to allow the periodic cleaning out of deposits and incrustations.

After reaching a city, some of the water was stored in vast cisterns, while the rest was brought to various baths, public fountains and private homes by means of a *castellum,* or water distribution center, which had conduits leading to each area of demand. In hard times these conduits could be shut down individually, so water would only go to those areas in the most need.[4]

A well-preserved section of the great aqueduct leading from Zaghouan to Carthage, showing supporting piers and the specus *or water channel on top. Roman, second quarter of the second century* A.D.

The most striking of the aqueducts built in Tunisia is that which delivered water to Carthage and other cities from a still excellent source high on Jbel Zaghouan, the ancient mons Zeugitanus. Situated some thirty-five miles south of Carthage, the aqueduct began near the top of the mountain and, to please the gods, a great sanctuary known as the Temple of the Waters was constructed there in the early second century A.D. under the emperor Hadrian (117–138). The sanctuary, which is still commonly used for international boy scout jamborees and other social events, consisted of a large semicircular court built over the water source, while a figure-eight-shaped basin below displayed the treasured water for all to see. A niche at the back of the semicircle may have harbored a statue of Neptune, the god who ruled over the sea and all water sources, and in the numerous niches which flanked this statue may have been images of nymphs.[5]

The Temple of the Waters is one of the most beautifully situated and elegantly designed examples of Hadrianic architecture in Tunisia, exhibiting that emperor's obsessive fondness for curvilinear geometric forms, precise symmetry and clear, shallow carving. From the sanctuary the waters continued down the slopes and crossed the plain of the Oued Miliane, finally being carried toward cities like Carthage and Oudna in enormous aqueducts on arches that are sometimes more than seventy feet high over an area of several miles.

This spectacular section of the aqueduct is the delight of tourists driving south from Carthage and gives the landscape much of the flavor of the Roman *campagna*. The *oued* in this area is crossed by a bridge two stories high and 440 feet long composed of eleven arches with openings up to 19 feet across. It attained a height of almost 120 feet across the water and 90 at the ends. Furthermore, great care has been taken to make the foundation as solid as possible and to create a powerful waterbreak against potential onrushing torrents.

At the end of the plain the aqueduct became subterranean, only to reappear about seven miles from Tunis and continue on to Carthage, meandering on for an estimated seventy-five miles—making it one of the longest aqueducts in the Roman world. With its ten miles of arcaded sections and giant piers supporting sections of still-preserved *specus,* it is also one of the world's most spectacular. A new engineering study, completed in 1988, has estimated its rate of flow at almost eighty gallons per second. At Carthage much of the water went into gigantic cisterns, from which it could then be fed into an enormous thermal complex, which had been erected on the waterfront about the middle of the second century.

The decision to build this incredible aqueduct was taken by the emperor Hadrian in A.D. 128; he had been deeply moved by the suffering endured by the people of Carthage during a terrible drought that lasted for five years. As a gesture of compassion, he visited the afflicted city personally, and at his entry into Carthage a cloudburst filled the city with rain. The aqueduct allowed Carthage to join the ranks of other capitals like Rome, which were bathing in hydraulic luxury.

The aqueduct remained in use until the end of antiquity before being abandoned, but it was once again repaired and reused in the thirteenth century. Impressed by its massive and imposing form, the renowned Tunisian historian of the fourteenth century, Ibn Khadoun, considered it to be the symbol of a powerful state, organized and brilliant. Repaired in modern times, it was still at least partly in use as late as 1950.[6]

In the regions of Tunisia where there were no rivers or readily accessible mountain springs, the Romans had to be extremely innovative to arrive at practical solutions. To supply Thysdrus, which became the second most important Tunisian city after Carthage, a large natural pool of brackish water and a sizeable well some twelve miles outside of town were pressed into service; the water was hardly suitable for drinking but it was good enough for domestic needs such as scrubbing floors, watering gardens and supplying the obligatory colossal baths. But this source could not provide drinkable water and for that, large public cisterns were built and home-owners supplemented them with small cisterns in their own houses.

At Bararus, near Thysdrus, a city of limited size and importance nestled in the Tunisian steppe, the same problems were experienced. Gigantic cisterns were erected here, with enormous interior supporting pillars that make the site today look like a sunken cathedral. It was capable of holding 250,000 gallons of water and seems to have been supplied by rain water and by having laborers continually hauling up water from a well some three hundred feet away. In short, no possible alternative was neglected in the quest for water. The entire Tunisian landscape, whether water-rich or arid, bears testimony to the spirit of innovation at work in exploiting every available water resource.

This same spirit infected other areas of city life as well, for although most cities followed Roman ideas in their basic makeup, there was room for experimentation and variety, and each community had its own distinct character. The pre-Roman city plans and the topography of the area often dictated what the Romans could do to a community, and a fascinating mixture of old and new ideas, a sort of syncretization, took place.

Wherever possible, the Romans chose sites not only near the water sources but also in places where the terrain was not too difficult for them to impose their elaborate city plans. They laid out their communities in a square or rectangular plan, usually around two principal axes, which crossed each other at right angles in the middle of the city. These became the principal roads. The one oriented north to south was called the *cardo maximus* and the east-west street was the *decumanus maximus*. At the limit of these streets were placed the four main gates of the city, often marked with a stately arch. After the principal roadways were marked out, it was possible to design the rectangular city blocks known as *insulae*. A city normally resembled a large chessboard, unless, of course, topographical, climatic or pre-Roman features intervened and altered the plan.

The idea of a gridded city plan was well known in the ancient Near East, Greece and Etruria and had undergone refinement and sophistication in the fifth century B.C. at the hands of the urban planner Hippodamos of Miletos (in western Anatolia).[7] The Roman plan, revolving around two principal cross-streets, may have derived also from Roman military camps known as *castra,* which frequently had such streets as well as small regular substreets, along which the soldiers would live in groups arranged by their title: allies, spearbearers, cavalry, *triarii,* etc. Since so many of the cities were settled by Roman veterans and laid out by military engineers, the strict legionary discipline of many of the overall plans is hardly surprising.

Carthage was another such city laid out in this manner, and the Byrsa hill became the central crossing-point for the principal streets of the Augustan community.[8] But other cities, such as Utica, followed this principal as well. The perfect planning of the colonies established at the end of the first century A.D. by the Flavian emperors (Vespasian, Titus and Domitian, A.D. 69–96) may still be seen at Sufetula (Sbeitla), Cillium (Kasserine), Ammaedara (Hydra) and Thelepte (Feriana).

Other sites which had well-established pre-Roman communities kept them, and the Romans built new, regularly planned quarters adjacent to the original center. This was the case at Thysdrus and Thuburbo Maius. But one must also admit that in Tunisia more than in Italy, asymmetry was tolerated and even at Sufetula regularity of plan is not always found. Certain streets have been truncated or set back because the wind from the steppe would have whistled down the right-angled streets and made life unbearable.

At Thuburbo Maius, the stately Temple of Baalat is situated in a beautiful but highly irregular open court. The colonnade of the court is quite asymmetrical, designed to line up to face two different major streets, which end in front of the temple. The view from the temple over its totally askew court is virtually unprecedented in Roman architecture and would have made Hadrian spin in his grave. The Temple of Mercury, which is located in the generally regular Roman forum of Thuburbo, has no reason to be asymmetrical, yet it has a round, colonnaded forecourt with the columns placed in an alignment unnecessarily out of kilter with the forum.

With the Roman cities becoming influenced so much by earlier Punic and Libyan cities, topography, climate and even, apparently, a taste for the askew, it is hard to apply hard-and-fast rules to all of the

The forum area of Sufetula (Sbeitla) with the remains of its three temples and porticoes. Roman, probably middle of the second century A.D.

urban plans, but a few generalizations may be attempted. First, it must be noted that with the Roman peace, cities no longer had to be located near the coast or on a hilltop for protection. The Libyan cities had been veritable fortresses on highly defensible heights; cities now could sprawl leisurely about in the plains near the water but, when hard times struck in the later empire, this made the new cities and their aqueducts much more vulnerable to attack.

Each city that the Romans took over was given an impressive forum ranging from 2,450 square feet to about one hectare in size. In this vast public place the political, judicial, commercial and religious life of the community was centered, and the people met to talk, hold funerals, listen to great and not so great speakers, offer public sacrifices, proclaim political support and swear allegiance. There were shops of all sorts, and all kinds of services were hawked in the colonnaded walkway around the forum. Statue bases proclaimed the virtues of leading citizens, while the central part of the forum was reserved for statues of the most important leaders, like the emperor himself. In addition, basilicas were large covered halls that not only protected people from bad weather but also were the scenes of discussion, trials and manumission of slaves.

The African forum took its inspiration not from the original Roman forum but from the large complexes built in Rome under Julius Caesar and later by the emperors Augustus, Domitian, Vespasian and Trajan, and known as the imperial *fora*.[9] Generally it was of rectangular, almost square shape and was surrounded on three sides by porticoes, which enclosed the facades of various important buildings such as temples, a *curia* (senate building), a basilica and buildings of religious and professional associations. At one end of the forum was placed the major temple, dedicated to Jupiter Capitolinus (and often to Juno and Minerva also) and known as the Capitolium, after the famous Temple of Jupiter on the Capitoline Hill in Rome.

Near this major temple were often other shrines dedicated to pre-Roman divinities or even to emperors, who were worshipped after their death because they were considered to have become divine and risen to heaven in an apotheosis.[10] The cult of the emperor Augustus was particularly extensive. At Althiburos (El Medina), near the Capitolium of the forum, was a temple dedicated to the Punic divinities Eshmoun (who had been assimilated in Roman times to Aesculapius, healing son of Apollo) and Ba'al Shamin (Jupiter). At Dougga most of the temples and other structures around the forum were destroyed in the Byzantine period, but inscriptions refer to Ba'al Hammon, who became syncretized into the Roman Saturn.

The city of Maktar, near Zama, was extraordinary in having two *fora*. The older one had no porticoes, was irregular in shape, and occupied the site of the center of the original Libyan community. Probably the temples of the original gods of the city were located here, and under the empire a temple dedicated to the cult of Rome and Augustus was installed. As the city grew, a completely new forum was added on, as had been done at Rome itself, which was much larger and more sumptuously appointed than its predecessor.

The form of the temples themselves could differ considerably in various cities. Many, particularly the Capitolia, or official main temples to Jupiter, Juno and Minerva, were built according to the Greco-Roman model, while others were more Punic in inspiration. The former featured a rectangular room harboring a cult statue (*naos*) and a second room or vestibule at the front (*pronaos*). The temple was raised up on a podium with steps only in the front. But there were also temples which consisted of an open, porticoed court at the front and one or more simple chambers (*cellae*) at the back. In these courtyards would take place the ritual assemblies and ceremonies which had been the rule since Punic times. Even under the Romans, architecture, as archaeologist Frank Brown used to say, had to be shaped by ritual. The best-known temples of this latter category are the Temple of Apollo at Bulla Regia and that of Saturn at Dougga, and one may also mention the Temple of Liber Pater at Maktar, which had its own crypt, a feature which appears also to be Punic in inspiration.

Spectacularly large, flamboyant baths were common in the coastal and northern regions of the country, where water was plentiful. Theaters and amphitheaters were built in virtually every major community and were similar in appearance to those constructed in Italy, but with one big difference: some of them were built using the Punic measuring system rather than the Roman and were constructed with more blocks of stone and less concrete than one would expect to find in Italy. Circuses were apparently also popular in many cities, although few physical traces of them have been uncovered. At Carthage, John Humphrey of the University of Michigan (joined by Naomi Norman of the University of Georgia) is now unearthing evidence of what was once a magnificent structure; its *cavea,* or seating area, had an elegant colonnade decorated with columns of Pentelic marble from Athens, Egyptian syenite and local pink limestone. The Carthage circus is apparently the fourth largest in the Roman world and the largest in Africa, having been able in its heyday to accommodate over sixty thousand spectators.[11]

Of the great cities of ancient Tunisia, Carthage itself was first and foremost, although it would be hard to prove it today since the traces of the Roman city are scattered among lavish villas filled with wealthy summer sunbathers. Obviously, the location of Carthage is still desirable, with its sharply rising hills offering beautiful vistas to the sea and to the sacred mountain, Bou Cornine, across the water.

Still, there are enough traces left to reveal something of the magnitude of the metropolis.[12] At the city limit are the remains of the enormous cisterns of La Malga, which so inspired the Islamic authors of the Middle Ages such as Ibn Khadoun, and nearby is the amphitheater, which some scholars believe to be the one in which the third-century Christian martyrs, Saints Perpetua and Felicity, were sacrificed. It was in Carthage too that Saint Cyprian was supposedly martyred as the crowd chanted "Cyprianus ad leones," or "Cyprian to the lions!" The celebrated theater, where St. Augustine wondered at the bizarre and artificial emotions of the actors and Apuleius recited poetry, has been partly rebuilt and is now used for modern performances of Greek plays as well as festivals.

Above the theater was the odeon, or covered hall, a type of building normally used for musical recitals; it was noted for the Pythian Games in honor of Apollo, which were associated with its inauguration. Perhaps the most impressive ruins are the so-called Antonine Baths, a complex of enormous size, comprising exercise areas (*palestrae*), promenade spaces, pools, hot and cold rooms, and club and reading centers.[13] The immense, curved public latrines were so vast that when they were first discovered they were taken for a theater.

Here and there around the city have been recovered traces of villas, many of them containing some of the most striking mosaics ever made. These sumptuous dwellings were often located on hills, such as the area around the odeon, from which could be enjoyed the incomparable panoramic view over the Gulf of Tunis. The Villa la Volière, for example, was more like a pleasure palace organized to delight the senses.[14] It contained a large reception room, which opened onto a little theater stage (*pulpitum*) complete with niches, which were alternately rectangular and semicircular. Behind this, three large basins appeared and the central one received a roaring cascade of water, while the walls behind glimmered with decorative mosaic featuring aquatic motifs. The other basins were planted with trees.

These are scant traces of a once great Roman city. The temples and forum area of the Byrsa are all apparently gone, and only the massive terracing walls and piers of the forum, which reach down and disfigure the Punic levels buried below, survive today. But Carthage was often referred to as the second Rome, and was considered by many to be the second greatest city of the Roman empire and the seat of a major university and numerous important schools. It was the "Colony of Concord," "most splendid Carthage," "happy Carthage" in the inscriptions, and Apuleius wrote:

> What subject for praise is greater and more worthy to
> celebrate than Carthage where I see among you in the entire
> city only cultivated men and where everyone is versed in all
> the sciences: children so they can learn them, young men to
> put them to good use, old men to teach them? Carthage—
> venerable school of our province; Carthage—celestial Muse of
> Africa. And finally Carthage—inspiring nymph Camoena of
> the people who carry the toga.[15]

By contrast, the small provincial city of Dougga, a Libyan center and former residence of kings, had a very different look. Under the Romans it had become the center of a rich agricultural region and was part of an administrative district under the control of Carthage. Like Carthage, it prospered enormously in the golden age of the second century under the Antonine emperors (138–192) and the Severan dynasty (193–235), but it never had more than about ten thousand citizens, whereas Carthage could boast a population in its region of perhaps ten times that figure.

The monuments of Dougga are surprisingly well preserved, situated among torturous, steep roads which wind up the hillside and ignore symmetry. One of the focal points of the city was the theater built in A.D. 168, containing thirty-five hundred seats. It was built by a *flamen*, or priest of the cult of the divine Augustus, a certain Publius Marcius Quadratus of the Amensi tribe. Its inscribed architrave is still

The Theater of Dougga, viewed from the cavea. *Roman,* A.D. *168–69.*

preserved, telling how he erected the theater with his own money along with the basilicas (halls flanking the stage), the porticoes, the *xystus* (statue platform), as well as the *scenae frons*, scene building with all its curtains and decoration.[16]

Another extraordinary public monument was the Capitolium, one of the best preserved in all of Africa, erected in A.D. 166 by the parents of our theater donor and featuring in its Baroque pediment the image of the emperor Antoninus Pius being carried up to heaven by the eagle of Jupiter in an apotheosis. It was dedicated to Jupiter Optimus Maximus, Juno (the queen of the gods) and Minerva. Nearby, the Temple of Juno Caelestis, another Romanized Punic divinity, was erected under the Severans in 222 A.D. It sits rather oddly in the midst of a semicircular court enclosed by a *temenos* wall, forming the shape of the crescent moon, popular Punic image of Tanit. An inscription reports that it had a cult image made of silver, while its cornice lists many Roman provinces and cities, perhaps cult centers of the goddess.

On the top of the hill is the precinct of Saturn of a type, as we have seen, which is pre-Roman in conception.[17] Near the forum are the

The Capitolium *of Dougga viewed from the market area. Roman,* A.D. *166.*

magnificent third-century Licinian Baths. Numerous houses line the hillside, some of them quite simple and few of them regular in plan. Most of them managed to have at least a few mosaics, and in some of the better buildings were mosaics of the highest quality.

Thysdrus, originally a town of no particular significance and known only as the center of a rapidly developing agricultural region, became by the time of the Antonines and Severans one of the great ancient centers of the province.[18] Like Carthage, it had a considerable circus, which was just about the size of the famous Circus of Maxentius in Rome, and its forum, of which few traces remain, was colossal.

Thysdrians, like Carthaginians and the people of all the other major cities, had a great fondness for the games of the amphitheater, and three such structures have been discovered there. Although the theater was dear to the heart of every civilized African, bloody games were the real joy of the masses. Originating either in South Italy (perhaps among the Samnites) or among the Etruscans in Italy, this form of entertainment required that spectators gather in a large oval around an arena (*harena* is the Latin word for sand) in which gladiators would fight—sometimes to the death. Gladiator fights in Rome were for a time held in the forum and were originally limited to funeral rites, as games which were ritualized human sacrifices for the dead.

This atrocious pastime was introduced to Tunisia when the Romans took over and was a huge hit with the native Berbers. It required no special training or education to enjoy it as the theater, on the other hand, did, and among groups whose tradition it was to be warriors and hunters, the combats had an instant and special appeal. Some sixty amphitheaters have been discovered in North Africa and of these fifty are in Tunisia. Wherever the Romans built cities, with few exceptions, amphitheaters were part of the urban African plan.

At Thysdrus the first amphitheater was, to put it simply, a mess. Dating probably to the time of Augustus, it was notable mostly for its lack of symmetry, the disquieting irregularity of its shape and the sharp variations in height from one part to another. In short, it was a primitive effort but it was at least functional. Built on a small hill, its seating too was rudimentary, the spectators having to sit on the cut-away bedrock that projected from the hillside. Probably this ad hoc structure was the result of a craving for the games by newly arrived Roman farmers, landholders and merchants, who had come to Thysdrus during the time of Julius Caesar's conquest of the area. Nostalgic for the delights of home, they improvised this inexpensive gathering place, which resembles early Republican amphitheaters known in Italy at Sutri and Luni. It is the earliest amphitheater known in Tunisia.[19]

Succeeding this embryonic prototype, a second amphitheater was erected on the same spot near the end of the first century, perhaps during the time of the Flavian emperors (A.D. 69–96). The first amphitheater was buried under a mound of earth and debris and quickly forgotten. Many different supporting walls were now constructed around the arena, on which were placed earth fill and then seats made of mudbrick, covered with a protective plaster coating. This second effort, despite all of its imperfections, was a lot better than the first. The arena area was more regular and functional, the steps and seats easier to maneuver. There were drains for runoff and special features such as

Views of the amphitheater of Thysdrus. Roman, first half of the third century
A.D.

a tribunal, or raised platform, for dignitaries. This type of amphitheater, built against a hill, resembles similar structures which have been
found throughout Tunisia at Thignica, Thuburbo Maius, Leptis Mi-
nus, Sufetula, Acholla and Bararus.

The third and final amphitheater at Thysdrus, one of the best surviving examples from all of antiquity, was built in a different location, and on flat ground, so that it conformed to the other great examples of this type, such as the Colosseum in Rome and the magnificent structures of Arles and Nîmes in the south of France, as well as the Tunisian examples at Carthage and Thapsus. It held twenty-seven thousand spectators as opposed to forty-three thousand for the Colosseum and thirty-five thousand for the Capua building. It was, along with that of Verona, the third largest amphitheater in the Roman world.

Constructed in the early/mid-third century A.D., one and a half centuries after the Colosseum, it differed from its predecessor in a number of aspects, for it had profited from all the technical progress which had been acquired during the interval. Its underground chambers, situated below the arena and containing the rooms for keeping wild beasts and stage machinery, were better organized. Just as in the Colosseum, the animals could be raised in cages up into the arena and released by using a pulley system. In the same manner, stage or arena decorations could also be raised up, so that the arena might be decorated as if it were set in the wild, with artificial hills camouflaging the openings in the floor of the arena. The spectator might be unaware of the raising and lowering going on behind the stage props, but amphitheater designers, like theater artists, were in great demand if they could come up with new and innovative ways to stage the games.

In this third Thysdrian amphitheater, the curve of the arena was made more flowing and rounded, avoiding dead angles, and the organization of the access corridors feeding people in and out of the building was simpler and less confusing than in the Roman Colosseum. Another difference dictated by local taste was that the large ashlar blocks of Punic building tradition were preferred to specially prepared Roman bricks. Although the Colosseum also used cut stone for its support skeleton (travertine and tufa), it had much more brick and concrete for its superstructure and vaults than was used at Thysdrus.

Yet another provincial manifestation was the fact that the Thysdrian amphitheater did not follow the traditional Roman system for exterior design as the Colosseum did. Normally the lower level of the exterior must be Doric, the next level Ionic, and the next Corinthian, following a natural progression that Vitruvius, the Augustan architect and writer, tells us goes from the most masculine to the most feminine type of column capitals. But at Thysdrus, traditional Roman decorum was violated. The amphitheater had Corinthian on its first and third stories and a composite capital (a combination of Ionic and Corinthian) on the second floor. It seems that in local taste, even though the basic ideas may have derived from Rome, propriety and decorum could be cast to the winds. In Rome, amphitheaters would be constructed using the Roman foot as a basic measurement, approximately thirty centimeters, but the Thysdrians used the fifty-centimeter Punic foot as their model, showing that old traditions die hard or not at all.

If the first Thysdrian amphitheater can be attributed to the passion of a few newly settled Italians (like British soldiers who, when they settle in foreign lands, quickly improvise soccer fields), the subsequent examples show that the local population at Thysdrus, as well as other Tunisian centers, took to the spectacle as if it were their own. It is interesting to note that Roman amphitheaters were not especially popular in the Near East, but then the citizens of that area did not have quite the same love of savage animals and hunting. There, hunting and even zoos were a delight reserved for the upper classes and especially royalty.

Whatever the reasons, amphitheaters sprouted everywhere like mushrooms, while *stadia,* which were structures designed for housing foot races and wrestling, held almost no appeal, and were relegated to obscurity.[20] Athletic contests, despite being encouraged by a number of emperors, lacked the violence and gore that the crowds demanded. Not every Roman or African was an enthusiast, and some emperors and writers railed against these blood games, but most of the emperors were themselves as fanatical as the masses. Attendance declined even at theaters in North Africa; they were either abandoned or sometimes transformed into amphitheaters themselves. Not even the popularity of Christianity, beginning to take root seriously in the later second century, could stop the popularity of the games.

The arena was a terrific diversion for a culture that had lots of holidays and a surprising amount of free time. A normal work day lasted only about six hours, and those with slaves or *coloni* were free whenever they wanted to be. Clients could easily get permission from their patrons or would accompany them. The poor found the games to be a fabulous spectacle they could see for almost nothing, and the wealthy could use it and the food dole to keep the rabble happy and keep their tiny ruling class in power.

At Rome the emperor Trajan (98–177) presented games involving 10,000 gladiators, and in A.D. 109, during 117 straight days of consecutive spectacles, 9,824 gladiators fought and fully half of them were killed. The same emperor did not hesitate to force into the arena some fifty thousand prisoners conquered in his Dacian campaign in Romania and he pardoned the winners. At the inauguration of the Colosseum (also known as the Flavian amphitheater) under Titus in A.D. 80, some five thousand wild beasts were killed in one day, creating a massive animal disposal problem.[21]

At Thysdrus, even if there is a lack of texts or inscriptions to re-create the frenzy of the crowd or the bloody ambiance of the arena, mosaic artists constantly depicted how major a role the amphitheater played in local life. There was a particular local taste for the *venationes,* or wild animal hunts, combats and spectacles. The dazzled spectator might witness savage beasts trained to do exotic things, such as one might see in a modern circus performance by Siegfried and Roy: panthers pulled chariots, lions pounced on hares and then released them alive on command, tigers licked the hands of their trainer, elephants (if we can believe it) wrote entire phrases on the sand with their trunks.

There were also humorous combats, or burlesques, featuring such curiosities as a bear fighting buffaloes, elephants taking on a rhinoceros, bull runs or *corridas* (as still occur in the Arles amphitheater). And there were moments of horrifying, gratuitous cruelty and sadism, as fully protected men taunted wild beasts by shooting arrows into them, intending to wound and enrage them, driving them mad and covering the arena with their blood even as the crowd roared. Another diversion was the more evenly matched but hardly less brutal fights in which men armed only with daggers, bows and arrows, lances, swords or firebrands risked their lives against ferocious beasts. Stake matches involved such ideas as a poorly armed man chained in one spot taking on an enraged leopard.

Crowds also flocked to gladiator combats, not very good ones in the small regional amphitheaters but frightening and thrilling matches in cities like Thysdrus. The events were preceded by a parade, where the gladiators clothed in Tyrian purple passed in review and saluted their emperor: "Hail Caesar. They who are about to die salute you" ("Ave Caesar morituri te salutant").[22]

These were combats designed, as Livy said, "sine missione munus gladiatorium dare," or "to exhibit gladiators who fought to the death."

Often after killing one man, the survivor had to face another opponent immediately and risk being killed again. The dead were evacuated at once, and the bloody sand of the arena turned over as the combats continued. Often a defeated gladiator, flat on his back, would raise his left hand and ask for clemency from his conqueror. If the emperor or a high official were present, it was he who would make the decision or he might ask the opinion of the crowd. If he waved his handkerchief or raised his thumb, the victim was spared, but if he turned his thumb down, the wretched loser was dispatched. It was a moment of great suspense and silence, which contrasted with the music that accompanied the combats. Partisans called for death or mercy at the top of their lungs, then all waited breathlessly for the final decision.[23]

A victorious gladiator was compensated right on the field. He might receive sacks of money, often gold coins, and he would make a victory turn around the arena as the crowd showed its approval. A unique mosaic found in a house at Smirat, located between Hadrumetum and Thysdrus, sheds some light on the question of compensation.[24] It shows an extraordinarily bloody combat between gladiators and beasts taking place in an amphitheater. The action sequences highlight four leopards being impaled by four *bestiarii* holding lances, as blood drips onto the arena. One of the men, Spittara, has each foot tied to a stake for a special handicap match as he defeats Victor the leopard. The scene is, appropriately, placed under the patronage of the goddess Diana, the huntress, and Bacchus.

In the center of the scene we see a rare image of the organizer of the games, a certain Magerius, who appears in a tableau that no doubt occurred at the end of the competition, even though it is shown as if it were in the midst of the struggle. He holds a tray with four sacks full of prize money, and each one is inscribed as to its amount.

A public announcer is prepared to reward the four victors and addresses the crowd by saying the words written to the viewer's left on the mosaic floor: "Spoken by the herald: Gentlemen, the *Telegenii* [one of the great gladiator associations of the region] troupe awaits its recompense; it is for you to accord to them some sign of your favor— give them 500 *denarii* per leopard."

An inscription to the viewer's right apparently gives the crowd's response in what appears to be colloquial Latin, which would not get high marks today in a university. It appears to be an *acclamatio* from the

Mosaic of the arena from Smirat showing Telegenii gladiators fighting wild beasts and Magerius offering 1000 denarii to each victor. Roman, probably circa A.D. 240.

crowd, informing us that since the contest has been particularly spirited, the shouting mob urges Magerius to make proof of his generosity and pay the money won by the gladiators. The crowd asserts that the reward should be equal to that given by the *quaestors* in Rome at the games. As the crowd continues to acclaim the proceedings until nightfall, Magerius, accustomed to offering abundant largess, agrees to pay the expenses of the games, and the money is placed in the sacks. But Magerius does not stop at paying only the five hundred *denarii* promised and demanded by the spectators. In a burst of generosity he offers one thousand *denarii* to each man.

This grand gesture elicits a delirious response from the crowd, which is at the height of its joy and acclaims Magerius. Obviously the day remained for a long time in Magerius' memory, for he immortalized the moment in this mosaic, which remains the pride of the Hadrumetum museum.

Apart from receiving financial rewards, a gladiator was considered someone worthy of adulation by the young ladies of the audience, even though he was normally of humble origin. Ancient writers have observed that the torment of the arena became the torment of hearts for the women, and a handsome, successful gladiator was called the "ornament of the ladies," or "the one who makes all the girls sigh." But his fame might not last long and he could die in a future combat.[25] If he showed mercy to someone, that same person might return another day to destroy him. The gladiators had a saying which went "moneo ut quis quem vicerit occidat," or "I warn you; show no pity for the conquered, whoever it may be."

In the tiny amphitheaters of the smaller cities, second-rate fights or even odd spectacles worthy of Ripley's *Believe It or Not* were the normal bill of fare: dwarf fights, dwarfs versus women, black against black. This type of event, which was considered humorous in its day by many, also filled the spare moments between contests at the big amphitheaters, for the show commenced at dawn and only stopped at nightfall.

In the beastly hot summertime of Tunisia, the heat and sun could be kept away by the rigging of a curtain over a good bit of the arena—a job usually given to ex-sailors, who knew all about rigging ships and needed work after they grew too old to stay at sea or had served their time in the military.

The star attractions at these games did not go on until the afternoon. The morning sessions might be reserved for the execution of criminals of all sorts or even, in later years, Christian martyrs. These hapless individuals would be delivered defenseless to ferocious and starved beasts. A startling, unnerving mosaic from a house in a late second-century residential district of Thysdrus reproduces one of these scenes. Some wild beasts, separated by arrows and scattered blood, move around an improvised structure, which may have been put in the arena to mask the animal elevators within. It has captured enemy trophies affixed to it. Although it is only partly preserved and had several later Roman graves cut through it before it was extensively restored in the 1970s, it shows two condemned men being devoured alive by beasts.

The men are of athletic build and quite muscular, and they wear nothing but short loincloths. One holds his feet together and stands rigidly; his hands are tied behind his back and a second person, perhaps an attendant who has bound him, flees. A menacing panther, which appears immense compared to its victim, prepares to deal the death

Section of a mosaic showing a prisoner being attacked by a leopard during games held in the amphitheater. From a house known as the Domus Sollertiana *at Thysdrus. Roman, third century (first half).*

blow, while the man's hair stands on end and his eyes bug out in terror. The rage of the beast contrasted with the agony of the man gives a pathetic and shocking air to this scene. In the second tableau, a panther plants its feet on the thigh, chest and shoulder of a bound prisoner. As the beast devours the man's face, blood gushes from the wound and trickles down onto the ground below.

The noon program was also reserved for those condemned to death and often took the form of a public execution of real criminals. Capital punishment was much more widespread in antiquity than it is now, and the execution of criminals in this manner was designed to send a clear message to those who might have thoughts of taking the law into their own hands.

The afternoon sequences were the most exciting. These were the great gladiator battles or fabulous hunts. But there was lots of action all around the amphitheater at all times: taverns, places to buy hot food and pastries, astrologers, magicians and prostitutes. Like the baths, the amphitheater was a bizarre world, where life and death existed side by side, along with joy and suffering, and the mobs felt the strange mass intoxication that came from feeding their passion for human blood sports. Unfortunately, this aspect of mankind's existence has not disappeared at all.

❦ X ❦

The Life of Ease

IN THE COMPLICATED social structure of Africa Proconsularis, only a very few people got to enjoy the good life to the maximum. Some of these elite lived in sumptuous houses in the city, while others played lord of the manor in lavish country estates. Many had a number of homes and could afford to be absentee landlords. Such an elitist society could not endure forever but while it lasted, the very rich certainly had a good time.

The focal point of social life for the wealthy was the house (*domus*) or villa, a center for entertaining, discussing business or relaxing in style.[1] The rich held frequent dinner parties for those in their employ: that is, the lesser people who managed their affairs or labored for them, or who were being supported by them in cultural endeavors. A formal client (*cliens*) was a free man who might entrust himself to a patron and receive protection and financial help in return. Former slaves, for example, when they became free but were still poor, might attach themselves to a former owner.

This unusual relationship was in fact a marriage of convenience, for the client helped the patron in his political ambitions or might function virtually as a servant, in exchange for which the patron offered legal and professional counseling, as well as food and, occasionally, some big nights out at his villa. During such evenings there was often a hierarchy of seating, and the quality of food might also vary according to who you were.[2]

The truly fine homes were well equipped for entertaining and were designed to provide visual surprises of all sorts for the guests:

perhaps someone cutting into a big pastry with a detachable upper crust to release birds to fly around the room. The architecture of the house too was intended to create a complete spatial and sensual experience for the visitor.

At Utica, where the Augustan city was laid out over the Punic one in a clear grid, the *insulae* (or rectangular city blocks) have twelve houses each, six on either side of a common border wall, which ran the length of the block. While most of the houses were occupied by lower-middle-class people and are nondescript—and dull as dishwater to excavate—one of them is exceptional in its flamboyance and pretentiousness, for the landowner bought up five of the twelve lots of the *insula* in the later first century A.D. and created a sumptuous villa right in the heart of the city. Known now as the House of the Cascade, it offers a valuable insight into how the other half lived.[3]

From the street a coachhouse offered a place to park your horse and carriage, and the stone door frames at its entry were curved to avoid serious damage from cart wheels. A monumental entry, which has been horrendously rebuilt by a French excavation team, was flanked by a reception room manned by a concierge, where perhaps a guard dog could either let you enter or urge you on your way with a growl.

If a visitor were lucky enough to gain admittance, he would begin to walk towards the center of the house and would pass by a basin spewing out water onto another rectangular basin below. The latter was floored with a mosaic showing popular Mediterranean fish. The placing of such a fountain along the principal entry route was no accident: the sight and sound of gurgling water (Pliny's *iucundissimum murmur*) were essential ingredients in fine homes. After Hadrian's aqueduct had brought water to Carthage, Utica and other centers before the middle of the second century, upper-class houses were remodelled to include water shows, fountains and *nymphaea*.

In the later first century A.D., the House of the Cascade was upgraded and had many of its mosaic floors ripped up to install lead pressure pipes and drains to evacuate water. This meant a lot of business not only for the firms that specialized in home remodelling and fountain installation but for mosaicists as well. However, in most cases at Utica the new floors lacked the precision and fineness of their first-century predecessors, while making up for them in the exuberance of the figural scenes. In the original first-century house, problems of level among the different sections had been solved by steps, but in the later second century, mosaic ramps were installed to make the transition.

Fish mosaics, especially mosaics depicting edible fish, were common choices to decorate fountain basins, and there were at least three such mosaics in this house alone. Laid in marble and limestone cubes known as *tesserae*, the mosaics often featured fish with their bodies highlighted in glass cubes so that they appeared to swim when water cascaded over them. Fish and crustaceans which regularly showed up on fish mosaics included jumbo shrimp (the *crevettes royales* of today's Tunisian restaurants), red mullet, sea bass, eel, spiny lobster, octopus, squid, sole, codfish, mackerel and a local fish known today as *daurade* (*sparus auratus*) and sometimes in English as gilt-head. *Garum,* the popular gooey fish sauce, was not depicted, but fishermen (or sometimes cupids) and their nets were.

Continuing up one of the two mosaic ramps, the client entered the peristyle or rectangular colonnaded walkway that surrounded an open-

Mosaic from El Alia showing a presumed Nilotic scene. Servants attend the wealthy and a drink is poured in front of a mapalia *or peasant hut while fish, shrimp, and crabs swim in a stylized body of water and a rustic shrine appears at the right on a hill. Roman, third century* A.D.

air garden, in the center of which was an enormous Baroque-style fountain. Lead pipes, no doubt perforated, wound around the center of it in a figure-eight pattern, so that the effect of dancing waters would have dazzled dinner guests. The fountain, moreover, was like the *pulpitum* of a Roman stage, with alternating rectangular and semicircular niches in front of a big pool of water, where real fish may have swum.

The garden and fountain were designed as the *pièce de résistance* of the house, for all of the main rooms opened out from them. There was a gargantuan dining room, or *triclinium,* furnished with couches on three sides. Originally paved in mosaic, it had been refloored in rich marble slabs of *opus sectile* about A.D. 160, in those golden years when money seemed to flow like the water. But dining was a special experience, for flanking the *triclinium* on two sides were open courts glimpsed through windows. Each court had a basin for water, so that a diner could be surrounded by circulating air and water on three sides. Such an arrangement was known to the Augustan writer and architect Vitruvius as a Cyzicene (from Cyzicus, in Asia Minor) *oecus,* the idea being that the aesthetics of fine dining required beautiful vistas, the gentle sound of water and elegant decor.

Nor was one dining room sufficient in the finest houses. Such an open arrangement as we have described above was only suitable in the summertime. For the winter months, a more secluded room, whose mosaic paving was replaced by handsome black and white *sectile* in the later first century, was reached from a bayonet-angled corridor, which was paved in mosaic with geometric designs. In some homes, although not in this one, dining areas had their floors and walls heated by a hypocaust system, which used pillars of stone to raise up the floor and allow the circulation beneath it of hot air, distributed from an oven (*praefurnium*) located in an open court.

After dinner, a short stroll down a corridor took one to a view of a fish mosaic laid on a slope, with a water jet at the top to create the cascade effect that gave the house its name. On the other side of the peristyle were small, squarish guest or family bedrooms, and farther away from the center of things were the simple servants' quarters—no mosaics here. A room with a rear area raised up about half a foot was either a master bedroom just off the peristyle (sleeping areas were often raised up to avoid scurrying things in the night), or a household shrine (*lararium*). Another exit at the far side of the house beyond the garden provided a second way out of the house for, as the first-century writer Petronius informs us in *The Satyricon*, fine houses had "one way in and another way out." It was considered gauche to have a single-entry home.

Because of the magnificent state of preservation of the House of the Cascade, it is not at all difficult to imagine what the good life was like in ancient Utica: the conviviality of the *triclinium* with its performing dancers and musicians, the superb seafood served by master chefs, and servants to wait on you hand and foot.

But up on the promontory beyond was a house (certainly that of the proconsul or a very high magistrate) that was at least three times as large as the House of the Cascade.[4] Built in the later first century also, it had a courtyard the size of a small football field and a *sectile* dining room over twice as big as that of the Cascade house; it also possessed an immense colonnaded room, more like a private basilica, with its own rooftop view over the entire harbor of Utica. In about A.D. 160, not to be outdone, the owner of this giant home, known as the House of the Great *Oecus,* added a private bath complex.

The mosaics which decorated the floors, walls and fountains of North African houses in antiquity were considered as essential as fine rugs are today in better homes. True mosaics, made with *tesserae* and not pebbles, were, as we have seen, a Carthaginian invention, but the Roman influence in ancient Tunisia used the art to make floor-filling black and white decorative tapestries of tiny stones. Gradually, by the later first century A.D., floors of a rich polychromy came into vogue, while the patterns became increasingly inventive.[5] The floor industry was considered a craft more than an art, and few floors were signed. This is in contrast to Greek mosaics, especially of the Hellenistic period, when there were a number of great masters, such as Sosos of Pergamon, renowned for their skillful work.

In the second century, when figural images became popular, the mosaic scenes were often produced from copybooks. Ideas, figural poses and whole scenes were borrowed, and often rethought and reordered, changing designs based on now lost Greek originals to suit local or at least contemporary tastes. Much of the originality of these floors lay in the inventive arrangements of figures and decorative patterns. Occasionally, particularly in scenes dealing with native pastimes like hunting, a truly original scene could be enthusiastically created.

The floor itself had to be placed on a firm foundation.[6] If a public monument was being erected and a strong floor was needed, the laborer would have to put down a *statumen* of cobbles set in a yellowish mortar. In houses and villas, the mosaicist used a sandy yellow mortar mixed with pebbles; this was tamped down into a layer perhaps six inches thick called the *rudus*. Over this was placed a layer of lime, sand and often crushed tile or pottery. This layer was about four inches thick and was called the *nucleus*. Once this was tamped down, rolled and dried, a rough outline could be drawn on the *nucleus* to show the desired pattern. This became known as the *sinopia,* and an example, sketched in red ochre, was excavated in one of the guest rooms (Room XXVI) of the House of the Cascade at Utica.

A setting bed, or *supranucleus,* of lime mortar, perhaps mixed with marble dust, was laid over the dry, levelled *nucleus*. It was just a fraction of an inch thick, and the relatively uniform *tesserae* could be pressed down into it as it dried, resting their bases on the *nucleus*. In this way a level floor was produced and then grouted. If the mosaic-making team (usually composed of a variety of specialists belonging to different guilds) did its job well, and the floors were not savaged by the hand of man in later centuries, the mosaic may survive to this day.

At the site of Thuburbo Maius, picturesquely situated thirty miles southwest of bustling, modern Tunis, the modern visitor can stroll amid middle-class houses built in the heart of the city between A.D. 150 and 200, the same date as the major public monuments of the burgeoning community. The houses were situated in the environs of the forum and just down the street from the huge public baths.

Although the homes were relatively modest, their mosaic floor decoration is surprisingly tasteful and elegant. These were not villas, but places where people lived simply and comfortably. The one preserved example of an elegant home in the area is the so-called House of Neptune, and, like the House of the Cascade, it is designed to showcase the only slightly less well-off patron at his best.[7]

Once again the visitor encountered that obligatory guardroom at the entry to the house, where the servant might greet and announce new arrivals. The guest could then be conducted to the interior, well isolated from the street, by descending a stately and broad staircase, at the bottom of which he turned left to gaze upon the vista of a splendid open rectangular courtyard, no doubt planted as a garden and surrounded by the usual peristyle with its twelve columns.

At the far side of the peristyle was the huge *triclinium* paved in *opus sectile* and in the garden in front of it, a large semicircular basin. Such basins or fountains, decorated with mosaics, were commonly put directly in front of major rooms to delight guests and usually featured elegant marine scenes. Here the god Neptune is shown in triumph, while shipboard anglers try to catch a host of fish scattered about the sea. The House of Neptune had two other dining areas, much more modest than this showpiece.

Another room of modest size seems to have served as an intimate, elegant living room. Its floor was covered with a rich "rug" of polychrome mosaic, featuring an interwoven floral pattern, elegant *rinceaux* (spiralling plant ornaments) and handsome crowns of laurel, filled inside with rosettes or different types of birds. Such a floor was typical of the rich, exuberant and colorful African mosaics of the first half of the third century. The House of Neptune also contained several bedrooms with lovely geometric and floral mosaics, and there were servants' quarters at the back of the house with kitchen, court and latrine, all with floors of beaten earth.

A glimpse at the kind of entertaining which went on in the *triclinia* soirees is afforded by a fragmentary mosaic showing a banquet scene: it was found in Carthage and is now in the Bardo Museum.[8] Although late in date (about A.D. 400), it shows that Carthaginians in the age of St. Augustine still knew how to have a good time. The mosaic is unusual in a number of ways: it has curved ends, the banqueters sit up instead of recline and the dining couches are placed on all four sides of the dining area instead of only three. A laurel garland frames the scene as diners seated in groups of three eat from elongated wooden tables, while servants hustle in food and drink. The much-damaged center of the scene shows a fat and balding musician blowing on pan pipes, while two dancing ladies accent the beat by shaking rattles.

Although times were hard for Africa Proconsularis in the second half of the third century, and there was considerably less building activity due to the instability of the Roman empire and the continuing economic difficulties, a revival of sorts—or at least an Indian summer—occurred in the fourth century after Constantine the Great's accession to leadership of the empire.[9] Many of the most fascinating Tunisian floors date to this later period, when African mosaicists were still in such demand that they even worked abroad in such locations as Piazza Armerina in Sicily.

One of the most famous mosaics from this period shows that the very rich still enjoyed the life of ease. It comes from the living room of a splendid Carthaginian house and shows the country domain of a certain Iulius, a man of considerable wealth. The detailed scenes on three registers allow us to view more closely the pursuits of the aristocracy of late antique Carthage. In the lower register, the *dominus* himself sits at the right, almost like a medieval Christ enthroned, wearing a long, elegant tunic. He extends his right hand to receive a parchment scroll, on which can be read the words *D[omi]no Iu[lio]* or "for Master Iulius."[10]

The servant presenting the scroll holds two cranes in his arms, perhaps intended as a gift to accompany the note. Another servant hurries in from the fields with a large basket brimming with autumn grapes; he passes through a quince and apple orchard, which is obscured by a handsome wooden screen, or *cancellum*. He is holding a

The "Seigneur Julius" Mosaic was found in 1920 in the excavations of a house in Carthage. It represents the domain of the wealthy Julius and illustrates his villa, pastimes, and activities during the four seasons of the year. Roman, fourth century A.D.

lively hare by the legs in the manner in which modern southern Tunisian hunters hold it after it has been killed by saluki hunting dogs.

Iulius' wife appears at the left of the lower register, reclining on a column in a pose borrowed from fourth-century-B.C. Greek sculpture. She wears a stunning embroidered tunic; a female servant hands her a necklace taken from an inlaid jewel box and a male servant offers a basket of spring roses and a perky canine looks on. Behind her is a soft chair with a curved top resembling a throne. The scene suggests someone to whom a refined life-style is extremely important and the operating maxim here seems to be "If you've got it, flaunt it."

The central register puts the emphasis on Iulius' villa, a handsome structure that looks more like a medieval manor than a house. It is built of solid ashlar masonry and flanked by tall tile-roofed towers; the facade possesses an arcaded and porticoed gallery upstairs and a monumental entranceway below. Behind this impressive facade can be glimpsed a series of domed rooms, which may indicate Iulius' private baths, and another, unidentified structure appears nearby, rendered at an angle to the rest of the building.

On either side of the central scene, the mosaicist has illustrated the departure for a hunt. As the fourth-century writer Ammianus Marcellinus tells us, the wealthy *domini* were obsessed with hunting and, even though their biggest conquest might be a good-sized rabbit, they enjoyed bragging about their prowess as if they were Alexander the Great. Iulius was apparently no different. He appears on his horse, jaunty and ready to go, attended by a personal valet and wearing a tunic which is the very latest in hunting fashions. Across the way two more servants with nets, spears and intelligent-looking greyhounds prepare to set out on the great adventure.

In the upper register a seated lady, possibly the patron spirit of the manor, appears in the middle of a cypress grove, holding a fan to help her keep cool. Attendants cannot wait to rush up and bring her offerings. To the left, warmly dressed children gather olives, and a male servant in tunic and cape (*chlamys*) hurries over with some ducks. A female servant brings a basket of olives in this winter scene, while across the way a shepherd sits near his hovel of a home by a field full of summer wheat as oxen plow and a servant woman offers the lady a goat. A feisty dog guards the shepherd's hut.

In scenes like this we see how the four seasons passed among the rich and famous. We can also see the things that Iulius and his ilk held dear to their hearts: a fabulous home, fine clothes and jewelry, private baths, fertility of the land and, of course, their aristocratic life-style. For although others rush and work feverishly around them (even children), they are the collectors who sit like Christian icons, live a life of ease, or deign to receive the offerings of their vast plantations. It is conspicuous consumption on a grand scale.

Even in the twilight of antiquity, when Carthage was supposed to be enduring severe economic hardship during the Vandal occupation of the fifth century, there were still many wealthy people and opulent houses to be found not only in Carthage but outside the capital as well. At Pupput, the ancient name of the popular seaside resort of Hammamet (about thirty-five miles south of Tunis) is the elegant House of the Figured Peristyle, unique in all of Tunisian art and architecture.[11]

Built in its final form in the second half of the fifth century, in the heart of the Vandal period, the mansion extended over some twenty-five hundred square feet. It had the bayonet entry so popular in North African houses as a windbreak. A small room led to the peristyle and was decorated in mosaic showing a ship at full sail in the middle of the sea, accompanied by the inscription "[Vela p]ansa non [a]bean[t]," or "The sails are set; may they not disappear." This is simply a plea for continued good sailing weather.

Once inside the colonnaded peristyle of the home, the visitor gets a surprise, for there is no central garden or even an open court. The central space is instead filled with mosaics. Next to each column is a mosaic-made "shadow" or imitation reflection of each column as it might look under water. The reflection of the arcades between the columns is also clearly indicated. In the center of this playful floor is the mosaic image of a functioning lighthouse, but the idea of a garden is kept alive by placing rose branches done in mosaic between the reflections of the columns.

This magnificent house contained many more rooms with magnificent floral and geometric mosaics as well as a good-sized private bath complex. Judging by the emphasis on sailing, it must have been connected with maritime commerce, and the owner must have been very successful at it, for his house is worthy of being placed among the very finest dwellings of the aristocracy of the province.

Theatrical scenes were particularly popular on Roman mosaics throughout the province. At Thuburbo Maius, for example, a floor of the third century depicts a poet or playwright seated on a shaft of

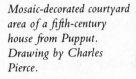

Mosaic-decorated courtyard area of a fifth-century house from Pupput. Drawing by Charles Pierce.

column and meditating over a scroll that has been placed before an altar, on which are set several theater masks. (Masks, known as *personae,* were worn by comic or tragic actors to help identify their particular types of characters for the audience; the characters always had the same traits.)[12]

Although these fabulous homes of the wealthy became popular gathering places for many levels of society, there were other haunts which the idle rich enjoyed visiting. One of the favorite places for the educated and semieducated to spend time was the theater. Admission was quite cheap, and even the poor could enjoy, if not always completely understand, the performances. The great tragedies and comedies of the famous Greek playwrights were performed with some success, as were plays by Roman writers such as Terence and Plautus.

The orchestra of the theater, originally circular, had been reduced to a semicircle, and much of the action now took place on a big, low stage called the *pulpitum.* The scene building behind the stage grew to enormous proportions in the first century, some three stories high, and was elaborately decorated. The Greek type of theater, formerly built on a hill with a commanding view over the countryside, was now in Roman times usually built on flat ground and turned into a self-contained world with no exterior views at all.

Particularly popular at the theater in North Africa were the performances by mimes and pantomimes. The mime performance, or *mimus*, had been developed in Greece and was a particular favorite of the lower classes.[13] Such performances featured lowlife characters in ragged dress and would include the use of gesture, dance, music and voice—and quite risqué dialogue or slapstick. Subjects were often taken from daily life and presented as satire or farce; the actors did not normally wear masks.

Less vulgar but equally popular were the pantomimes. These were performed by dancers, who might be accompanied by a chorus and music and who were often highly renowned for their skillful interpretations of religious stories or historical subjects. The North African writer Apuleius described his own visit to such a performance about the middle of the second century and reported seeing wonderfully attired handsome young men and lovely young ladies dancing. He also recorded an elaborate example of set design: a mountainous landscape, planted with greenery, where unfolds the story of the Judgment of Paris, in which the young son of King Priam must decide who is the most beautiful of all the goddesses.[14]

Paris appears, a handsome young shepherd; then Mercury, the messenger god; next follows Juno, queen of the gods, who is accompanied by the *Dioskouroi*: Castor and Pollux. Then comes Minerva, and finally Venus, whose arrival astonishes everyone because of her stunning beauty, which sets her apart from the other goddesses.

Descriptions like this suggest that these pantomimes, unlike the mimes, were huge spectacles, costly to produce and of very high quality. Only big cities would be able to produce a full-blown show, while the mime performances often thrived in lowbrow, rustic surroundings. An individual pantomimist could be a true superstar, as the epitaph of one Vincentius of Timgad (in Algeria) attests:

Consecrated to the Manes is Vincentius, the most honored of
pantomimes. He lives forever in the thoughts of the people,
not only for the art in his performances. This was a man
whom everyone loved: just, good and in his every relationship
with each person irreproachable and sure. There was never a

day when, during his dancing of the famous pieces, the whole
theater was not captivated enough to reach the stars. Here
now under the earth he rests before the ramparts; 23 years he
has lived in his prime, pious and even more eloquent in his life
than he was in his movements.[15]

The dedicants' deep sense of loss and their reverence for this
talented, delightful man are obvious. While it is true that many writers
condemned such dancers, many intellectuals enjoyed the performances
enormously. Only the Christians were unanimous in their condem-
nation of all spectacles inspired by pagan religion.

Many upper-class citizens enjoyed not only plays and theatrical
performances of all sorts but fine literature as well; *The Aeneid* was
apparently a must on the reading lists of the province. A famous
mosaic, found in a house in Hadrumetum and dating from the later
third or early fourth century, shows the great poet Virgil himself,
flanked by Clio, the muse of history, and Melpomene, muse of
tragedy.[16] The former holds a scroll and the latter a theater mask, while
the poet is seated in a high-backed chair, with that same air of importance we have seen in the Iulius mosaic from Carthage.

Dressed in a toga, he meditates over a scroll on which we can read
the eighth line of *The Aeneid* and part of the ninth, "Musa mihi causa
memora quo numine laeso quidve," or "Muse, tell to me the reasons,
by what deity offended or . . ." The mosaic reveals the literary sophistication of the owner of the house but may have to take a back seat
to another mosaic from fifth-century Sufetula for obscurity of literary
reference.

This mosaic represents the four seasons, each of which is labelled
by inscription. But there is also a mosaic portrait, around which is
written "Autor Xenofonte."[17] A recent article has identified this individual as the fourth-century-B.C. Athenian Greek philosopher, author and adventurer Xenophon. Such an interest in not only Latin but
also Greek works shows the level of culture which permeated the
African aristocracy.

The sophistication of a surprisingly large section of society seems
a bit unusual at first glance, but Africans, both boys and girls, were
unusually well educated until they were sixteen. Latin and Greek might
be taught in the numerous schools, and Virgil was one of the most
widely read authors. An extraordinary structure was found at Maktar

Mosaic of Virgil the poet surrounded by the Muses Clio and Melpomene and holding the manuscript of The Aeneid. *Found in a Roman house in Hadrumetum in 1895. Roman, third to early fourth century A.D.*

in 1944, which may have been the center of a youth organization or official society. It had a large porticoed courtyard, an assembly room that resembled a basilica and an apsidal end like a Christian church, also office and storage spaces and even a bath with pools.[18]

At such institutions, teenagers might spend a year or two in required or strongly suggested service to the community, collecting and storing grain, olive oil and other products and building *horrea,* or warehouses. In a society that lacked formal police or a national guard for emergencies, such a group could almost function as a paramilitary organization, and indeed when the city of Thysdrus revolted against the emperor, such youth organizations were among the most ardent of the rebels. In fact, Mars was their patron divinity. But these groups were also centers for the diffusion of Hellenic and Latin culture; rhetoric and philosophy were taught there and the precepts that Rome wanted to instill in young men would be emphasized.

As the Iulius mosaic from Carthage informs us, no aspect of the good life delighted the landed aristocrats as much as the chance to participate in a great hunt, and they were not the only ones to enjoy it. The Roman historian and politician Sallust, author of *The War Against Jugurtha*, the definitive work on the Libyan chieftain, wrote that the hunt was essential to the African mentality and to the *virtus,* or feeling of manliness, of Jugurtha himself. Sallust believed that the valiant African horsemen were as passionate for the hunt as for war.

Of course the land of Africa was tailor-made for a people with a taste for hunting.[19] Great pride was taken in the breeding of powerful, hardy horses and in the training of greyhounds, and there was a seemingly endless natural reserve of game to stalk. Hunts were often major undertakings requiring the services of professional hunting associations, to track down the wild beasts destined for the amphitheater. Hunters were equipped with decoy animals, spears, shields and firebrands to trick the animals into nets or cages. Sometimes parent animals were diverted while cubs were snatched by hand.[20]

As we have seen, the smaller scale hunts—in which hunters followed on horseback as trained dogs tracked small game such as hares— were tremendously popular too. Great and small hunts were among the most popular subjects shown in the African mosaics, on funerary *stelae* and even on the walls of sarcophagi.

A famous mosaic of the third century from Althiburos, about 140 miles southwest of Tunis, documents some of the most exciting details of a great hunt—or perhaps several great hunts thrown together in a fury of narrative excitement. Although the mosaic, which measures well over 5.5 square meters, is severely damaged, it still gives an idea of the scale of mosaic work not uncommon to huge villas or public buildings, in this case the Monument of the Asclepieia, named after a Greek mosaic inscription that was found there.[21]

This floor was the centerpiece of a *triclinium,* which opened into a peristyle. The figural scenes were enclosed by an elegant *rinceau* border of acanthus leaves. Inside each circle of the *rinceau* pattern is a motif relating to the hunt, including all sorts of game (plumed larks, ducks, thrushes, etc.), instruments of the hunt (snares, game sacks) and heads of wild animals.

The central scene is divided into four distinct registers separated by gray-yellow ground lines. In the top register near the center is the departure scene, set in a flat countryside with a few patches of grass and occasional trees. The stars of the show, the beautifully dressed leaders of the hunt, canter on horseback and are attended by their valets. As the signal to begin is given, the masters ride tall in the saddle, carrying themselves in a stately manner, one riding a handsome steed called Faunus, after the woodland deity. As the hunt begins, two hunters with a stick dislodge a small beast hidden in a lair.

In register two, the slow buildup of the first register bursts into action: a wild beast hunt with every animal participant labelled in Latin.

The Hunt Mosaic from Althiburos. This illustrates the falling rider sequence and the release of dogs to chase down wild animals such as hares and jackals. Roman, third century A.D. (late).

The horseman riding Bracatus, a name meaning "wearing breeches like the Gauls," falls at full gallop, landing on his neck while still clutching the reins. A servant rushes up to help, while another informs the master, who has been engaged in trapping a creature with the aid of his dogs, among them one named Spina (the word means thorny, full of anxiety and so perhaps a problem animal). Another rider rushes along, helping to make the pattern of the whole sequence form a circle, a tribute to the mosaicist's ingenuity at planning a complex scene.

The unfortunate destruction of the central section of the mosaic interrupts the story here, but one can still observe some equipment for catching birds and a horseman goading along his steed, named Suriaca. In the next register down, two horsemen ride Perdix (Greek for partridge) and Plumeus (literally, downy or, as used by the poet Martial, "light as a feather"), the former galloping right and the latter prancing left. Below, a servant tries to overtake the dogs Pinnatus (here almost living up to his name, "winged") and Lecta ("chosen one"), who are tearing into an exhausted jackal; the pathetic creature bleeds profusely from the abdomen. Again the composition is circular.

To the far right is another circular composition, showing a hare hunt. A pair of speedy greyhounds, Polifemus (possibly a one-eyed or odd-eyed creature named after the Cyclops in the *Odyssey*) and Bois, hem in the creature, which looks like a huge Sonoran desert jackrabbit. Another horse gallops up although only its legs remain visible. A third dog, named Atalante, moves in (perhaps named after the Greek maiden of Boeotia renowned for her incredible running speed). Below all this are two riders, who come at the gallop on Miniatus (an ancient Iberian word for native cinnabar and by extension something vermilion-colored) and Cucia. At the left, a servant tends to the leg of a fallen rider.

The fourth and final register shows a greyhound attacking a hare, while a servant tries to remove the hapless animal and a second servant gestures wildly. Two horsemen ride up from either side. The rider to the right pulls the horse up short by its reins. This creature is Eventus ("occurrence," "experience," "success"), while the other horse is Auspicator ("taker of the auspices" and, by extension, "fortunate one"). Before the hunt ends, several of the participants, still on horseback, talk briefly. One of their horses is Icarus, named for the son of the Athenian craftsman Daedalus, who built the labyrinth of Knossos in Crete. The mythological Icarus drowned in the Aegean sea while trying to fly with wings made by his father.

Finally, to the viewer's left, the weary band returns home, content with their triumph in the hilly countryside, the captured animals trussed up to long poles carried over the shoulders of the heroes while the horse Amor ("Love") looks on.

From such a mosaic can be understood not only the techniques employed and logical progression used in organizing a hunt for small wild animals, but also something of the excitement generated by such an event. The *domini* are true *GQ* gentlemen, with their embroidered riding tunics and stylish striped sleeves, their bare thighs pressing hard against the horses' flanks. Their shoes resemble elegant *cothurni* or buskins with leggings. (The valets all wear simpler tunics and sandals.)

The Althiburos hunt mosaic has something of the character of a *National Geographic* documentary (only the sound is missing), providing a direct reportage of all the thrills and spills.

There are numerous other documents, less ambitious than this to be sure, but nonetheless of a great realism and liveliness. A handsome mosaic decorates the threshold of a main room of the House of the Laberii family at Oudna, about fifteen miles southwest of Tunis.[22] On this early-fourth-century floor we are not given the complete story of a hunt. Instead we join the hunt already in progress, literally at its peak of excitement: two horsemen ride at full gallop, their valet rushes up on foot and two saluki dogs (Ederatus and Mustela) nip at a hare and a fox who run ahead. Ederatus has a remarkable yellow coat slashed with black like a zebra.

Another intriguing floor comes from the House of the Hunt in Utica.[23] The mosaic panels, which date to about the middle of the fourth century, reveal the variety and techniques used by a wealthy estate owner and his retinue in the hunt, and the great pleasure they get from it. The scenes are not of high artistic merit but they have a theme that is worthy of an elegant imperial villa, even though they come from the peristyle of a slightly run-down, middle-class place in a big city *insula*. The situation is a little like a dweller in a modest row house enjoying "Life-styles of the Rich and Famous."

Panel one, for example, shows not the House of the Hunt but a country estate, or *villa rustica,* with pedimented upper story, towers, and roofs with *acroteria* (decorative objects or statues) placed on them. Trees in the background suggest the countryside. Panel two takes the viewer from the general to the particular: the apparent occupants of the villa, two men, perhaps servants, try to catch birds—there are three blatantly perched in a tree. Armed with thin yellow reeds and long flat-ended poles studded with what look like black nails, the men attack their prey and indeed a fallen bird is speared by one of them. The catch can then be stashed in the sacks suspended from the belts of the birdcatchers. Such a technique, still known in Tunisia, requires quickness, a sure aim and, at least at first, a high tolerance for frustration. This subject is extremely rare on Roman mosaics, but birdcatching was ardently pursued in antiquity and was the subject of a poem by Oppian, a Greek from southwest Turkey living in the second century A.D.

Panel three is a more common scene on North African hunt mosaics and is rendered in the characteristic shorthand style of the time. In this scene, two hunters oversee the driving of two stags into a prepared net. The intense lower figure, dressed in a tunic, herds the beasts inside and makes sure the stake will hold firm against the force of the animals.

The same technique can be seen on a mosaic from Hippo Regius, not far from the Tunisian border in northeastern Algeria. Beasts destined for the amphitheater are driven into nets by men using firebrands, while others surround the beasts by holding up rows of shields. All does not go well however, for a panther gets free and ends up chewing on a hunter's face. [24]

In panel four of the House of the Hunt mosaic, the chase has finally ended and, as usual in these hunting scenes, the booty is proudly displayed. Two hunters pose happily, the first with a rolled-up net, and the second with a hare dangling in front of a most interested African greyhound on a leash. Panel five, although fragmentary, suggests another staple scene: the *dominus* as the great hunter. No hares or stags for him, for the tail of what was no doubt a lion shows that while others can net the small stuff, he pursued the sport of ancient kings.

In panel six the *dominus* returns from his triumph on horseback led by a valet on foot. He is dressed in a blue cloak featuring glass mosaic *tesserae* of green and red and he carries a two-pronged, animal-spearing fork. Panel seven shows two hunters holding batons and a heavy net, which seems to have a captured animal inside. They wear flashy boots tied with black laces just below the knee.

Hunts were not only exciting pastimes full of unpredictable high adventure. They were also considered to have religious overtones, and proper sacrifices had to be made before the festivities could begin. A fifth-century mosaic from Carthage, known as the Offering of the Crane, once covered the floor of a Roman house in the district of Salammbô. In the center of the floor is the facade of a Roman temple, in which are placed two statues of the brother and sister divinities Apollo and Artemis, the patron divinities of hunters. Each is fitted out with hunting accessories, while a crane is offered before them as a sacrifice. The second-century Roman historian Arrian recommended such a required act of piety in order to obtain good luck, for the hunt was considered a gift from the gods.

Although the hunt was a test of manhood and a source of plea-surable relaxation and sport, a few hardy citizens were, as we have mentioned, professional hunters who belonged to big game-hunting organizations; it was their job to prepare and lead expeditions into the hinterland, trap wild animals and, as explorer Frank Buck used to say, "bring 'em back alive" for the amphitheaters. This is the subject of the fabulous Carthaginian hunt mosaic found in the Dermech district of Carthage. It documents scenes of stunning realism: hunters trap lions using a stuffed goat mounted on a wheeled cart to lure the beasts from their rocky lairs into a large box cage with sliding vertical trapdoors.[25] Tigers and wild boar are encountered too, some of the fierce beasts being pierced with spears. But other creatures are wanted alive and are whisked onto an animal transport ship for delivery to the arena. Such animals would then be well cared for until the time of the games; then they would be goaded and starved.

Hunting organizations needed large ships, a supply of cages, snares, protective gear, weapons of all sorts, nets and lures. It was big business, and the painted decorations on the walls of a bathing estab-lishment at Lepcis Magna in Libya indicate it may have been a head-quarters for such an organization. One can barely imagine the tall tales that must have circulated between those walls![26]

Besides the great and not so great hunts and the exciting contests of the amphitheater, a number of Africans enjoyed the games of the circus, or the *ludi circenses*. Documents illustrating the games are nu-merous in Tunisia; over two dozen mosaics celebrate the subject.[27] In addition, astrology was extremely widespread in Roman North Af-rica, and devotees often emphasized that the circus itself was a meta-phor for the heavens and had celestial significance. In later antiquity it was thus possible to think of the circus as representing the universe, with the twelve *carceres* (starting gates) symbolizing the twelve months of the year, and the four different-colored factions or teams standing for the four seasons. The conquering charioteer, or *auriga*, represented the sun or moon.

One of the best known of the circus mosaics comes from the odeon of Carthage and gives an idea of the architecture of such a structure. The form of the circus is elliptical, with the exterior facade shown as ranges of arcades placed in two stories. The *velum*, which is a sort of tent or covering to protect spectators from sun and heat, is lowered. On the right side are the *carceres*, while the *spina*, or spine around which the charioteers raced, occupies the center of the field and divides it. On the mosaic only a part of the *spina* is preserved, ending in a curve which was the scene of many pileups and crashes as drivers jockeyed for position. Around the *spina* race four *quadrigae*, or four-horse chariots, three moving in the same direction and one in another.

The latter may be intended to represent the winner of the contest and he is preceded by a horseman who may be the *iubilator*, or individual charged with encouraging the driver during the race. Also present, on foot, is the *sparsor*, who holds a whip and an amphora with

Circus mosaic from odeon of Carthage. Third century A.D.

water to sprinkle on and revive tired horses. The mosaic also depicts a basin and other dedicatory monuments, including a statue of the goddess Cybele, who makes a gesture to indicate the finish line.

The victorious driver and horses had the right to honors and recompense and they were cheered and revered like modern football players. They were also the subject of a number of mosaics, most notably one from Dougga that shows a driver in his chariot holding a palm branch (symbol of victory), a whip and a crown, while the presence of the circus is indicated by five arches behind him. Two of the victorious horses still bear their names, Amandus ("well loved") and Frunitus ("gay"), while next to the charioteer's head is the in-scription "Eros Omnia Per Te," or "Eros, all things because of you." This is a glorification of the victor, whose name was Eros and, perhaps, a little joke in that love in general may be said to produce all things worthwhile. Eros apparently belonged to the green faction, if one can believe the tunic he wears. (Factions were the various teams [originally the white and the red] which competed and engendered enormous partisan support from the fans.)

Winning was extremely important in the circus competitions, and participants did not hesitate to use magic to hex a rival. Some *tabellae defixionis,* or specially made lead sheets used for casting magic spells, have been recovered, inscribed with the names of demons and riddled with curses just like those of Punic times. These might be placed at night in a tomb; several have been found in the circus area, including one actually nailed to the arena. One such tablet, found at Carthage, had this to say:

> I conjure you up, prematurely dead demon, such as you are
> able to be, by the powerful names Salbal, Bathba,
> Authierotabal, Basutatheo, Aleo, Samabethor, bind the horses
> whose names and images I place for you on this tablet. . . .
> [the horse names are given] . . . Paralyze them in their course,
> destroy their power, their soul, elan and speed. Take victory
> away from them. Make them stumble and be unnerved, so
> they will not be able today in the hippodrome to run, walk, or
> win, or leave the stables or traverse the arena and the track or
> to make it around the markers. But make them fall along with
> their chariot . . . [more names are given of horses and then of
> demons]."

Obviously some competitors took their sports seriously indeed.[28]

The appeal of the *tabellae* is not hard to see. How wonderful it would be for us today to simply write up a good curse, bury it and wait for our enemies to crumble into dust. Indeed, in numerous areas of the United States, including recently in Fresno, California, similar practices are still carried out. And for those of us who may need more subliminal but equally effective elimination of our worst enemies, there is always Sylvester Stallone as Rambo or Clint Eastwood as Dirty Harry. The cinematic exorcism may be less obvious but it stems from the same basic need to overcome potential inadequacy.

☙ XI ☙

The Realm of Saturn

THE BLOODY GAMES of the amphitheater and circus and the cultural life embodied by literature and the theater provided ways for the Roman, Libyan and Punic citizens to share common interests, but a special kind of syncretization or intercultural mixing occurred on the spiritual plain as well.

By the later first century A.D., the province of Africa Proconsularis was becoming a place where the Near East met the Greco-Roman west, while the persistent Libyan substratum, with its own spiritual and artistic statements to make, helped to ensure that the ancient Tunisian culture would have its own stamp.

When Punic Carthage was finally destroyed and buried under layers of ash and salt in 146 B.C., the Roman conquerors who laid waste the land believed that they had forever exorcised the ghost of Hannibal. How surprised they would have been to find the Punic gods still flourishing four centuries later in cities where Romanization had taken over completely. But the Romans themselves were partly to blame, with their tradition of respecting as much as possible the customs of all conquered peoples. Getting the enemy's gods on your side was always a Roman goal, and it was an effective way to win new friends and influence people. This fusing together of old and new traditions gradually allowed North African religion to take on a unique, hybrid aspect.

To be sure that the major divinities of Rome were omnipresent in the newly conquered or founded communities, the Romans saw to it that Jupiter, his wife, Juno, and Minerva (the so-called Capitoline triad) were the focus of attention in the major temple, or Capitolium, in the heart of every city. The other principal gods were honored in temples and shrines as well.[1] Apollo was a patron of the arts; Bacchus, who was often shown as a youth, could look after the fecundity of crops and people—and enjoyed an enormous popularity; Neptune watched over the hazardous seas with their storms and shipwrecks; Venus looked after affairs of the heart and took over many duties of Astarte; Diana was the patroness of the beloved hunt and amphitheater games, where she was sometimes known as Diana-Nemesis; Mercury kept a watchful eye on the markets; and Aesculapius tried to make sure everyone stayed in good health. The goddess Cybele, who had been brought to Rome from Phrygia (Turkey) in the Second Punic War, was often associated with the cult of the emperors and her major temple, the Metroon in Carthage, featured the rite of the *lavatio,* a yearly procession and ceremony to ritually bathe her cult statue.[2]

The images of these divinities bombarded the province in a propaganda campaign to Romanize the souls of the natives. One of the most popular Roman divinities was Saturn, whose sanctuary usually occupied the greatest height of a city or town.[3] He became the Romanized version of Ba'al Hammon, the chief Punic divinity and creator of the universe, in many cases even replacing him. Although in earlier times his image was almost never seen, this important deity was abundantly visible under the Romans, when taboos about depicting him seem to have been lifted.

Now Saturn began to appear with lions, bulls and rams, sometimes seated on a great throne flanked with animals. He was often associated with a consort, known now as Caelestis or Juno Caelestis, but who may be the Romanized form of the Punic goddess Tanit. Under the Romans, Saturn as harvest divinity appeared with a sickle for the first time, but his Punic solar emblem still remained with him.

Despite the Roman attempt to fuse Saturn and Ba'al Hammon (and other attempts to turn Ba'al Hammon into Jupiter), the ancient rites of child sacrifice continued in the hinterland right into late antiquity, although offerings such as the first fruits of the season, birds, and animals such as rams or goats were much more common. But inscriptions honoring the god were increasingly written in Latin as Punic gradually died out in the high empire.

Even in modern Tunisia, some of the ancient sacrificial practices may still be observed in the more remote areas of the countryside. It is still common to see Arab men and women bringing offerings of a bull, lamb, cock or just a simple candle to sacrifice to a *marabout,* a male or female saint whose tomb is considered a magical place with special positive properties. The saint, a privileged being in the afterlife, could then intercede with Allah to fulfill the supplicant's vow.

Ba'al Hammon and Tanit were not the only legacy of Punic Carthage to Roman religion. Egyptian divinities, which had long been popular, continued to exert great influence. Isis worship in particular was widespread, and devotees fasted and abstained from sensual pleasures.[4] At his capital city of Iol (now Cherchel in Algeria), the Libyan leader Juba II is said to have kept a sacred crocodile captured in the southern Atlas Mountains. He also issued coins with Egyptian imagery.

Among the most exceptional sources of information which have come down to us from Roman times are a series of twelve tombstones—probably dating to the third century—from La Ghorfa, south of Dougga.[5] Now in the Bardo Museum, they illustrate the survival of Punic and Libyan religion and show how natives of a rural community attempted to come to grips with the advent of Roman religious concepts. They are also important not just because they all come from one location but because they are naive, stylized efforts to interpret and redefine classical imagery and iconography. They are, in short, genuine folk art.

Each *stele* consists of a slab in obelisk form sculpted on one side in three registers. The lowest register is generally reserved for images of the lower world—heroes, gods or a scene of sacrifice of an animal such as a bull. Here, for example, a very stiff and stylized Hercules with overlarge head and hands confronts the Nemean lion as one of his legendary twelve labors. The central register is more commonly reserved for the image of the dedicant, dressed in a Roman toga and enthroned in an ornate temple with a Greco-Roman facade of pilasters, a coffered and rosette-decorated frieze and a triangular pediment, in the center of which is a goddess with her hair unfurled. The mysterious deity is none other than Tanit-Caelestis. Atop the pediment is an eagle, the attribute of the supreme sky god, who here is not Jupiter but Saturn.

The top register follows the same hierarchic arrangement and shows the popular gods of the region as if they are hovering in the sky above the temple. Venus appears with a dove and Bacchus has a pine cone. In the center of the proceedings, towering over the pediment, is

Saturn, the great giver of all blessings, brandishing two horns of plenty. Above him may be seen, surprisingly, a head of the Egyptian goddess Hathor. At the very highest part one might find a crescent moon under a garland surrounding the head of Caelestis.

Through tombstones such as these it is possible to glimpse something of the richness of the African pantheon, where Roman, Punic and Libyan divinities divided up the sky and ruled in harmony over the world of the living.

Following along in this same tradition is the charming Boglio *stele* (named for its finder) from the region of Siliana, south of Jama.[6] Its forms are stylized and naive in the manner of the folk art of La Ghorfa. The proportions of the figures are squat, the figures themselves doll-like and frontal, and the heads, hands and feet are too large; there is little plasticity of form. But the artist has taken these simple elements and arranged a composition that is not only of the highest narrative and religious interest, but is as pleasing to the eye as a modern Tunisian rug from Gafsa, with its carefully presented simplified forms.

This important votive *stele* contains five registers, of which once again the lowest is the most humble. Here wheat has been loaded onto three chariots, and the horses begin to gallop away while the drivers crack their whips to urge them along. It is a wonderfully rendered scene with the horses, wheat, drivers and chariot wheels all forming a stylized, repetitive pattern that delights the eyes and gives a feeling of naive order.

In the panel above this scene, two yoked bulls pull a simple plow of a type which can be seen throughout Tunisia today (sometimes pulled by camels!). A puppetlike man keeps a hand on the plow and whips the beasts forward. Behind him we see a stylized harvest scene as two men cut wheat with their sickles and move through the deep field. The wheat is of enormous size, indicating its importance not only to the narrative here but to the community in general.

The harvesting and carrying-off of the wheat for distribution is of great importance to the dedicant, but it is because this is a scene of human labor that it is relegated to the bottom of the *stele* and placed in two very narrow panels. But in the next panel up we see a sacrificial scene of more importance where a man, perhaps the dedicant, sacrifices before an altar. His fancy robe lets us know he is someone of stature in the community.

As incense burns on the altar, a woman in what certainly looks like

Votive stele *to Saturn from the region of Siliana. Roman period, probably third century* A.D.

a turban brings a basket bursting with fruit. She appears to be the stylishly dressed wife of the sacrificing man, and the two flank the central altar as if they are intended to be the centers of attention. At each end of the scene, vertical balance is provided by two young girls bringing offerings, which they carry on their heads in the fashion of Berber women, who can be seen carrying baskets in this same way as they walk the roadsides of Tunisia today. The young lady on the right has a jar or pitcher for a libation, and the two girls may be the daughters of the sacrificer.

Flanking the altars are two reclining animals, a ram and a bull, and two more charming creatures than these one can hardly imagine. The bull stares out as if to lament his fate, while his summarily indicated tail swirls up behind him. The coat of the ram is magnificently cross-hatched in a pattern of lozenges, which fairly dances across the surface of the *stele*.

Before the next register is reached, a space or ground line appears on which is crudely carved an inscription: "PN Cuttinus Votum Solvit Cum Suis." This informs us that the sacrificer is "our patron," a rich proprietor named Cuttinus, who has offered this monument together with his own family.

Then in the next register we finally arrive at the chief subject matter, and the space allowed is larger than for any of the other scenes. In the very center, in the place of honor, is the great god Saturn, patron of the great patron Cuttinus, smiling down from the heavens, first onto Cuttinus and his family, who honor him in the register below and are large in his eyes, and then onto the entire realm of Cuttinus and all of his much smaller-sized workers.

Saturn rests on a reclining bull. He is the largest of all the figures and the most classically rendered, with a tiny measure of Greco-Roman plasticity that makes him stand out from the puppetlike forms around him. His chest is bare, with his mantle flung over his right shoulder and draped around the lower torso in a style borrowed, stiffly, from Hellenistic Greek prototypes. In his right hand he holds the sickle, indicating his power to help Cuttinus with his harvest. His left hand pulls aside his mantle so his vision is not obstructed.

On either side of Saturn are unusual companions: the *Dioskouroi*, Castor and Pollux, who were the brothers of Helen of Troy and would seem to have nothing to do with Ba'al Hammon or Saturn. They were, however, special divinities to the Romans and were thought to have helped fight for Rome's independence. The Temple of Castor and Pollux in the Roman forum was one of the very first structures built there—along with the Temple of Saturn. They were often present in North African art and may have been honored for their association with the constellation Gemini; their cult was famous for producing miracles. Here they may help to proclaim the celestial power of Saturn and they appear, as always, with their horses, and wearing military cuirasses.

Appropriately, Saturn and the *Dioskouroi* are enshrined, framed between columns and under an arch (the arc of the heavens?). Above Saturn and his friends flutter two victories, a classical idea but very stiffly done here, holding palms and flanking a handsome cartouche that says: "Saturno Aug[usto] Sacrum." It leaves no doubt that the revered Saturn has been given this sacred offering. At the very top of the *stele,* in the pediment, an awkward-looking regal eagle spreads its wings. Normally the bird of Jupiter, the creature is here once again the attribute of Saturn.

This amazing *stele* is a vision of the world offered by a rich proprietor of the countryside. He sees himself in finery above his workers, the have-nots who labor steadfastly in the fields. He loves and seeks to protect his dear family but he is nothing compared to his beloved god from whom all blessings flow. It is a scene of popular art that one would never see in Rome.

That is not to say that religious art, especially in the big cities, couldn't be downright classical and up-to-date. On the Byrsa hill in Carthage was found an extraordinary altar that dates to the time of the emperor Augustus, or shortly thereafter.[7] The figures are rendered with a suppleness and fullness of form and proportion that are worthy of Rome, and the iconography of the monument is in keeping with ideas promoted by Augustus himself.

One face shows the figure of the goddess Roma in her war attire, surrounded by symbols of conquest and prosperity. On another side is Aeneas, that brave Augustan ancestor, leading his son Ascanius/ Iulus and carrying his aged father, Anchises, on his shoulder. On another panel a sacrificial procession of toga-clad Romans and a *camillus* (religious attendant) participate in the sacrifice of an ox. On the fourth side Apollo, one of the patron divinities of Augustus, sits with his lyre and his prophetic tripod.

A far cry from the naive religious art of La Ghorfa and Siliana, these images are connected to official imperial propaganda and appear separately and in various combinations in other works of sculpture of the Augustan age, as well as in *The Aeneid* itself. When this altar was made, the legend of Aeneas was already well established: that the Trojan prince left Troy at the time of its destruction and made his way to Italy, where he founded Rome and the Julian family line, to which Gaius Julius Caesar Octavianus Augustus, the emperor, belonged.

Even before Augustus, the Julian clan had been making political and religious hay out of the legend that the Iulii were descendants of Iulus, son of Aeneas, son of Venus, daughter of Jupiter.[8] Julius Caesar had used the occasion of the funeral of his aunt Julia, wife of Marius, to enhance his own public image. He delivered the eulogy and in it reminded the audience that she was a descendant of the goddess Venus and so, necessarily, was the rest of the family.

It is not surprising then that the image of Aeneas should show up on the most important spot in Carthage. In fact, Virgil's poem about Aeneas is easily read as an epic dealing at least indirectly with Augustus. Their lineage connects the two, but as Virgil developed the heroic figure in *The Aeneid,* Aeneas became the legendary embodiment of virtues considered important in Augustan Rome, and to that extent he became a symbol for what Augustus expected from the Roman people and wanted them to believe about himself.

Aeneas' primary virtue is *pietas,* an all-encompassing loyalty that views the self in the light of responsibility towards things larger than the self, such as the family, state and gods.[9] The figure of Aeneas on the Altar of the Gens Augusta from Carthage, carrying his father Anchises and leading little Iulus, suggests concern for the continuity of the line, which will culminate in the birth of Augustus.

Another aspect of *pietas,* which might not be lost on the people of Carthage, was Aeneas' necessary rejection of Queen Dido of Carthage. In Virgil's eyes, that rejection ultimately triggered the conflict known as the Punic wars, but at the same time it symbolized the denial of one's own desires out of regard for the greater needs of the state. The story is particularly appropriate, for Augustus himself had also rejected a queen, Egypt's Cleopatra, who had detained two latter-day heroes, Julius Caesar and Mark Antony, with some danger to the Roman state.

In his obedience to the will of the gods, who hastened him on to meet his destiny, Aeneas embodied the concern for religious matters that Augustus wished to emphasize and reflect. To this end, the Roman emperor revived a number of vacant priesthoods and built and renovated a great number of temples and altars.

In the Augustan outlook, prosperity and success in war follow when the gods and the state are thus honored. The figure of Roma on the Altar of the Gens Augusta is the personification of such ideals; she is shown dressed in military gear like Minerva, holding an image of victory in an upraised hand. An overflowing cornucopia rests precariously on a stand nearby and reminds one of another Augustan altar, the Ara Pacis Augustae (Altar of Augustan Peace) in Rome, with its similar symbols of productivity, power and fertility.

Apollo too has his place in the Aeneas story and the Augustan family, for Aeneas, dressed for hunting on that fateful day when the only game he took was Dido herself, is said by Virgil to be as handsome as Apollo. And it is Apollo as the god of prophecy, the lord of Greek Delphi, who advises Aeneas of the route to take. And it is Apollo's Sibyl at Cumae in South Italy who accompanies Aeneas on his trip through the underworld, and before his descent Aeneas prays to Apollo and vows a temple in honor of the god of prophecy and his prophet the Sibyl. (Such a temple was actually built in Rome by Augustus himself near his own house on the Palatine Hill.)

Furthermore, Aeneas carries into battle a shield crafted by Vulcan, and among the figures on it is Apollo drawing his bow in support of Octavian (Augustus) at the Battle of Actium, the battle that resulted in the defeat of Antony and Cleopatra and the removal of Octavian's major rivals. Without the success of Actium, Octavian would never have become Augustus, and he acknowledged Apollo's support at Actium by renovating an old temple to Apollo at that location.

Apollo seems to have been a kind of patron saint for Augustus, which accounts for Apollo's prominence in *The Aeneid*, his appearance on our altar and his general popularity in Carthage. According to the historian Suetonius a century later, Augustus once gave a dinner party to which the twelve principal guests came dressed as Olympian divinities. Augustus, of course, came as Apollo, reflecting the special position that Apollo held in his life and regime. This divine figure of rationality, foresight and creativity in the arts, a symbol of civilization itself, was a very apt guardian angel for the Rome that Augustus and his court produced and attempted to export. Augustus was a leader who turned mudbrick into marble, created the new Carthage and turned Republican literature into a new Augustan golden age of writing.

Suetonius recorded a legend that Atia, the mother of Augustus, once fell asleep in a temple of Apollo and was impregnated by a serpent. Nine months later she gave birth to the future Augustus.[10] For Augustus, Apollo was not just another pretty Olympian face, and the altar found at Carthage reveals much of the master plan to Romanize Carthage and the province. It represents a conscious effort to promote concepts and divinities in harmony with the current vision of the Roman state. In execution and intent, it is a far cry from the art of the hinterland, but it is an important illustration of the range of religious and political ideas afoot in Roman Tunisia.

The Libyans, of course, continued in many cases to worship their own pantheons, which might vary from region to region or tribe to tribe. They might erect votive *stelae* to their seven or eight major divinities, who were sometimes rendered in a purely naive style and sometimes showed traces of syncretization (the Libyans too seemed to like the *Dioskouroi* and adopted them early on). We know very little about many of these gods, and names like Bonchor and his consorts Vihinam and Varsissima seem extremely alien to us.[11]

Alongside the traditional deities there was the darker side of religious practice: terrifying demons who could snatch babies away in the night and death-dealing curses and potions that could catch you unawares. We have already seen how magic was used to hex a circus participant, but the use of magic was enormously widespread; the entire province, especially the rural areas, was racked with fears and superstitions, and craved protection and security. Every phenomenon, natural or man-made, was ripe for a fantastic or miraculous interpretation. Individuals and families needed a complex system of defense to protect them from the evil eye, or *invidus*. Demons had to be placated and steps had to be taken to ensure that the evil dead stayed in their tombs.

Some of these practices were very simple and took the form of amulets or rings with prophylactic decorations or magic formulae. House thresholds often contained special charms or apotropaics rendered in mosaic such as a fish, an eye or a phallus. It is still the practice in Carthage today, when building a new villa, to throw a fish or a representation of a fish into the foundations, and the fish is given as a good luck token in the souks of Tunis.

But these were simple precautions. Real magic came in when an individual called on someone to intercede for him with the forces of the supernatural by using formulae and secret rites. Magicians did thriving business all over the Roman world, endeavoring to help people get ahead, win in the arena or circus, attract a lover or cast an evil spell. To fulfill these wishes, the conjurer would often call on the spirits of those who had died violently or of children who had died particularly young.

Something of these magic practices is known because of the discovery of many of the *tabellae defixonis* already mentioned. On these lead leaves one could place all sorts of wishes and appeals to demons with names impossible to pronounce. On one example found in Hadrumetum, a frustrated and unrequited lover turned her desires over to a magician hoping for better luck:

I ask . . . by the great god and the Anteros and by the one
who has a falcon on his head and by the 7 stars, that at the
moment when I have composed this Sextilius, son of
Dionysia, will sleep no more, that he burn up and be made
mad, and that he neither sleep nor be able to sit nor speak, but
that he has me in his mind, me Septima, daughter of Amoena,
that he is consumed, mad with love and desire for me, that the
soul and heart of Sextilius, son of Dionysia, be consumed with
love and desire for me Septima, daughter of Amoena. And
you, Abar, Barbarie, Eloe, Pachnouphy, Puthiemi, grant that
Sextilius, son of Dionysia, never find any sleep but be
consumed with love and desire for me, that his spirit and body
be burned up and every part of the entire body of Sextilius,
son of Dionysia. And if not I shall descend into the cave of
Osiris and I will destroy the mummy and send it into the river
which carries it for I am the great Decan of the great god
Achrammachala.[12]

This jawbusting collection of demon names and requests repeated
over and over to make sure they would stick are typical of these written
incantations. The suffering woman wanted to leave no possible loop-
holes or ways that Sextilius could avoid his fate.

Lest this tale seem fantastic, it must be stated that witchcraft of all
sorts is still practiced in Tunisia today, following traditions that step
right out of the *tabellae*. In the ruins of Thuburbo Maius, people still
invoke charms against the Arbetha, who carries off children on windy
nights, and still fear that the djinn will emerge from under the ground
if archaeologists dig too deeply.

But a more unusual event illustrating the continuity of magic
practices occurred in 1969, in the small village which surrounds the
ancient Punic and Roman site of Utica, between Tunis and Bizerte. A
group of families became embroiled in a serious controversy. A young
girl fell deeply in love with a young man from another nearby village,
but the two families did not get along.

The father of the girl accused the boy's mother of baking a potion
into a pastry and forcing the girl to fall hopelessly under the mother's
spell. The father thereupon decided to hire someone to drive them all
to El Fahs, near the ancient site of Thuburbo Maius, to visit one of the
most important "doctors," or magicians, of Tunisia. The doctor heard
the girl's story and quickly tied a tiny piece of lamb to a string and made

the girl swallow it, while he continued to hold the end of the string. He then pronounced a spell over and over again, which nobody present could fully understand. Next he asked the girl if she were still in love with the boy, and she replied that she was. He pulled the string and the girl gagged and became violently ill from the choking, only regaining her breath with difficulty. Twice more the same question was asked, with the same response.

Finally the girl, becoming seriously ill, agreed that the cure had worked and she never wanted to see the boy again. The doctor said that if the girl had a relapse, the ceremony would be repeated. The girl then returned home and the father was delighted and told everyone of the incredible power of the doctor. More objective witnesses to this event were left to wonder if the girl had not finally realized that she would probably choke to death if she did not give in.

As we have seen in the case of the Boglio *stele* from Siliana, the safeguarding of the harvest was critically important for the people of the country. Magic obviously filled a great need in this domain. Scarecrows—frequently in the form of the god Priapus, with all sorts of ripe fruits covering up his private parts—were sometimes used, but often strange demons were called upon to do the trick.

An inscription written in Greek on a stone from Bou Arada, about ninety miles southwest of Carthage, may serve as an example. After some magic letters it begins:

> Oreobazagra, Oreobazagra, Abrasax, Makhar, Semeseilam,
> Stenakhta, Lorsakhthe, Koriaukhe, Adonaie, lord gods. Turn
> away from this domain and from the fruits which grow on the
> vines, the olive groves, the fields sowed with seeds, and keep
> away the hailstorms, mildew, the wrath of the hurricane
> winds, the multitude of evil-doing locusts, so that none of
> these nefarious things can attack this domain and the fruits in
> their totality which are found here. Instead, protect them,
> intact and healthy, for as long as these stones on which are
> inscribed your sacred names will be placed under the
> surrounding earth.[13]

This inscription has been dated by its discoverers to about A.D. 200 and represents the work of a magician of Greek origin serving the demands of the superstitious proprietor of a field. It is from a highly agricultural region, where, apparently, magicians were considered as necessary as, say, insurance today. Hail is a particular problem in the regions where the climate is semicontinental and hailstorms are infrequent but still occur there today, often causing panic.

Mildew seriously affects wheat and grape raising, and, according to the Augustan poet Ovid, an annual festival used to be held on April 25 to ward off its deleterious effects. High winds are known to be capable of destroying a harvest in a few hours, while locusts are still considered one of the most dangerous hazards to Tunisian crops and in recent years have been particularly irksome.

Magicians did not always have an easy life. They might be feared for their powers, and there were laws, such as the *Lex Cornelia de Veneficiis* (the Cornelian law against sorcerers), which tried to protect individuals and communities from their harmful influence. In accordance with this law, the famous writer and orator Apuleius of Madaurus, who had been educated at Carthage, was accused of sorcery about A.D. 155.[14]

He had been travelling through North Africa and had reached Oea in Tripolitania (Libya), when he fell ill and was visited by his friend Sicinius Pontianus, who was concerned that his widowed mother would marry a bounder named Sicinius Clarus, his uncle. Pontianus fixed up Apuleius with the widow and they were married, but Sicinius Clarus' brother was outraged and accused Apuleius of using magic to ensnare the woman, virtually the same accusation made in our modern Utica tale. The case actually came to trial in the coastal city of Sabrata (now Sabratha) and Apuleius defended himself in a famous *Apologia,* making his opponents seem ridiculous, and was acquitted. Nonetheless, the story illustrates how seriously magic and sorcery were taken in North Africa.

Even in elegant homes there was a long-standing tradition that after the major meal of the day the food scraps should be left in the *triclinium* as an offering to the spirits of the dead, the *manes,* who were believed to be able to return under certain circumstances.[15] A number of mosaics have been recovered that illustrate the remnants of a sumptuous meal—including fish bones, lentils, shrimp shells, and eggshells—and these were no doubt designed to remind the owner to leave his food scraps or to represent a symbolic and therefore good-luck offering to these dangerous spirits of the dead. This practice, which was also known to the ancient Greeks, continued into the twentieth century in the south of France and may be behind the tradition of leaving something for Santa Claus and his reindeer. The particular type of mosaic floor came to be known in Greek as an *asarotos oikos,* or unswept floor.

To the agricultural communities of the hinterland, the one thing that seemed to prove the harmony of the universe and to show that all was following an orderly divine plan was the regular changing of the seasons. The seasons came to symbolize the hope for a joyous afterlife, for man too had a role in the cosmos, some part in the eternal life of the universe, just as Cuttinus had shown on his *stele*.[16] Personified seasons are among the most common figural images on Tunisian mosaics and are usually, but not always, female. They may appear in conjunction with divinities such as Bacchus, Jupiter or Apollo, or just by themselves as symbols of good luck, hope and tranquility.

What appears to be a simple mythological scene is illustrated on a late-second-century mosaic from a house at Thysdrus, but its significance may be deeper than is apparent a priori.[17] The subject is the story of Marsyas, a woodland divinity of ancient Phrygia (Turkey), an area noted for great flute playing at religious festivals. The goddess Athena appears on the floor as well; she invented the instrument but quickly cast it aside, whereupon Marsyas took it up and challenged the great lyre-playing god Apollo to a musical contest. Of course, Marsyas lost and was flayed alive for his hubris, while Apollo was crowned as victor.

In this scene the naked Marsyas has just stopped playing and his face is contorted, partly from playing and partly from the fact that Apollo is blocking his path with his foot. In the corners of the floor are the four winged seasons, each framed with garlands. Spring is appropriately young and floral-crowned, while Summer is crowned with wheat. Autumn wears a vine crown and Winter, dressed warmly, is crowned with roses. Between them elegant kraters contain the flowers and fruits of the season.

By the later second century, mosaics such as this had strong symbolic meanings. Apollo might be the sun god and hope of salvation and his seven-stringed lyre could equal the seven mystical spheres espoused by such groups as the Neo-Pythagoreans, who believed that man's celestial soul might rise from the earth after death. The seasons became the symbols of harmony and renewal in the universe.

Originally the Marsyas story seems to have glorified the Dorian

Greeks and their lyre music, ridiculing the uncivilized, wavering flute of Asia Minor, which disfigured the face, prevented singing and contaminated ancient Athens with effeminate Ionian influences in the fifth century B.C. But by late Roman times this story had a new meaning, showing not only the great power of the gods but also the need for mortals to know their place if they wish to rise after death to the spheres and dwell in Apollo's realm.

The gods and goddesses could also play a direct role in the protection of the family. Images of Venus were commonly used as talismans and kept in the home, or appeared in baths to remind people to think chaste thoughts and not be tempted by the sight of nudity. Among her talents was the ability to revive the dead and break the spells of sorcerers. Cities were protected by patron deities: Mercury, for example, was the special god of Thysdrus, while Bacchus looked after Lepcis Magna in Libya. Natural phenomena, such as comets or a halo around the sun, were considered to have the highest significance and might be related to the birth of great leaders.

Finally, there was a whole host of magical signs and symbols, not all of which are even now understood. A crown might be a symbol of victory but also a good-luck image against evil. Arrows and chameleon images could be evoked against the evil eye, as could the tail eyes of a peacock. Even horses were seen as valuable talismans, and their images often appeared in tombs.[18]

Perhaps the most genuinely strange example of religious imagery and syncretization that has come down to us from Africa Proconsularis is a statue of a man found at Bordj-el-Amri, about twenty-five miles from modern Tunis.[19] Believed to be the image of a deceased person of middle age, the figure has been given a variety of attributes associated with divinities. The head is rendered in a style popular about the middle of the third century A.D. and known to art historians as Neo-Verism, in which the face is extremely realistically depicted. It seems to portray a particular individual, complete with prominent nose, wrinkled forehead and a stubbly beard typical of the era. The face is modelled with extreme care and is one of the most naturalistic heads in all of ancient Tunisian sculpture of any period.

The figure wears a lion skin, the head of which surrounds his own head so that a deep pocket of shadow is created. The lion's paws dangle from the section of the animal skin knotted around the man's neck, and the rear paws hang from the skin belted around the waist. Under the

Statue of a (deceased?) man from Bordj-el-Amri with attributes of Ceres and Hercules. Roman, middle of the third century.

lion skin, the man wears a long-sleeved tunic that comes down to just above the knee. Lion skins arranged in just this way are traditionally associated with Hercules, and a similar arrangement on a famous portrait bust of the emperor Commodus now in Rome suggests the desire to syncretize an emperor with the great hero/god. In addition,

Hercules was assimilated by the Romans to the Punic deity Melqart, as we have seen earlier.

But the divine attributes do not stop there. The figure holds the club of Hercules in his left hand, while in the right hand is a bouquet of poppies and wheat, popular symbols of the goddess Ceres and traditionally connected to the Greek cult of Demeter and Kore, known in Carthage since the fourth century B.C. The fusion of a female divinity or divinities with a male who looks as if he has five-o'clock-shadow may seem quite bizarre at first sight, and even more so when one notices that the sculptor seems to have rendered female breasts under the man's tunic.

To complete the picture, the figure wears sandals that look more like buskins, and a slim dog sits next to him. The dog is usually identified as Cerberus, the hound of hell and guardian of the under-world, whom Hercules is said to have captured during one of his labors. The style of the statue (excluding the head) is of a remarkable stiffness and stylization, and the piece has no thickness at all, although from the front it appears to be a sculpture; it must have been placed in a niche.

If this is a portrait of a dead man, the artist apparently wished to emphasize a number of points. The association of the deceased with a hero and a goddess could indicate that he was a worshipper of traditional cults which, in the troubled third century, still held out hope of a peaceful life beyond the grave. Both Hercules and Ceres had long-standing Punic antecedents, but what seems new here is the literal grafting of their attributes, whether male or female, onto a man. What is important is not the physical features or sex of a divinity or hero, but the idea and the power of the divinity.

It does not matter here that a man has breasts. Indeed, as the artist clearly demonstrates, realistic or classical form on this statue does not matter in the slightest. The body is a symbolic mass of attributes crudely rendered in the popular art tradition. Only the head, which gives us an indication of a specific individual, is rendered in realistic detail. It isn't that the artist is not capable of making the entire statue look classical or realistic; he does not choose to do so because mere physical reality is no longer important. The subject is not a man with the breasts of Ceres; he is a man infused with her spirit and protection for the afterlife.

But who is the man? Is he some forgotten magistrate or wealthy farmer? Such honors would be reserved only for persons of the greatest

252 ♨ CARTHAGE ♨

importance, such as an emperor, and indeed the face bears a vivid resemblance to that of the soldier-emperor Trajan Decius, whose strongly anti-Christian attitude would make him a prime candidate to be honored in just this way. In the troubled age in which he lived, he would have needed all the divine help he could get. Perhaps this was a posthumous statue honoring him as if he were among the divine, but scholars still disagree on just who and what is shown here.

The religion and superstition of Africa Proconsularis was a fascinating combination of Punic, Libyan and Roman official religions, mixed with a generous sprinkling of the unofficial beliefs of these cultures (particularly a widespread belief in the power of the occult).[20] Lest we find these beliefs naive and ridiculous, it is necessary to remember that our own supermarkets can barely keep in stock a wide variety of newspapers that proclaim miraculous births, regular visits from aliens and the anti-Christ, and people coming back from the dead. And a couple of years ago a nationally syndicated television talk show held what purported to be a serious conversation about the possibility of miraculous sightings of the ghost of Elvis Presley.

Epilogue

❧

NO CIVILIZATION endures forever. It is not really surprising that the golden age of Roman North Africa and the *pax Romana* came to an end. What is more startling is that, with all its gross inequities, it lasted as long as it did.

The zenith of this extraordinary civilization occurred between A.D. 150 and 225.[1] At this time, fully fifteen percent of the senators and *equites* of Rome were African in origin, and many rose to the highest ranks of the imperial administration. The honor roll of distinguished North Africans from this period is long indeed. Marcus Cornelius Fronto, a Numidian born at the former Berber capital of Cirta, became the foremost orator of the mid-second century; his influence at Rome was so considerable that he was entrusted with the education of the future emperor Marcus Aurelius, who became one of the most erudite of all Roman rulers.

Salvius Julianus, a contemporary of Fronto and a brilliant jurist, may have been born at Pupput and, before he was thirty years old, was entrusted by the emperor Hadrian to revise the edicts, or sets of rules of office, for the Roman high magistrates known as *praetores;* his work won him empire-wide acclaim.[2] The Numidian Antistius Aventus was one of the best generals serving under Marcus Aurelius, while Lucius Quietus, a Mauretanian, was one of the emperor Trajan's greatest generals. But these are just a few names among many who attained the highest levels of achievement.

If one had to pick two areas where the legacy of the Roman empire in Africa was most distinctive, they would certainly be the areas of letters and religion. Africa Proconsularis was fairly covered with schools, and it is due to the zeal of African educators that manuscript writing involving the use of a lowercase cursive was developed. Carthage became one of the greatest university towns of the empire and produced numerous fine writers and scholars.

Lucius Apuleius, for example, whom we have already met a number of times, was a Numidian. Born to a wealthy and distinguished family, he was educated in Carthage and Athens, then travelled far and wide, becoming an initiate in the religious mysteries of various regions. Considered by many to be the most original Latinist of his age, he lived in Carthage and wrote the extraordinary *Metamorphoses,* in which a man turned into an ass observes the bizarre behavior of mankind and gives valuable insights into the morals and unusual religious beliefs of his time.

North Africa, particularly Africa Proconsularis and the province of Numidia, became known as a land of powerful and opinionated Christian leaders, who combined the African genius for producing fine literature with a passion for the teachings of Jesus. In a society used to the syncretization of religious beliefs, Christianity made great headway, and communities which had supported Ba'al Hammon and then Saturn found hope in a transcendant faith and dogma that reached out to rich and poor alike. By the second century A.D., when the Christian church was having only limited success in the west, mostly with citizens of Near Eastern origin, mass conversions occurred throughout North Africa.

While Rome was often tolerant of Christian beliefs and practices, it was not until the emperor Constantine's conversion to Christianity in A.D. 312 that a Christian could practice his faith with a minimum of fear. For centuries the discreet practice of the religion was the rule in Rome, and members of a Christian community had to protect each other from outsiders.

There were already persecutions under the emperor Commodus (A.D. 180–192), and twelve of the victims became the first African martyrs. The intermittently repressive practices of Rome only served to increase the ardor of the faithful and the number of converts. By the beginning of the third century A.D., the Christian apologist Tertullian, a Libyan born in Carthage to pagan parents, could boast, not without exaggeration, that Christians were more numerous than pagans. As the countryside became rapidly Christianized, basilicas sprang up and a major struggle and schism known as the Donatist controversy soon began. It was to rock the church of North Africa to its foundations, but before discussing it in some detail it is necessary to know a little about the relationship of the province to Rome at the end of the second and beginning of the third centuries.[3]

By this time Africa Proconsularis was no longer a mere province but a major political and economic force in the empire. With such power, Africans were in the position to make and unmake emperors themselves, without having to wait on the whims of Rome. And so in A.D. 192 the praetorian prefect, a powerful man who functioned as a sort of prime minister, used his influence to precipitate a crisis of food distribution designed to undermine the Roman state. The prefect was the African Aemilius Laetus of Thaenae (near the modern city of Sfax) and his actions opened the way for a North African compatriot to become emperor, Septimius Severus of Lepcis Magna (which at that time was still the jurisdiction of Africa Proconsularis). In this age of numerous pretenders to imperial power, Severus' greatest rival was Decimus Clodius Albinus, a noble who had been governor of Britain but whose family was from Hadrumetum (modern Sousse).

Severus won out, but in Rome the members of the old Roman families considered the accession to power of a North African to be Hannibal's revenge. Severus quickly opened up the praetorian guard to citizens from all over the empire, and his son Caracalla issued an edict in A.D. 212 that provided citizenship for all the inhabitants of the empire.[4] The old guard of Italy had been overrun from within the system. The monster created in Africa had become as strong as the mother city and had come back to rule the roost. The Severans became the first true African dynasty to rule in Rome, even though Severus himself never managed to speak Latin without a heavy accent. No friend to Christians, Severus was emperor when two of North African Christianity's most beloved saints, Perpetua and Felicity, were martyred in a Carthage amphitheater.

The role played by the province in Roman politics took a shocking turn in A.D. 235 because of one Maximinus Thrax, an uneducated Thracian peasant who had been promoted by Severus to the rank of centurion. Maximinus participated in a mutiny instigated while he was military commander on the Rhine. His troops declared him emperor and repudiated then ruler Alexander Severus. Severus and his wife were murdered in a military camp near Mainz as he was preparing to fight threatening German tribes on the frontier. The harsh fiscal policies of the new emperor soon inflamed the Africans, and the center of rebellion focused on Thysdrus, where an imperial fiscal procurator was killed. There, possibly in the renowned amphitheater, the seventy-nine-year-old African proconsul, Gordian, was proclaimed emperor of Rome (he then made his son, Gordian II, co-emperor). The senate endorsed him, but Capellianus, the legate of Numidia, remained loyal to Maximinus and defeated Gordian's forces, which were simply volunteers, near Carthage. The rule of the Gordians had lasted twenty-two days.[5]

The Age of the Soldier Emperors is the term given to the middle two thirds of the third century, and it is an appropriate one, as emperors were made and then overthrown at an alarming rate.[6] Even those who endured faced barbarian hordes, mutinies and general unrest in virtually every part of the empire. Persians threatened in the east, Goths in the north, and the defenses of the Rhine frontier were a shambles. There were dangerous new rulers in Palmyra, and usurpers controlled Gaul, Spain and Britain.

In these difficult times it is hardly a wonder that people sought alternative solutions, especially in the area of religion. The traditional gods seemed to have abandoned mankind, and although North Africa remained better insulated than some areas, times were certainly hard for many people.

To control the seemingly cancerous spread of Christianity and to ensure the continuity of imperial influence in North Africa, the emperor Trajan Decius stepped up the persecutions and also saw to the issuing of a decree (in A.D. 250) requiring that all Christians sacrifice to the official gods of the Roman state and that they do so in front of state-approved witnesses. To many Christians, regardless of their particular sect, this was too much to ask, and those who did it were accused of selling out their faith and ideals to Rome.

Carthage was by now the site of an important bishopric, and its influential bishop was the diplomatic and forceful Cyprian.[7] Born in A.D. 210, he had converted to Christianity at the age of thirty-five after a fine classical education, and had become bishop in A.D. 249. Strong-minded but with a reputation for fairness, he struggled against the lack of discipline and high moral standards in the church and frequently clashed with the Bishop of Rome regarding the autonomy of the African church.

Despite his tactful efforts, he became caught in an impossible situation. He criticized those selling out to Rome as *lapsi* (or lapsed Christians), but agreed to pardon them so long as they had not actually sacrificed at the imperial shrines (such people were the unpardonable *sacrificati*). With this distinction, Cyprian was able to walk a fine line between his congregation, his Numidian church colleagues and the feared Roman authorities. He succeeded in this balancing act for almost a decade and kept the church from falling apart despite its increasing factionalism.

But the Roman emperors, who had periodically used Christians as scapegoats for the myriad problems of the empire, continued to persecute the church, and Cyprian was arrested in A.D. 258, during the reign of the emperor Valerian. Although allegedly given ample opportunities to escape, he refused. As a regular reader of the Christian apologist Tertullian, he understood the value of martyrdom and met his death in A.D. 258. The Sainte Monique hill of Carthage contains the impressive remains of a basilica believed by many scholars to be the one built at the site where the imperial authorities took his body after his death. Here too may have been the site where Saint Monica herself, the mother of Saint Augustine, prayed for her son when he left Carthage for Italy. Three basilicas were named for Cyprian after his death, and the Christian community of Carthage celebrated a festival in his honor right up to the last days of antiquity.[8]

With Cyprian dead, the factionalism generated by the decree of A.D. 250 increased; other Christian leaders lacked his tolerance and political skills. But Christianity still continued to attract an enormous following, especially among the poor, who had good reason to believe that life on earth held out little hope for them. The quality of life had fallen off, and the patron-client relationship had been weakened. The poor found themselves increasingly at the mercy of the rich landholders and Roman authorities. Some of those down on their luck sometimes joined outlaw bands, while others preferred to look beyond the problems of this world to new hope and salvation.

The persecutions continued during the early fourth century under the Dalmatian (Yugoslavian) emperor Diocletian. By this time the empire had become a maze of warring factions and was rapidly becoming too unstable to govern.[9] Diocletian wisely created an administrative tetrarchy, whereby he and three loyal colleagues would divide the empire and try to govern it effectively. For Africa Proconsularis this meant subdivision: the north retained the original name, but the south and southeast areas became Byzacenia.

Now Christian gatherings were sought out and broken up with brute force, churches were defaced and sacred relics and documents were seized. Mensurius, the Bishop of Carthage, sought to circumvent these problems by substituting phony scriptures so they could be taken by the Roman authorities. For a time he fled the city and waited for things to cool down. This action so infuriated the hard-core Christians of North Africa (and especially of Numidia) that when the new bishop, a certain Caecilius, succeeded Mensurius after his death, the Numidians rebelled, protesting that Caecilius was a Roman collaborator. At the Council of Carthage held in A.D. 312, the Numidians carried the day, declaring a new Bishop of Carthage, Majorinus, who, unfortunately, rather promptly died. His replacement, Donatus, was to create the famous Donatist controversy of the fourth century.[10]

Little is known about this mercurial and powerful man, but his advent produced a schism in the church that the emperor Constantine was now called upon to solve. Trying to moderate the dispute and especially anxious to not lose the coveted resources of Africa, Constantine delayed in announcing his opinion on the controversy and allowed the Donatists to gain a good measure of support in the African provinces. By the time he was prepared to calm things down in A.D. 313 with his Edict of Milan, which proclaimed religious tolerance throughout the empire and an end to the persecutions, it was too late.[11]

Constantine believed that the only hope for the survival of the empire lay in officially embracing Christianity and he became the first emperor to do so. But by now a virtual class struggle was intensifying and when Constantine finally took several stands against Donatus, the provinces erupted. The Caecilians wanted collaboration with Christianized Rome; most of them did not want to rock the boat, for they were often wealthy people who had a lot to lose if the empire should take a stand against them.

The more devout, hard-line Christians, with copies of Tertullian in hand, tended to be poor *coloni,* Libyans, slaves, runaways and the like, who had little to lose. Their protests to the emperors, landlords and tax gatherers normally went unheeded, and since Diocletian's time they had been virtually frozen in their positions; the mobility of society—the hallmark of the high empire—had evaporated. Taxes were collected on the basis of a person's productivity, and *coloni* had to stay in the fields indefinitely or face harsh penalties. Many simply fled.

Of course, not everyone suffered. Throughout the fourth century the wealthier classes continued to enjoy considerable prosperity. Trade was still booming in Carthage and new warehouses were put up at the commercial port. Utica's House of the Hunt was completely refloored in fine mosaic but its courtyard was paved in reused *opus sectile;* apparently the various imperial marble quarries were not readily accessible or were no longer being worked. Public baths, which had fallen into neglect in the third century, were extensively remodelled later in the fourth. The *latefundia,* or huge estates of the wealthy, began to resemble feudal manors, where the rich protected themselves and their supporters from the incursions of the dissatisfied poor. In a way it was a continuation of the earlier patron and client system, but with individual areas becoming more like true fiefdoms.

Church building for all sects went on at a truly staggering rate in the fourth century, with most of the buildings of a conservative nature, taking the form of Roman-style basilicas with an apsidal short end and a large central nave. Unlike the pagan basilicas, these had an altar in the central nave just before the apse. The largest church in all of North Africa was built at Carthage perhaps around the middle of the fourth century A.D. Known as the Damous-el-Karita or House of Charity, it was 215 feet long and had eight aisles and a transept. Sacred objects and martyrs' relics were already being deposited in such churches, and the graves of martyrs were especially revered.[12]

The Damous-el-Karita was an ecclesiastical complex which, by the sixth century A.D. Byzantine revival, had become quite sizeable and gone through many phases. About fifteen hundred feet to the north lay the ruins of the Basilica Majorum Arearum and a large cemetery, where an inscription referring to the sepulchre of martyred saint Perpetua was recovered. The Douimès Basilica, located near the Antonine Baths, was a five-aisled church and may have been the seat of a fourth-century religious association or school.

When Constantine relocated the seat of empire from Rome to Constantinople, the African provinces began to seem even more isolated to many of its inhabitants, even farther away from the center of power. And Christianity, which was to have been the hope for salvation, was now pitting brother against brother, master against slave, parents against children and rich against poor.

By the later fourth century, the Catholic church and its proimperial supporters managed to severely cripple most of the Donatist resistance, and the church was dominated by the forceful writings and leadership of a Numidian Bishop, Saint Augustine, considered by the Donatists to be a *lapsus* and collaborator. The son of a pagan father and

Christian mother (Saint Monica), he had passed a tumultuous youth in Carthage, where he studied and taught at the university before leaving for Milan.

In his shockingly frank *Confessions,* which deal with his errant boyhood, Augustine has left a scathing indictment of his life in the African metropolis, with comrades who would think nothing of lying, cheating, fornicating, stealing and wasting their time at the games or in the theater. Clearly in his day Carthage was still bustling and cosmopolitan, both a center of learning and refinement and a place of wild living and decadent morality, "a hotbed of sinful desires."

There he took a mistress and abandoned himself to hedonism, although at the same time he did begin his search for the meaning of life. Once converted to Christianity, he added his voice to that of other Christians complaining of the depravity of the age:

> At Carthage . . . the licentiousness of the students is odious
> and without limit. They cynically force their way and like
> madmen disrupt the established order to suit their own
> interests. They commit 1,000 insolent acts with an incredible
> stupidity which the law should punish if it didn't have a
> tradition of protecting them.[13]

Augustine left to posterity over one hundred works, including *The City of God,* which remains a highly influential religious treatise to this day. In addition, his life remains a high water mark for Christianity in North Africa, for immediately following his death in A.D. 429 came the Vandal invasions.

The most renowned general of North Africa at this time was Boniface, a highly controversial figure and, surprisingly, a good friend of Augustine. He was married to an Arian, a member of an heretical Christian sect. This group followed the teachings of Arius, himself a Libyan priest with a considerable following in Alexandria, Egypt. According to Arian ideas, God had begotten a son, but that son was neither equal to the father nor immortal.[14] The spread of this idea caused great consternation for an African church already racked by the Donatist controversy.

The emperor Constantine, moving away from the Edict of Milan, finally took steps to condemn the movement as a heresy; the Arians themselves split into three groups, which despised each other. Despite the failure of Arianism to gain a foothold among the Christian masses in ancient Tunisia, it had much more success at the northern frontiers of the empire, where Goths and Vandals embraced it in surprisingly large numbers.

Boniface was confronted with the task of supporting an imperial family that had been enjoying no particular success. Theodosius I had been a powerful ruler who had briefly managed to unite the crumbling empire, but his sudden death of dropsy in A.D. 395 had left no capable leaders to succeed him. His sons, Arcadius and Honorius, divided the empire but ruled without distinction. Now, with imperial Africa falling apart, Theodosius' daughter, Galla Placidia, was the regent for her tiny son Valentinian III. Rome had been sacked by Alaric and the Visigoths in A.D. 410 and Galla Placidia had been wed to Alaric's successor, then after his murder she was ransomed for six hundred thousand measures of African corn and returned to her brother Honorius.

In these dark days, Boniface took matters into his own hands and made a deal with the Vandals, a Baltic tribe that despite its name had been driven out of its homeland and pushed from the Rhine to France and ultimately to Spain.[15] Boniface needed help and the Vandals wanted a new home. In exchange for Vandal support for his own bid for power (he was refusing to follow the empress regent's recall order of A.D. 427), Boniface granted Vandal leader Gunderic two thirds of Roman North Africa. In A.D. 429, under King Gaiseric, the Vandals spread through Tunisia, bringing with them their dreaded religion of Arianism. Boniface, threatened by the Vandal expansion, reunited with Galla but realized too late that he had exchanged one unwanted master for another.

After Gaiseric defeated Boniface, Carthage itself was severely threatened. A massive fortification wall had already been built there between A.D. 423 and A.D. 425 by Theodosius II, the grandson of Theodosius. (Recent Canadian and British excavations have uncovered traces of it running through the amphitheater district, the cisterns of La Malga and the circus area.) But in A.D. 439, Carthage, despite its prepared state, fell quietly to Gaiseric and brought an end to many centuries of Roman control.

In A.D. 441 a feeble attempt at liberation was launched from imperial headquarters in Constantinople, but to no avail; it only underscored how weak the ravaged, eastern–based Roman empire had become. The Vandals, in the meantime, expanded their power into Sicily, Sardinia, Corsica and the Balearic Islands and took control of a sizeable portion of western Mediterranean trade, while using much of the captured Carthaginian fleet for nasty pirate raids in Italy and Sicily that helped to give them their bad name. Gaiseric even succeeded in looting Rome itself, capturing the empress Eudoxia and her two daughters, a crowning insult.

Although many of the traditional basilica churches now fell into disrepair and the standard of living generally declined, Carthage survived the century of Vandal control, and a number of communities even prospered. At Pupput, as we have seen, a magnificent home was constructed, and the small Bath of the Stars at Thuburbo Maius was completely repaved and shored up.

However, the gridded plan of Carthage that had been imposed by the Romans began to unravel as new houses sprawled into what had once been major arteries, a sure sign of the decline of order.[16] A circular ecclesiastical monument of the later fourth century, built southwest of the theater of Carthage, lay in disrepair. There were drainage and sewage problems at the ports and maintenance problems at the odeon and theater, even though some individuals continued to live very well indeed. In fact, because of their abundant raw materials, the Tunisian provinces were better able to resist the falling standard of living and the constant problems which had beset the empire since A.D. 250. Even in the fifth century, Carthage was a refuge for senators and members of the aristocracy fleeing from the Visigothic sack of Rome, and to the Germanic conquerors of Rome, Africa still seemed like a promised land.

The Vandals proved to be less than capable administrators and their tenure in Tunisia was a brief one. When, in the early sixth century, King Hilderic promoted religious tolerance, the Christian church was able to recover and to reestablish a presence in Carthaginian life, all the time making overtures to Constantinople to rescue Africa.

It would be wrong to think of the Vandals as an incredibly powerful and efficient war machine. They took over an area already bedeviled by Libyan raids, internal religious dissension, social unrest and a debased standard of living. Many witnesses have documented their brutality, especially their penchant for mutilation, but the sixth-century A.D. Byzantine historian Procopius, not without prejudice, gave a far different portrait of the later Vandals:

Of all the nations I know, the most effeminate is that of the
Vandals. They spend all their days in the baths and in taking
sumptuous repasts where they enjoy the most exquisite
produce of land and sea. Covered with gold ornaments and
with clothes of Oriental silk, they pass their time in the
spectacles, circus games and all amusements. They especially
like to hunt. Dances [pantomimes?], mimes, music, all the
pleasures of the eyes and ears delight them. They like to locate
their homes in the middle of well irrigated orchards where the
trees grow in abundance. Finally, being lovers of the earth,
they deliver themselves without reservation to the pursuit of
love-making. [17]

As the above would suggest, the Vandals did little to resolve the
confusion that the African provinces had fallen into. Many of the cities
of ancient Tunisia declined seriously in the latter years of Vandal rule.

The situation was chaotic, with the people rebelling against their
overlords and the Arian heresy and with frequent raids from the
Libyans of the Aures mountains and the Tripolitanian camel-driving
nomads. In A.D. 534 the Byzantine general Belisarius followed the
emperor's example and led another attempt from Constantinople to
oust the Vandals. This time Carthage was successfully liberated. [18] It
seemed for a time that Roman control had returned permanently and
that a new golden age would soon begin. The Byzantine conquerors
reinstituted the *annona,* an annual tax payable in wheat that could be
used to feed the poor, and the domains which the Vandals had conquered were returned wherever possible to the families of the ancient
masters.

Economic life began to prosper again, though not like before.
Still, trade revived and stabilized, and the standard of living at Carthage
seems to have improved for a time. At Thuburbo Maius a whole new
village sprang up over the ruins of the old city, often completely
disregarding the original city plan. But old public baths lay in ruins. A
column base from the destroyed Bath of the Stars was turned upside
down and used as a grinding stone. Architraves were recycled into
feeding troughs for mules, sometimes with their once-proud inscriptions still visible.

In Carthage the harbor walls were rebuilt, streets were repaired
and the sewage problems improved. Churches once again received

particular attention and in Sufetula, long an ecclesiastical center with numerous churches, the sixth century represents a boom period. Most notable was the Cathedral or Basilica of Vitalis, a vast building with five aisles and two apses. Behind one of the apses was a baptistery, the font of which is still decorated with mosaic floral patterns, garlands and a cross.

The Byzantine golden age began to wane in the later sixth century, as Libyan tribes pressed hard on the frontiers, and there were serious internal controversies as well. A former Byzantine soldier named Stozas led a scruffy group of Libyans, Byzantines and Vandals in a rebellion against Carthage that appropriated much of the arable land of the region, and Hadrumetum also fell—despite having been renamed Justinianopolis after the Byzantine emperor. Doctrinal disputes racked the leadership of Constantinople and Carthage, and not until the reign of the Byzantine usurper Heraclius (A.D. 610–641) did a measure of stability return. The heavy financial burdens, many of them military, the excesses of power and corruption, the disunity of the people, the repressive actions against multiple heresies and the endless revolts of mountain tribes and desert nomads perpetuated the atmosphere of insecurity.

The Byzantine leaders were forced to cover the country with a network of fortresses, which were hastily erected by using material stripped from earlier, more stately monuments that were in disrepair. Many of the fortresses may still be seen at sites like Ain Tounga (near Dougga) and Sufetula.[19]

While the Byzantines failed to resolve their religious differences and wasted valuable time and money in debate over whether Christ's true nature was human, divine, or human *and* divine, the followers of the prophet Mohammed were on the move attacking Byzantine communities. Syria, Palestine and even Egypt fell before their onslaught, while Constantinople was once again ruled by an infant. Like Boniface before him, the exarch Gregory, whose responsibility it was to hold the line in the two Tunisian provinces, faced a desperate situation and a crisis of loyalty. The bishops of North Africa now felt more closely tied to the religious beliefs of the Pope in Rome than to those of leaders in remote Constantinople.

In the middle of the seventh century Gregory rebelled and allied himself with Pope Theodorus and the North African bishops, but it was already too late. Switching his center of operations from Carthage to Sufetula, he made a heroic last stand but was killed by Arab invaders from Tripoli. Carthage held out longer from the incursions of leaders such as Ugba Biennafi and Hassan Ben Al Nu'man, but the latter finally captured the city once and for all in A.D. 705, marking the end of Roman Carthage.[20]

Under numerous Islamic dynasties and later Turkish and French domination, the face of Tunisia would change again and again before independence was achieved in 1957. As the Punic and Roman cities faded from memory and became forgotten ruins, colorful mosques with their minarets, massive rabats, twisting souks of the *medinas,* old city areas bustling with shoppers and finally palaces of the Beys with stunning glazed tiles colored the new landscape over the passing centuries. French culture provided a slight Western overlay, and today there are abundant signs of a modern, international architectural style that has yielded everything from baby blue skyscrapers to hotels that look like upside-down triangles.

With an administration barely three years old, Tunisia looks eagerly to the future, but unlike many modern countries, it takes great care of its past and is concerned that generations to come be able to see as well as read about the golden days of Carthage. Ancient Tunisia had been profoundly marked by the superposition of many different civilizations: Libyan, Phoenician, Greek, Roman, Vandal, Byzantine. This was largely due to the country's central position in the Mediterranean, critically located between Europe and Africa, Phoenicia and the Pillars of Hercules. And beyond this, Tunisia was fertile and virtually without natural barriers, while still possessing a number of major interior waterways.

For all the comings and goings of great civilizations, the conquerors failed to impose their values completely, for the natives only accepted from them what was workable and could be assimilated into their own traditions and beliefs. Rather than imposing, the invading cultures tended to become themselves partially assimilated. By the time of the Roman golden age, the feeling of unity in Tunisia went quite deep, despite the fact that the land had been settled and conquered by so many diverse people.

Nonetheless, by the Middle Ages the splendor of ancient Carthage had gone forever. Hassan Ben Al Nu'man and his successors used the ancient stone blocks, columns and pillars to build their mosques, palaces and souks. In A.D. 1270 the sultan El Mostaneir, following the Crusade led by St. Louis, ordered the last vestiges of antiquity destroyed. Many beautiful marbles were plundered, sold and carried away on ships to foreign countries, their contexts never recorded in the rush.

Sir Grenville Temple, a distinguished British traveler of the eighteenth century, lamented when he climbed the Byrsa Hill and looked out over the vast region that was Carthage:

> . . . my heart sank within me, when, ascending one of its hills
> (from whose summit the eye embraces a view of the whole
> surrounding country to the edge of the sea), I beheld nothing
> more than a few scattered and shapeless masses of masonry.

N. Davis, visiting and reporting on the site of Carthage in 1861, experienced the same feeling. "[The traveller] pushes on until he reaches an elevation, and looks eagerly in every direction for the ruins of temples, and amphitheatres, and palaces; but, alas! he looks in vain."[22]

At such a moment, Davis was moved to recall the Edward Fairfax translation of the sixteenth-century poet Torquato Tasso's *Jerusalem Delivered:*

> Great Carthage low in ashes cold doth lie,
> Her ruins poor, the herbs in height can pass;
> So cities fall, so perish kingdoms high,
> Their pride and pomp lie hid in sand and grass.

In Davis' time, humble shacks dotted the fields of ruins; it was not until well into the nineteenth century that the area began slowly to revive and not until after World War II that it blossomed as a true tourist metropolis. As the crowds gather today at the Cinéma Carthage for an international, celebrity-studded film festival, the ultra-modern theater auditorium slides open its massive roof to reveal the twinkling stars of a summer night. Amid such refinement it is easy to forget the now legendary human dramas that took place all those centuries ago, as Carthage rose and fell—twice. But to the historian and archaeologist, Carthage will never be forgotten, or destroyed.

Notes

❧

Introduction

1. Virgil I (tr. W. F. J. Knight). 496–500.
2. Ennabli and Slim 1982, 26–27, 76–77; Fantar 1973, foldout plan.
3. For the ancient sources dealing with Dido, see Pease 1935; Schmitz 1960.
4. The authors wish to thank Professors Richard Jensen and Norman Yoffee of the University of Arizona for these interpretations.
5. Virgil IV. 193–197.
6. Gordon 1969, 270–271.
7. Virgil I.496.
8. On Cleopatra, see Solomon 1978, 41–52.
9. Theme or programmatic painting as a Roman tradition is discussed in Thompson 1961.
10. The ancient sources on Dido are presented and discussed in Pease 1935, 11–21.
11. The character of the Phoenicians is discussed in Herm 1975, 73–74.
12. Karageorghis 1976.
13. Maier and Karageorghis 1984, 81–102.
14. Herodotus I.198–202.
15. On the "Woman at the Window" and the cult of Aphrodite Parakyptousa, see Akurgal 1968, 144, 147.
16. Warmington 1960, 130.
17. Stager and Wolff 1984, 38; Moscati 1988, 113–114.
18. Bisi 1964–65.
19. Bass 1972, 41–48.
20. The British excavations are published by Hurst and Roskams 1984. See also Hurst and Stager 1978, 341; Hurst 1974, 20.
21. Virgil IV.642–647.
22. For this account see Charles-Picard and Charles-Picard 1965–66, 296.
23. Krahmalkov 1981.

Chapter I

1. On the Canaanites, see Cross 1980; Dever 1980; Kamp and Yoffee 1980; Dever 1985; Knapp 1988, 168–169; and Rogerson and Davies 1989, 70–77. Most recently, see Sandro Filippo Bondi, "The Origins in the East," in Moscati 1988, 28–32.
2. On the Canaanite expansion and Amorite invasion, see Herm 1975, 25–26, 33–34.
3. Kamp and Yoffee 1980; Kenyon 1964, 159–160; Dever 1980.
4. For the complexity of the question of the character of third and early second millennium settlement in the area of Palestine, see Dever 1980; Kamp and Yoffee 1980; Harden 1962, 21; all with extensive bibliographies.
5. Herm 1975, 35–38.
6. Kenyon 1964, 206–208; Kemp 1984–85.

7. Katzenstein 1973.
8. Bass 1987.
9. See Giovanni Garbini, "The Question of the Alphabet," in Moscati 1988, 86–103.
10. Gordon 1949.
11. For a survey of Ugaritic mythology, see Hooke 1983, 79–94.
12. Sandars 1985.
13. For the connections between Canaanite mythology and Hebrew epic, see Cross 1980.
14. Mosca 1975 discusses the origins of the term *moloch* and the rite of human sacrifice among Canaanites, Pho-enicians and Carthaginians. See also Herm 1975, 119–120. The presumed Canaanite-Phoenician-Carthaginian connection is discussed and challenged in Green 1975, 179–187, 199–203.
15. Sandars 1985, 164–166; Dothan 1985.
16. On ancient technology, see Muhly 1982.
17. Special thanks to Norman Yoffee for advice on this particular section.
18. Whittaker 1974.
19. Isa. 23:8.
20. 1 Kings 5:6. For the biblical references to Hiram, Tyre and Sidon, see Odelain and Séquineau 1981; Dow 1983.
21. 1 Kings 5:9.
22. Massa 1977, 121.
23. For Albright's views, see Albright 1956, Albright 1961 and Albright 1968.
24. Julien 1961, 61.
25. On the difficulty of giving precise answers to the Berber question, see Camps 1984–87; Bousquet 1957.
26. Ben Abed Ben Khader and Soren 1987, 18–24, 85–87.

Chapter II

1. Whittaker 1974, 58 (plan).
2. Lancel 1985b, 728–736.

3. Moscati 1973, Moscati 1988.
4. Cintas 1950.
5. Wolff 1986.
6. For useful general histories of Carthage, see Warmington 1960; Charles-Picard 1956; Charles-Picard and Charles-Picard 1965–66.
7. On Syracuse, see Drögemüller 1969; Guido 1980. On the Greeks overseas, see Dunbabin 1948; Finley 1968; Boardman 1973.
8. Biers 1980, 94.
9. Whitaker 1921.
10. A recent survey of the history and archaeology of Sicily is Coarelli and Torelli 1984.
11. On the history and coinage of Gela, see Jenkins 1970.
12. The history of the Greek tyrants is recounted in Berve 1967.
13. Pindar *Pythian Ode* XII. 1–3. See also Kininmonth 1972, 178.
14. Herodotus VII. 168.
15. Herodotus VII. 158.
16. On the Temple of Zeus, see Riemann 1964.
17. For the fifth-century-B.C. Carthaginian recovery and fortifications, see Rakob 1984.
18. Herodotus VII. 168.
19. Wentker 1956; Green 1971.
20. Thucydides VII. 87.
21. Special thanks to Lawrence Stager and Joseph Greene for sharing the results of their population studies.
22. Diodorus Siculus XIV. 70–71. The authors wish to thank Dr. Kenneth Iserson of the Arizona Health Sciences Center for reviewing this section.

Chapter III

1. Pliny *Natural History* II.67.
2. Various dates for the voyage are offered by Piero Bartolini, "Ships and Navigation," in Moscati 1988,

74–75 (late fifth century B.C.), and 81 (625 B.C.); and also in Charles-Picard 1968, 91–100 (470–455 B.C.).

3. On the voyage of Hanno, see Demerliac and Meirat 1983; Oikonomides 1974.

4. On Spanish Phoenician settlements, see Maria Eugenia Aubet Semmler, "Spain," in Moscati 1988, 226–242; also Whittaker 1974, 58–64.

5. Herodotus IV.38.

6. Herodotus IV.40–44.

7. Herodotus IV.40.

8. Pliny *Natural History* II.67, 169

9. For the text, translation and useful maps, see Oikonomides 1974.

10. On Himilco's voyage see Avienus *Ora Maritima* 114–134, 380–389, 406–415.

11. Caputo 1937 and Cornevin 1967, 127–131 discuss the history of the region.

12. For Tripolitania, see Haynes 1965.

13. Bartoccini 1927; Carter 1965; Ward 1970.

14. On Lepcis and Tripolitania, see Merighi 1940; Goodchild 1954; Caffarelli and Caputo 1966; Bakir 1968; Squarciapino 1966.

15. Parke 1967; Larsen 1988.

16. Herodotus IV.168–196.

17. Herodotus II.32–35.

18. Ben Abed Ben Khader and Soren 1987, 138. On pygmies, gorillas and explorers, see Oikonomides 1974, 65–67, 75–76. On pygmies, see Homer *Iliad* III.6.

19. Such a hut is depicted on a Roman mosaic from El Alia, Tunisia. See Daniels 1970, 41.

20. For background on this region, see Page 1969.

21. For the Garamantes, see Herodotus IV. 174–183; Pliny *Natural History* V.26–46.

22. Bovill 1968, 42.

23. Daniels 1970, 43–44.

24. These tall tales are from Herodotus (see note 16).

Chapter IV

1. On Demeter, see Ben Abed Ben Khader and Soren 1987, 142; Delattre 1923, 361.

2. The development of Carthage and its trade in the fourth century is discussed in Wolff 1986.

3. Appian *Libyca* VII.96; Hurst and Stager 1978, 341.

4. Hurst 1975, Hurst 1978; Hurst and Stager 1978.

5. Wolff 1986, chap. 2.

6. Morel 1981.

7. Wolff 1986, 136–165.

8. Blackman 1982, 207; Isserlin and du Plat Taylor 1974.

9. Aristotle *Politics* II.2.

10. Justin *History* XXI.4. On this period, see also Charles-Picard and Charles-Picard 1965–66, 138–139.

11. Charles-Picard and Charles-Picard 1965–66, 210.

12. Diodorus Siculus XX.8, 1–4.

13. For the various interpretations of silphium, see Apicius *De Re Coquinaria* I, 16; Solomon and Solomon 1977, 44.

14. Athenaeus III.100—quoted in Tannahil 1973, 99.

15. Ben Abed Ben Khader and Soren 1987, 159.

16. On the materials traded by Carthage in the fourth century, see Wolff 1986, 171–207.

17. *30 Ans* 1987, 57.

18. Katzenstein 1973.

19. Esther 8:15. For the other biblical citations, see Negev 1986, 121.

20. Tillyard 1908.

21. On this area, see Ciaceri 1928–49.

22. Iacopi 1953, 27.

23. See the account in Roussel 1970.
24. Frost 1976.
25. Bass 1972, 67.
26. Frost 1987, 67.

Chapter V

1. Polybius I.1.
2. Polybius III.11.
3. Polybius III.12 insists that Antiochus was convinced the story was true.
4. For Hannibal in Spain, see Sutherland 1940, 22–43. Excellent maps of the campaigns can be found in Lazenby 1978.
5. Polybius II.1. On Hamilcar, see Lloyd 1977, 129–134.
6. On the life of Hannibal, see the ancient account of Livy and more recently de Beer 1969; Dorey and Dudley 1972; Proctor 1971.
7. The history of Marseilles is discussed in Clébert 1972, 157–176; Busquet 1945.
8. For the military ability and character of Hannibal, see de Beer 1969, 95–97.
9. On elephants, see Scullard 1974.
10. For the leading Roman political families of this period, see Scullard 1973, 31–82; Eckstein 1987, 233–267; Epstein 1987.
11. Polybius V.118.
12. Livy XXII.57.
13. For the accomplishments of Archimedes, see Heath 1958.
14. On this Scipio, see Haywood 1933; Scullard 1970.
15. On Syphax and Masinissa, see Walsh 1965.
16. Polybius XV.5–9.
17. However, his family burial place on the Via Appia was sadly neglected in the third century A.D. See Coarelli 1988, 34–36. On the downfall of the Scipios, see Haywood 1933, 86–105.

18. Lancel 1985, 743.
19. Appian, *Libyca* 67. On the Carthaginian revival, see Wolff 1985, 240–243; Greene 1986, 110.
20. Rose 1960, 51–52.
21. For Puteoli, see Ostrow 1977; Ingrassia 1981, 80–89.
22. On this period, see Maroti 1983.
23. Plutarch *Cato* 26; Scott-Kilvert 1965, 149.
24. Plutarch *Cato* 27. On Cato, see Astin 1978, 125–130; Scullard 1973, 240–245.
25. For this period, see Adcock 1946; Astin 1967, 48–60; Dorey and Dudley 1972, 165–166.
26. Polybius XII. 509–510.

Chapter VI

1. Matthews 1974, 166.
2. de Prorok 1926, 87.
3. de Prorok 1926, 88.
4. Kelsey 1926, vii.
5. A survey of the ancient accounts appears in Brown 1986, 12–33.
6. Diodorus XX.14.
7. Plutarch *De Superstitione* 171C–D.
8. Scholia to Plato's *Republic* 337 A: F Gr H IIB, 745, frag. 91.
9. On Sanchuniathon, see Attridge and Oden 1981, 63.
10. Stager and Wolff 1984.
11. Ribichini 1976, 148.
12. The history of the tophet is summarized with bibliography in Ben Abed Ben Khader and Soren 1987, 40–43, 149–154.
13. Harden 1937b.
14. Stager and Wolff 1984.
15. Kelsey 1926, 50; Hvidberg-Hansen 1979.
16. For the *stelae* and their symbols, see Barteloni 1976 (for the earlier periods) and Brown 1986, 89–194 (circa 400 B.C. and after).

17. For animal sacrifice, see Sergio Ribichini, "Beliefs and Religious Life," in Moscati 1988, 120.
18. For the controversy, see Benichou-Safar 1982, 7–9; Ribichini in Moscati 1988, 120.
19. Mosca 1975.
20. Brown, personal communication. On the development of the tophet area in Punic times, see Brown 1986, 51–63.
21. For inscribed tophet *stelae,* see Ben Abed Ben Khader and Soren 1987, 150–151.
22. Weinfeld 1972.
23. Moscati 1988, 120.
24. Brown 1986, 88.
25. Whitaker 1921.
26. Cintas 1947.
27. Acquaro 1987, 172–181.
28. Benichou-Safer 1982.
29. Stager and Wolff 1984, 51. On the surprising numbers of references to sacrifices in the ancient Greek world, see Henrichs 1980.
30. Tertullian *Apology* IX. 2–4.
31. Ben Abed Ben Khader and Soren 1987, 49.

Chapter VII

1. Caven 1980, 294.
2. For a discussion of this section of Diodorus Siculus (Book X), see Hurst and Stager 1978, 340.
3. Rakob 1984.
4. Polybius XXXIX.3. On the architecture and urban development of Carthage during this period, see Lancel 1985b, 743–751.
5. On the French Byrsa excavations, see Lancel 1979–85, Lancel 1983, 19–44.
6. On Kerkouane, see Fantar 1984–86, Fantar 1987.
7. *30 Ans* 1987, 57.
8. Poinssot 1983, 58–61, with bibliography.

9. For an introduction to Punic ceramics, see Cintas 1950.
10. A wide range of Punic artifacts is discussed in Ben Abed Ben Khader and Soren 1987; *30 Ans* 1987; and *De Carthage à Kairouan* 1983, with bibliography.
11. See Charles-Picard 1965–66, 14.
12. Astruc 1957.
13. Seefried 1982, 6, 26.
14. Acquaro 1971.
15. Egyptian imagery in Carthage is discussed in Vercoutter 1945; Leclant 1968–69.
16. Jewelry is discussed in Quillard 1983.
17. Ben Abed Ben Khader and Soren 1987, 146; Quillard 1970–71, 10.
18. Acquaro 1977, with bibliography; Ben Abed Ben Khader and Soren 1987, 143–145.
19. *30 Ans* 1987, 109.
20. Ben Abed Ben Khader and Soren 1987, 155.
21. *De Carthage à Kairouan* 1983, 46–48.
22. Moore 1905, 148.
23. Jenkins and Lewis 1963.
24. Fouchet 1962 offers a brief, highly negative survey of Punic art; his sentiments are echoed by Charles-Picard and Charles-Picard 1965–66, 162.

Chapter VIII

1. Camps 1960; Saumagne 1966. On Berber history, see Camps 1980.
2. Baradez 1949.
3. On centuriation, see Saumagne 1924b; Davin 1930; Wightman 1980.
4. On the administration of Carthage during this period, see Broughton 1968, 1–87; Gsell 1927.
5. On the Gracchi, see Boren 1969; Bernstein 1978; Stockton 1979; Shochat 1980.

6. For Jugurtha, see Saumagne 1966.
7. Mommsen 1974, 306.
8. For Caesar in Africa, see Gelzer 1961, 261–272; Fuller 1963, 261–276; Greenbalgh 1981, 266–268.
9. On Utica, see Lezine 1970.
10. Broughton 1968, 54–56, 67–68.
11. For Haidra, see Baratte and Duval 1974.
12. On Tacfarinas, see Marsh 1931, 148–150; Kornemann 1960, 152–156; Shaw 1982, 29–50.
13. Tacitus *Annales* III.73.
14. Baratte and Duval 1974, 7.
15. On African agriculture, see Slim 1984b, 156–162.
16. Pliny *Natural History* XV.III, 8.
17. Pliny *Natural History* XV.V. On olives, see Camps-Fabrer 1953.
18. On the abundance of olive oil in ancient Tunisia and Augustine's lighting problems, see Raven 1984, 102.
19. Juvenal V.86–91.
20. On African red slip ware, see Hayes 1972, 1–299.
21. On the lamps of Carthage, see Deneauve 1969.
22. For basilica plaques and Roman statuettes, see *De Carthage à Kairouan* 1983, 128–137, 187–189.
23. Pliny *Natural History* XXXI.94 and Martial XIII. 102. See also Curtis 1978.
24. For Roman ships in Tunisia, see Foucher 1957.
25. For life in second century Tunisia, see Slim 1984b, 177–184.
26. Slim 1984b, 173–176. On Roman social structure generally, see MacMullen 1974.
27. On *latifundia*, see Raven 1984, 88; for *villae*, see McKay 1977, 222–237.
28. The baths of Carthage are discussed in Lezine 1969b. On Roman African baths, see also Mahjoubi (n.d.), 91–107.
29. For discussion, see Charles-Picard 1954, 14; Raven 1984, 90–91, 99; M'Charek, 207–208.
30. Charles-Picard 1954b, 15.
31. Broughton 1968, 36, 157; Raven 1984, 88–89.
32. The Lex Manciana is discussed by Slim 1984b, 160–161. For African estate management, see Broughton 1968, 157–175.
33. For conditions of slaves on the African estates, see Gsell 1932.
34. Ben Abed Ben Khader and Soren 1987, 229–230.
35. For Apuleius, see LeGlay 1966b, 47–61, with bibliography.

Chapter IX

1. Wheeler 1964, 46.
2. On water in Roman times, see Gauckler 1897–1901.
3. On water problems at Dougga, see Poinssot 1983, 20, 48, 70–71.
4. On Roman hydraulic engineering generally, see White 1984, 162–172.
5. For the Temple of the Waters, see Rakob 1971.
6. Slim 1984b, 191–197.
7. On the history of city planning, see Martin 1956; Castagnoli 1968.
8. For the history of Carthaginian gridded planning, see Wightman 1980, with bibliography.
9. Slim 1984b, 184–189.
10. Poinssot 1983, 35.
11. For circuses, see Humphrey 1986, Humphrey 1988.
12. Guides to Carthage include Fantar 1973; Ennabli and Slim 1982.
13. Lezine 1969.
14. Ennabli and Ben Osman 1983.
15. Apuleius *Florida* XX.
16. Poinssot 1983, 27–32.
17. On the Saturn cult, see LeGlay 1966a.
18. Slim 1985.
19. Slim 1984a, Slim 1986.

20. On Tunisian amphitheaters, see Slim 1984b, 200–203.
21. For the Colosseum, see Pearson 1973.
22. Suetonius *Claudius* XXI.
23. The character and types of combats are discussed by Cozzo 1971, 11–12, 54–56; Savi 1980.
24. Beschaouch 1966.
25. Despite momentary fame, gladiators were considered to be at the bottom of society and are compared to prostitutes by Highet 1962, 62–63.

Chapter X

1. Clavel and Lévêque 1971.
2. On class and social distinctions, see MacMullen 1974, 88–120.
3. Alexander and Ennaifer Vol. I, Fasc. 1 1973, 19–56.
4. Alexander and Ennaifer Vol. I, Fasc. 2 1974, 1–18.
5. Ben Abed Ben Khader and Soren 1987, 132–135.
6. Moore 1968; Vitruvius VII.I, 1–3.
7. Alexander and Ennaifer Vol. II, Fasc. 1 1980, 141–162.
8. Dunbabin 1978, 124.
9. Soren 1972, 105–127, 140–141; Albertini 1950, 116.
10. Dunbabin 1978, 119–121.
11. On Pupput, see Ben Abed Ben Khader 1983.
12. Yacoub 1970, 117.
13. On mime and pantomime, see Bieber 1971, 159–160, 165, 227–237.
14. Apuleius *The Golden Ass* X.46.
15. Bayet 1955, 103–121. Performances of mime and pantomime are discussed by Nicoll 1931.
16. Foucher 1960, 49–50.
17. Dunbabin 1978, 132–133; Parrish 1983.
18. Charles-Picard 1954b, 12–13; Romanelli 1964.

19. On ancient Roman hunting, see Aymard 1951.
20. Ben Abed Ben Khader and Soren 1987, 213–217; Dunbabin 1978, 46–64.
21. Ennaifer 1976.
22. Yacoub 1978, 139–142; Prêcheur-Canonge (n.d.) 80, 83.
23. Alexander and Ennaifer Vol. I, Fasc. 1 1973, 67–82.
24. Marec 1954, 104–105, 109.
25. Ben Abed Ben Khader and Soren 1987, 215.
26. Ward-Perkins 1985, 382.
27. Dunbabin 1978, 88–108.
28. On the *tabellae defixiones*, see Audollent 1904. For this curse, see Charles-Picard 1954a, 244.

Chapter XI

1. For Roman religion in North Africa, see Charles-Picard 1954a.
2. On Cybele generally, see Vermaseren 1977.
3. LeGlay 1966a.
4. Benabou 1982, 13–21.
5. Bisi 1978.
6. Yacoub 1978, 40–45.
7. Poinssot 1929.
8. Galinsky 1969, 51–53, 225–227.
9. Moseley 1975.
10. Suetonius, *Augustus* 94.
11. Ben Abed Ben Khader and Soren 1987, 139–140.
12. Charles-Picard 1954a, 245.
13. Gabillon 1983, 109. On the use of magic formulae to protect family and field, see Charles-Picard 1954a, 236–238; for the role of magic and the occult in Greek and Roman religion, see Luck 1985.
14. Apuleius, *De Magia*.
15. Deonna and Renard 1961, 118–119.
16. For the role of the seasons, see Hanfmann 1951.
17. Dunbabin 1978, 147.
18. Signs and symbols to ward off the

evil eye are discussed by Charles-Picard 1954a, 237–240; Audollent 1901, 426–427.

19. Charles-Picard 1946, 453–459.
20. For Roman religion generally, see Ferguson 1970. For the North African sources, see Février 1972; Charles-Picard 1954a.

Epilogue

1. Ben Abed Ben Khader and Soren 1987, 59–67.
2. Slim 1984b, 214–215.
3. For this period in North Africa, see Lepelley 1979.
4. On the Severans, see Birley 1972.
5. Julien 1961, 132–133.
6. Brauer 1975.
7. Raven 1984, 165–170.
8. On the influence of Cyprian, see Warmington 1954, 76–102.
9. On this period, see Warmington 1954, 5–7. MacMullen 1988, 29–30 believes that Carthage remained essentially prosperous until the seventh century.
10. Frend 1952; Jones 1962, 91–108.
11. On toleration and persecution, see Guterman 1951. For Constantine and the lack of effectiveness of the Edict of Milan, see MacMullen 1984, 44.
12. For the Damous-el-Karita, see Krautheimer 1967, 144–145.
13. Augustine, *Confessions* III.1. On Augustine in Carthage, see Charles-Picard 1965; Hamman 1979; Romanelli 1981, 161–180.
14. For the subtle complexities of Arianism, see Jones 1986, 86.
15. On the Vandals in Africa, see Courtois 1955.
16. On Late Roman Carthage, see Humphrey (ed.) 1975, Humphrey 1980; Ellis 1985, Ellis 1988.
17. Procopius IV. vi, 5–10. But for a more frightening portrait, as a group feared by the Roman army, see III. xix, 27.
18. Pringle 1982.
19. On this period, see Wells 1982; Slim 1984b, 362–368.
20. Julien 1961, 271–279; Slim 1984b, 386–392.
21. Fradier 1970, 34–45.
22. Davis 1861, 35–36.

Selected Bibliography and Reading of General Interest

❦

Acquaro, Enrico. *I rasoi punici*. Rome, 1971.
———. *Amuleti egiziani ed egittizzanti del Museo Nazionale di
Cagliari*. Cagliari, Sardinia, 1977.
———. *Cartagine: Un impero sul Mediterraneo*. Rome, 1987.
Adcock, F. E. "Delenda est Carthago." *Cambridge Historical Journal*
8 (1946): 117–128.
Akurgal, Ekrem. *The Art of Greece*. New York, 1968.
Albertini, E. *L'Afrique romaine*. Algiers, 1950.
Albright, W. F. *Archaeology and the Religion of Israel*. Baltimore,
Md., 1956.
———. "The Role of the Canaanites in the History of Civili-
zation." In *The Bible and the Ancient Near East,* edited by
G. Ernest Wright. Garden City, N.Y., 1961: 438–487.
———. *Yahweh and the Gods of Canaan*. London, 1968.
Alexander, Margaret, and Mongi Ennaifer. *Corpus des mosaïques de
Tunisie*. Tunis, 1973–.
Anderson, J. K. *Hunting in the Ancient World*. Berkeley, Calif.,
1985.
Apuleius. *The Golden Ass*. Translated by William Adlington (1566)
and edited by Harry C. Schnur. New York, 1962.
Astin, Alan. *Scipio Aemilianus*. Oxford, 1967.
———. *Cato the Censor*. Oxford, 1978.
Astruc, M. "Exotisme et localisme. Étude sur les coquilles d'oeufs
d'autruche decorées d'Ibiza." *Archivio de prehistoria Levantia*
(1957): 47–112.
Attridge, H. W., and R. A. Oden. *Philo of Byblos, the Phoenician
History*. Washington, D.C., 1981.
Audollent, A. *Carthage romaine*. Paris, 1901.

———. *Defixionum Tabellae*. Paris, 1904.

Aymard, J. *Essai sur les chasses romaines*. Paris, 1951.

Bakir, Taha. *Historical and Archaeological Guide to Lepcis Magna*. Tripoli, 1968.

Baradez, Jean. *Fossatum Africae*. Paris, 1949.

Baratte, François, and Noël Duval. *Haidra*. Tunis, 1974.

Barnes, T. D. *Tertullian, A Historical and Literary Study*. Oxford, 1971.

Barnett, R. "Phoenician and Punic Arts and Handicrafts. Some Reflections and Notes." *Atti del I Congresso internazionale di studi fenici e punici, Roma, 5–10 novembre, 1979* 1 (1983): 19–26.

Barteloni, P. *Le "stele" arcaiche del tofet di Cartagine*. Rome, 1976.

Bartoccini, P. *Guida di Sabratha*. Milan, 1927.

Basch, Lucien. "When Is a Ram Not a Ram? The Case of the Punic Ship." *The Mariner's Mirror* 69 (1983): 129–142.

Bass, George. *A History of Seafaring*. London, 1972.

———. "Oldest Known Shipwreck." *National Geographic* (December 1987): 693–734.

Bates, O. *The Eastern Libyans*. London, 1914.

Bayet, J. "Les vertus du pantomime Vicentius." *Libyca* 3 (1955): 103–121.

Belkhodja, K., Ammar Mahjoubi, and Hedi Slim. *Histoire de l'antiquité de la Tunisie*. Tunis, 1968.

Ben Abdallah, Zeineb. *Catalogue des inscriptions latines païennes du Musée du Bardo*. Rome, 1986.

Ben Abed Ben Khader, Aicha. "Une mosaïque à pyramides végétales de Pupput." In *Mosaïque, receuil d'hommages à Henri Stern*, 61. Paris, 1983: 61–64.

Ben Abed Ben Khader, Aicha, and David Soren, eds. *Carthage: A Mosaic of Ancient Tunisia*. New York, 1987.

Benabou, Marcel. *La résistance africaine à la romanisation*. Paris, 1975.

———. "Les survivances préromaines en Afrique romaine." In *L'Afrique romaine*, edited by Colin Wells, 13–27. Ottawa, 1982.

Benichou-Safar, Hélène. *Les tombes puniques de Carthage*. Paris, 1982.

Bernstein, Alvin. *Tiberius Sempronius Gracchus: Tradition and Apostasy*. Ithaca, N.Y., 1978.

Berve, H. *Die Tyrannis bei den Griechen*. 2 vols. Munich, 1967.

Beschaouch, Azzedine. "La mosaïque de chasse à l'amphithéâtre découverte à Smirat." *Comptes rendus de l'Académie des inscriptions et belles-lettres* (1966): 134–157.

Bieber, Margaret. *The History of Greek and Roman Theater*. Princeton, N.J., 1971.

Biers, William. *The Archaeology of Greece*. Ithaca, N.Y., 1980.

Birley, Anthony. *Septimius Severus: The African Emperor*. Garden City, N.Y., 1972.

Bisi, Anna Maria. "Une figurine phénicienne trouvée à Carthage." In *Mélanges de Carthage* (1964–65): 43–53.

———. "A proposito di alcune *stele* del tipo della Ghorfa al British Museum." *Antiquités africaines* 12 (1978): 21–88.

Blackman, D. J. "Ancient Harbors in the Mediterranean, Part 2." *International Journal of Nautical Archaeology* 2 (1982): 185–211.

Boardman, John. *The Greeks Overseas*. Harmondsworth, England, 1973.

Boren, Henry. *The Gracchi*. New York, 1969.

Bousquet, G. H. *Les Berbères*. Paris, 1957.

Bovill, E. W. *The Golden Trade of the Moors*. Oxford, 1968.

Brauer, George. *The Age of the Soldier Emperors*. Park Ridge, N.J., 1975.

Bright, J. *A History of Israel*. Philadelphia, Pa., 1981.

Broughton, T. R. S. *The Romanization of Africa Proconsularis*. New York, 1968.

Brown, Peter. *Augustine of Hippo*. London, 1967.

———. *Religion and Society in the Age of St. Augustine*. London, 1972.

Brown, Susanna Shelby. *Late Child Sacrifice and Sacrificial Monuments in their Mediterranean Context*. Ph.D. diss., University of Chicago, 1986.

Busquet, Raoul. *Histoire de Marseilles*. Paris, 1945.

Caffarelli, Ernesto, and Giacomo Caputo. *The Buried City: Excavations at Lepcis Magna*. New York, 1966.

Camps, Gabriel. "Massinissa ou les débuts de l'histoire." *Libyca* 8, no. 1 (1960).

———. *Berbères*. Paris, 1980.

Camps, Gabriel, et al. *Encyclopédie Berbère*. 4 vols. Aix-en-Provence, France, 1984–87.

Camps-Fabrer, H. *L'olivier et l'huile d'olive dans l'Afrique romaine.* Algiers, 1953.

Caputo, Giacomo. "Fezzan e oasi di Gat," in G. Caputo and others, *Il Sahara italiana,* 243–330, Rome, 1937.

Carter, Theresa Howard. "Western Phoenicians at Lepcis Magna." *American Journal of Archaeology* 69 (1965): 123–132.

Cary, M. *A History of Rome.* London, 1962.

Castagnoli, Ferdinando. *Topografia e urbanistica di Roma antica.* Bologna, Italy, 1968.

Caven, Brian. *The Punic Wars.* London, 1980.

Charles-Picard, Gilbert. "Le mysticisme africain." *Comptes rendus de l'Académie des inscriptions et belles-lettres* (1946): 453:459.

―――. *Les religions de l'Afrique antique.* Paris, 1954a.

―――. "Mactar." *Bulletin économique et sociale de la Tunisie* 90 (1954b): 1–18.

―――. *Carthage.* London, 1956.

―――. *La civilisation de l'Afrique romaine.* Paris, 1959.

―――. *La Carthage de Saint Augustin.* Paris, 1965a.

―――. "Sacra Punica." *Karthago* 13 (1965b): 14–62.

Charles-Picard, Gilbert, and Colette Charles-Picard. *The Life and Death of Carthage.* London, 1965–66.

Chelbi, Fathi. "Quelques aspects de la civilisation carthaginoise à l'époque hellénistique." *Cahiers des études anciennes* 16 (1985): 79–88.

Chevallier, Raymond. *Roman Roads.* Berkeley, Calif., 1976.

Ciaceri, E. *Storia della Magna Grecia.* 3 vols. Milan, 1928–49.

Cintas, Pierre. "Le sanctuaire punique de Sousse." *Revue africaine* 91 (1947): 1–80.

―――. *Céramique punique.* Paris, 1950.

―――. *Manuel d'archéologie punique.* 2 vols. Paris, 1970–76.

Clavel, M., and P. Lévêque. *Villes et structures urbaines dans l'occident romaine.* Paris, 1971.

Clébert, Jean-Paul. *Provence antique.* 2 vols. Vol. 1, *Des origines à la conquête romaine.* Paris, 1972.

Coarelli, Filippo. *Il sepulcro degli Scipioni a Roma.* Rome, 1988.

Coarelli, Filippo, and Mario Torelli. *Sicilia.* Rome, 1984.

Cornevin, Robert. *Histoire de l'Afrique.* 3 vols. Vol. 1, *Des origines au XVI siècle.* Paris, 1967.

Courtois, Charles. *Les Vandales et l'Afrique.* Paris, 1955.

Cozzo, Giuseppe. *The Colosseum*. London, 1971.

Cross, Frank Moore. *Canaanite Myth and Hebrew Epic*. Cambridge, Mass., 1980.

Cumont, Franz. *After Life in Roman Paganism*. New York, 1959.

———. *Astrology and Religion Among the Greeks and Romans*. New York, 1960.

Curtis, R. I. *The Production and Commerce of Fish Sauce in the Western Roman Empire*. Baltimore, Md., 1978.

Daniels, Charles. *The Garamantes of Southern Libya*. North Harrow, England, 1970.

Davin, Paul. "Étude sur la cadastration de Colonia Julia Karthago." *Revue tunisienne* (1930): 74–85.

Davis, N. *Carthage and Her Remains*. London, 1861.

de Beer, Sir Gavin. *Hannibal*. New York, 1969.

De Carthage à Kairouan. Paris, 1983.

Decret, François. *Carthage ou l'empire de la mer*. Tours, France, 1977.

Delattre, Paul. "Une cachette de figurines de Demeter et de brûle-parfums votifs à Carthage. *Comptes rendus de l'Académie des inscriptions et belles-lettres* (1923): 361.

Demerliac, J. G., and J. Meirat. *Hannon et l'empire punique*. Paris, 1983.

Deneauve, Jean. *Lampes de Carthage*. Paris, 1969.

Deonna, W., and M. Renard. *Croyances et superstitions de table dans la Rome antique*. Brussels, 1961.

de Prorok, Court Byron Khun. *Digging for Lost African Gods*. New York, 1926.

De Roch, Serée. *Tébessa*. Algiers, 1952.

Desanges, J., and Serge Lancel. *Bibliographie analytique de l'Afrique antique*. Paris, 1962–.

Dever, William. "New Vistas on the EBIV ("MB I") Horizon in Syria-Palestine." *Bulletin of the American Schools of Oriental Research* 237 (1980): 35–58.

———. "The Impact of the 'New Archaeology' on Syro-Palestinian Archaeology." *Bulletin of the American Schools of Oriental Research* 242 (1981): 15–30.

———. "Relations Between Syria-Palestine and Egypt in the Hyksos Period." In *Palestine in the Bronze and Iron Ages: Papers in Honour of Olga Tufnell,* edited by J. Tubb, 69–87. London, 1985.

Diodorus Siculus. *Biblioteca. (Library of History)*. Translated by R. M. Geer. Cambridge, Mass., 1962.

———. *Library of History (Biblioteca)*. Translated by C. H. Oldfather. Cambridge, Mass., 1950.

Dorey, T. A., and D. R. Dudley. *Rome Against Carthage*. New York, 1972.

Dothan, Trude. "The Philistines Reconsidered." *Biblical Archaeology Today* (1985): 165–176.

Dow, Reverend James. *Dictionary of the Bible*. London, 1983.

Drögemüller, M. P. *Syrakus*. Heidelberg, Germany, 1969.

Dunbabin, Katherine. *The Mosaics of Roman North Africa*. Oxford, 1978.

Dunbabin, T. J. *The Western Greeks*. Oxford, 1948.

Duval, Noël. *Les églises africaines à deux absides*. 2 vols. Paris, 1971–73.

Duval, Noël, and F. Baratte. *Les ruines de Sufetula-Sbeitla*. Tunis, 1973.

Eckstein, Arthur. *Senate and General*. Berkeley, Calif., 1987.

Ellis, Simon. "Carthage in the Seventh Century: An Expanding Population?" *Cahiers des études anciennes* 17 (1985): 31–42.

———. "Carthage Sewers Project—1986." *CEDAC* 9 (1988): 6–38.

Ennabli, Abdelmajid, and W. Ben Osman. "Étude des pavements de la villa de la volière." In *Mosaïque, receuil d'hommages à Henri Stern*, 147–148. Paris, 1983.

Ennabli, Abdelmajid, and Hedi Slim. *Carthage*. Tunis, 1982.

Ennaifer, Mongi. *La cité d'Althiburos et l'édifice des Asclepieia*. Tunis, 1976.

Epstein, David. *Personal Enmity in Roman Politics 218–43 B.C.* London, 1987.

Fantar, Mhamed. *Carthage, la prestigieuse cité d'Elissa*. Tunis, 1970.

———. *Visite de Carthage*. Tunis, 1973.

———. *Kerkouane I–III*. Tunis, 1984–86.

———. *Kerkouane, une cité punique au cap-Bon*. Tunis, 1987.

Février, J. P. *Les sources épigraphiques et archéologiques et l'histoire religieuse des provinces orientales de l'Afrique antique*. Ravenna, Italy, 1972.

Février, P. A. "Notes sur le développement urbain en Afrique du Nord." *Cahiers archéologiques fin de l'antiquité* 14 (1964): 3–4.

Finlay, M. *A History of Sicily*. London, 1968.

Foucher, Louis. *Navires et barques*. Tunis, 1957.

———. *Inventaires des mosaïques: Sousse*. Tunis, 1960.

———. *Hadrumetum*. Paris, 1964.

Fouchet, Max-Pol. *L'art à Carthage*. Paris, 1962.

Fradier, Georges. "Tunis—A Jewel of Islam." *The Unesco Courier* (December 1970): 34–45.

Frankenstein, Susan. "The Phoenicians in the Far West: A Function of Neo-Assyrian Imperialism." In *Power and Propaganda,* edited by Mogens Trolle Larsen, 278–286. Copenhagen, 1979.

Frend, W. H. C. *The Donatist Church*. Oxford, 1952.

Frost, Honor. *Lilybaeum (Marsala). The Punic Ship: Final Excavation Report*. Rome, 1976.

———. "How Carthage Lost the Sea." *Natural History* (December 1987): 58–67.

Fuller, J. F. C. *Julius Caesar: Man, Soldier and Tyrant*. London, 1963.

Gabillon, Aimé. "Une inscription magique de la région de Bou Arada (Tunisie)." *Bulletin archéologique du Comité des travaux historiques et scientifiques* (1983): 109–125.

Galinsky, Karl. *Aeneas, Sicily and Rome*. Princeton, N.J., 1969.

Gascou, Jacques. *La politique municipale de l'empire romain en Afrique Proconsulaire de Trajane à Septime Severe*. Paris, 1972.

Gauckler, Paul. *Enquête sur les installations hydrauliques romaines en Tunisie*. 5 vols. Tunis, 1897–1901.

———. *Inventaire des mosaïques de Tunisie*. Paris, 1910.

Gelzer, Matthias. *Caesar: Politician and Statesman*. Cambridge, Mass., 1961.

Goodchild, R. G. *Lepcis Magna. Tabula Imperii Romani*. London, 1954.

Gordon, Cyrus H. *Ugaritic Literature*. Rome, 1949.

———. "Vergil and the Near East." *Ugaritica* 6 (1969): 267–288.

Green, Alberto. *The Role of Human Sacrifice in the Ancient Near East*. Missoula, Montana, 1975.

Green, Peter. *Armada from Athens*. London, 1971.

Greenbalgh, Peter. *Pompey: The Republican Prince*. London, 1981.

Greene, Joseph. *The Carthaginian Countryside: Archaeological Reconnaissance in the Hinterland of Carthage*. Ph.D. diss., University of Chicago, 1986.

Gsell, G. "Esclaves ruraux dans l'Afrique romaine." In *Mélanges Gustave Glotz,* Vol. 1, 397–415. Paris, 1932.

Gsell, Stéphane. *Histoire ancienne de l'Afrique du Nord.* Vol. 4, *La civilisation carthaginoise.* Paris, 1920.

———. "Les premiers temps de la Carthage romaine." *Revue historique* (November 1927): 228.

Guéry, R., C. Morrison, and Hedi Slim. *Recherches archéologiques franco-tunisiennes à Rougga.* Rome, 1982.

Guido, Margaret. *Syracuse.* Syracuse, Sicily, 1980.

Guterman, S. L. *Religious Toleration and Persecution in Ancient Rome.* London, 1951.

Hamman, A.-G. *La vie quotidienne en Afrique du Nord au temps de saint Augustin.* Paris, 1979.

Hanfmann, George. *The Season Sarcophagus at Dumbarton Oaks.* Cambridge, Mass., 1951.

Harden, Donald B. "Punic Urns from the Precinct of Tanit at Carthage." *American Journal of Archaeology* 31 (1937a): 297–310

———. "The Pottery from the Precinct of Tanit at Salammbô, Carthage." *Iraq* 4 (1937b): 59–89.

———. *The Phoenicians.* New York, 1962.

Hayes, John. *Late Roman Pottery.* London, 1972.

Haynes, D. E. L. *The Antiquities of Tripolitania.* Tripoli, 1965.

Haywood, Richard. *Studies on Scipio Africanus.* Westport, Conn., 1933.

Heath, T. L. *The Works of Archimedes.* New York, 1958.

Henrichs, Albert. "Human Sacrifice in Greek Religion: Three Case Studies." In *Le sacrifice dans l'antiquité,* edited by Olivier Reverdin and Bernard Grange, 195–242. Geneva, 1980.

Herm, Gerhard. *The Phoenicians.* New York, 1975.

Herodotus. *The Histories.* Translated by Aubrey de Selincourt. Baltimore, Md., 1965.

Highet, Gilbert. *Juvenal the Satirist.* New York, 1962.

Hooke, S. H. *Middle Eastern Mythology.* New York, 1983.

Humphrey, John. "Vandal and Byzantine Carthage: Some New Archaeological Evidence." In *New Light on Ancient Carthage,* edited by John Griffiths Pedley, 85–120. Ann Arbor, Mich., 1980.

———. *Roman Circuses.* London, 1986.

———. *The Circus and a Byzantine Cemetery at Carthage.* Ann Arbor, Mich., 1988.

————, ed. *Excavations at Carthage*. Ann Arbor, Mich., 1975–.

Hurst, Henry. "Excavations at Carthage 1974. First Interim Report. *The Antiquaries Journal* 55, no. 1 (1975): 11–40.

Hurst, Henry, and S. P. Roskams. *Excavations at Carthage: The British Mission*. Vol. 1, no. 1. Sheffield, England, 1984.

Hurst, Henry, and Lawrence Stager. "A Metropolitan Landscape: The Late Punic Port of Carthage." *World Archaeology* 9 (1978): 334–346.

Hvidberg-Hansen, F. O. *La déesse Tanit*. 2 vols. Copenhagen, 1979.

Iacopi, G. "Messina nell'antichita." *Messina* 3 (1953): 277.

Ingrassia, Anna Maria Bisi. *Napoli e Dintorni*. Rome, 1981.

Isserlin, B. S. J. "Some Common Features in Phoenician/Punic Town-Planning." *Rivista di studi fenici* 1 (1973): 135–154.

Isserlin, B. S. J., and Joan du Plat Taylor. *Motya*. Leiden, The Netherlands, 1974.

Jenkins, G. Kenneth. *The Coinage of Gela*. Berlin, 1970.

Jenkins, G. Kenneth, and R. B. Lewis. *Carthaginian Gold and Electrum Coins*. London, 1963.

Jones, A. H. M. *Constantine and the Conversion of Europe*. New York, 1962.

————. *The Later Roman Empire*. 2 vols. Baltimore, Md., 1986.

Julien, Charles-André. *History of North Africa: Tunisia, Algeria, Morocco*, translated by John Petrie. London, 1970. Originally published as *Histoire de l'Afrique du Nord: Tunisie, Algérie, Maroc*. Paris, 1961.

Kamp, Kathryn, and Norman Yoffee. "Ethnicity in Ancient Western Asia During the Early Second Millennium B.C.: Archaeological Assessments and Ethno-archaeological Prospectives." *Bulletin of the American Schools of Oriental Research* 237 (1980): 85–99.

Karageorghis, Vassos. *Kition*. London, 1976.

Katzenstein, H. J. *The History of Tyre*. Jerusalem, 1973.

Kelsey, F. W. *Excavations at Carthage, 1925: A Preliminary Report*. New York, 1926.

Kemp, B. J. *Amarna Reports*. 2 vols. London, 1984–85.

Kenyon, Kathleen. *Archaeology in the Holy Land*. New York, 1964.

Kininmonth, Christopher. *The Travelers' Guide to Sicily*. Indianapolis, Ind., 1972.

Knapp, A. Bernard. *The History and Culture of Ancient Western Asia and Egypt*. Chicago, Ill., 1988.

Kornemann, Ernst. *Tiberius*. Stuttgart, Germany, 1960.

Krahmalkov, Charles R. "The Foundation of Carthage, 814 B.C.: The Douimès Pendant Inscription." *Journal of Semitic Studies* 26 (1981): 177–191.

Krautheimer, Richard. *Early Christian and Byzantine Architecture*. Baltimore, Md., 1967.

Lancel, Serge. *Byrsa I–III*. Rome, 1979–85.

———. *La colline de Byrsa à l'époque punique*. Paris, 1983.

———. "Les *pavimenta punica* du quartier punique tardif de la colline de Byrsa." *Cahiers des études anciennes* 17 (1985a): 157–170

———. "La renaissance de la Carthage punique." *Comptes rendus de l'Académie des inscriptions et belles-lettres* (1985b): 727–751.

Larsen, Torben. "Siwa, Oasis Extraordinary." *Aramco World* 39, no. 5 (1988): 2–7.

Law, R. C. C. "The Garamantes and Trans-Saharan Enterprise in Classical Times." *Journal of African History* 8 (1967): 181–200.

Lazenby, J. F. *Hannibal's War*. Warminster, England, 1978.

Leclant, Jean. "Egyptian Talismans in the Cemeteries of Carthage." *Archaeologia Viva* 1, no. 2 (1968–69): 95–102.

LeGlay, Marcel. *Saturne africaine*. Paris, 1966a.

———. "Les religions de l'Afrique romaine au IIe siècle d'après Apulée et les inscriptions." In *L'Africa romana,* edited by Attilio Mastino, 47–61. Rome, 1966b.

Lepelley, Claude, *Les cités de l'Afrique romaine au bas empire*. Paris, 1979.

Lewis, Naphtali, and Meyer Reinhold. *Roman Civilization: Sourcebook I*. New York, 1966.

Lezine, Alexandre. *Architecture romaine d'Afrique*. Tunis, 1961.

———. *Thuburbo Maius*. Tunis, 1969a.

———. *Les thermes d'Antonin à Carthage*. Tunis, 1969b.

———. *Utique*. Tunis, 1970.

Livy. *The War with Hannibal*. Translated by Aubrey de Selincourt. London, 1965.

Lloyd, Alan. *Destroy Carthage*. London, 1977

Luck, Georg. *Arcana Mundi: Magic and the Occult in the Greek and Roman Worlds*. New York, 1985.

McKay, Alexander. *Houses, Villas and Palaces in the Roman World.* London, 1977.

MacKendrick, Paul. *The North African Stones Speak.* Chapel Hill, N.C., 1980.

MacMullen, Ramsey. *Roman Social Relations.* New Haven, Conn. 1974.

————. *Paganism in the Roman Empire.* New Haven, Conn., 1981.

————. *Christianizing the Roman Empire.* New Haven, Conn., 1984.

————. *Corruption and the Decline of Rome.* New Haven, Conn., 1988.

Mahjoubi, Ammar. *Les cités romaines de Tunisie.* Tunis, n.d.

Maier, F. G., and Vassos Karageorghis. *Paphos.* Nicosia, Cyprus, 1984.

Marec, Erwan. *Hippone la Royale.* Algiers, 1954.

Maróti, E. "On the Causes of Carthage's Destruction." *Oikumene* 4 (1983): 223–231.

Marsh, Frank Burr. *The Reign of Tiberius.* Oxford, 1931.

Martin, Roland. *L'urbanisme dans la Grèce antique.* Paris, 1956.

Massa, Aldo. *The Phoenicians.* Geneva, 1977.

Matthews, Samuel W. "The Phoenicians: Sea Lords of Antiquity." *National Geographic* (August 1974): 149–189.

M'Charek, Ahmed. *Aspects de l'évolution démographique et sociale à Mactaris aux IIe et IIIe siècles ap. J.C.* Tunis, 1982.

Merighi, A. *La Tripolitania antica.* 2 vols. Verbana, Italy, 1940.

Merlin, Alfred. *Inscriptions latines de la Tunisie.* Paris, 1944.

Mommsen, Theodor. *The Provinces of the Roman Empire.* Vol. 2, Chicago, Ill., 1974.

Moore, Mabel. *Carthage of the Phoenicians.* London, 1905.

Moore, R. E. "A Newly Observed Stratum in Roman Floor Mosaics." *American Journal of Archaeology* 72 (1968): 57–68.

Morel, Jean-Paul. *Céramique campanienne.* Rome, 1981.

Mosca, Paul G. *Child Sacrifice in Canaanite and Israelite Religion.* Ph.D. diss., Harvard University, 1975.

Moscati, Sabatino. *The World of the Phoenicians.* London, 1973.

————, ed. *The Phoenicians.* Milan, 1988.

Moseley, N. "Pius Aeneas." *Classical Journal* 10 (1975): 398–400.

Muhly, James D. "How Iron Technology Changed the Ancient

World and Gave the Philistines a Military Edge." *Biblical Archaeology Review* (November–December 1982): 40–54.

Negev, Abraham, ed. *The Archaeological Encyclopedia of the Holy Land*. Jerusalem, 1986.

Nicoll, Allardyce. *Masks, Mimes and Miracles*. London, 1931.

Niemeyer, Hans Georg, ed. *Phönizier im Westen*. Mainz, Germany, 1982.

Norris, H. T. *The Berbers in Arabic Literature*. London, 1982.

Nostrand, J. J. "The Imperial Domains of Africa Proconsularis." *University of California Publications in History* 14 (1925–26): 1–88.

Odelain, O., and R. Séguineau. *Dictionary of Proper Names and Places in the Bible*. Garden City, N.Y., 1981.

Oikonomides, Al. N. "Hanno the Carthaginian: *Periplus.*" *Antipolis* 1 (1974): 43–76.

Ostrow, Steven. *Problems in the Topography of Roman Puteoli*. Ann Arbor, Mich., 1977.

Page, J. D. *History of West Africa*. Cambridge, 1969.

Page, Thomas Ethelbert, ed., with Introduction and Notes. *"The Aeneid" of Virgil*. 2 vols. London, 1967.

Parke, H. W. *Ammon*. Chap. 9 in *The Oracles of Zeus: Dodona, Olympia, Ammon*. Cambridge, Mass., 1967.

Parrish, David. "The Mosaic of Xenophon from Sbeitla." In *Mosaïque, receuil d'hommages à Henri Stern*. Paris, 1983: 297–306.

Pearson, John. *Arena: The Story of the Colosseum*. New York, 1973.

Pease, Arthur Stanley. *Publi Vergili Maronis Aeneidos liber quartus*. Cambridge, Mass., 1935.

Pedley, John G., ed. *New Light on Ancient Carthage*. Ann Arbor, Mich., 1980.

Petit, Paul. *La paix romaine*. Paris, 1967.

Poinssot, Claude. *Les ruines de Dougga*. Tunis, 1983.

Poinssot, Louis. *L'autel de la gens Augusta*. Tunis, 1929.

Polybius. *The Histories*. Translated by Alvin H. Bernstein. South Bend, Ind., 1980.

Prêcheur-Canonge, Thérèse. *La vie rurale en Afrique romaine*. Tunis, n.d.

Pringle, Denys. "The Defense of Byzantine Africa from Justinian to the Arab Conquest." *British Archaeological Reports International Series* 99 (1982).

Proctor, Dennis, *Hannibal's March in History*. Oxford, 1971.

Quillard, Brigitte. "Les étuis portes-amulettes carthaginois." *Karthago* 16 (1970–71): 10.

———. *Bijoux carthaginois I: Les Colliers*. Louvain-la-Neuve, Belgium, 1979.

Rachet, Marguerite. *Rome et les Berbères*. Brussels, 1970.

Rakob, Friedrich. "Le sanctuaire des eaux à Zaghouan." *Africa* III–IV (1971): 133–176.

———. "Allemagne. Campagne de travail 1981." *CEDAC* 4 (1981): 12–14.

———. "Deutsche Ausgrabungen in Karthago." *Römische Mitteilungen* 91 (1984): 1–22.

Raven, Susan. *Rome in Africa*. New York, 1984.

Ribichini, Sergio. "Un episodio di magia a Cartagine nel III secolo av. Cr." In *Magia,* 148. Rome, 1976.

Riemann, H. "Zum Olympeion von Syrakus." *Römische Mitteilungen* 71 (1964): 229.

Rogerson, John, and Philip Davies. *The Old Testament World*. Englewood Cliffs, N.J., 1989.

Romanelli, Pietro. *Storia delle province romane dell'Africa*. Rome, 1959.

———. "A proposito della *Schola Juvenum* di Mactaris." *Les cahiers de Tunisie* 45–46 (1964): 11–20.

———. "Topografia e archeologia dell'Africa romana." *Enciclopedia classica* 10, no. 7 (1970).

———. *In Africa e a Roma*. Rome, 1981.

Rose, H. J. *A Handbook of Latin Literature*. New York, 1960.

Roussel, D. *La Sicile entre les Romains et les Carthaginois à l'époque de la première guerre punique*. Paris, 1970.

Salama, P. *Les voies romaines de l'Afrique du Nord*. Algiers, 1951.

———. *Bornes milliaires d'Afrique Proconsulaire*. Tunis, 1987.

Sandars, N. K. *The Sea Peoples*. London, 1985.

Saumagne, Charles. "Notes de topographie carthaginois. La colline de Saint-Louis." *Bulletin archéologique du Comité des travaux historiques et scientifiques* (1924a): 177–193.

———. "Colonia Iulia Karthago." *Bulletin archéologique du Comité des travaux historiques et scientifiques* (1924b): 131–139.

———. *La Numidie et Rome: Massinissa et Jugurtha*. Paris, 1966.

Savi, Fabrizio. *I gladiatori*. Rome, 1980.

Schmitz, Alfred. *Infelix Dido*. Paris, 1960.

Scott-Kilvert, Ian. *Makers of Rome: Nine "Lives" by Plutarch*. London, 1965.

Scullard, H. H. *Scipio Africanus: Soldier and Politician*. Ithaca, N.Y., 1970.

———. *Roman Politics 220–150 B.C.* Oxford, 1973.

———. *The Elephant in the Greek and Roman World*. Ithaca, N.Y., 1974.

Seefried, Monique. *Les pendentifs en verre sur noyau des pays de la Mediterranée antique*. Rome, 1982.

Sempère, S. *Archéologie de l'Afrique antique*. Paris, 1963.

Shanks, Hershel, ed. *Ancient Israel*. Englewood Cliffs, N.J., 1988.

Shaw, Brent. "Fear and Loathing: The Nomad Menace and Roman Africa." In *L'Afrique romaine*, edited by Colin Wells, 29–50. Ottawa, 1982.

Shochat, Yanir. *Recruitment and the Programme of Tiberius Gracchus*. Brussels, 1980.

Slim, Hedi. "Recherches préliminaires sur les amphithéâtres romains de Tunisie." *L'Africa romana* (1984a): 129–165.

———. *Histoire de la Tunisie: l'antiquité*. Tunis, 1984b.

———. "Nouveaux témoignages sur la vie économique à Thysdrus." *Bulletin archéologique du Comité des travaux historiques et scientifiques* (1985): 63–85.

———. "Les amphithéâtres d'El Jem." *Comptes rendus de l'Académie des inscriptions et belles-lettres* (July 1986): 440–469.

Solomon, Jon. *The Ancient World in the Cinema*. New York, 1978.

Soren, H. D. *Roman Pottery from Utica, Tunisia*. Ph.D. diss., Harvard University, 1972.

Squarciapino, Maria Floriani. *Leptis Magna*, Basel, Switzerland, 1966.

Stager, Lawrence, and Samuel Wolff. "Child Sacrifice at Carthage—Religious Rite or Population Control?" *Biblical Archaeology Review* 10, no. 1 (1984): 30–51.

Stockton, David. *The Gracchi*. Oxford, 1979.

Sutherland, C. H. V. *The Romans in Spain*. London, 1940.

Talbert, R. *Timoleon and the Revival of Greek Sicily*. Cambridge, 1974.

Tannahill, Reay. *Food in History*. New York, 1973.

Thompson, L. A., and J. Ferguson. *Africa in Classical Antiquity.*
  Ibadan, Nigeria, 1969.
Thompson, Mary Lee. "The Monumental and Literary
  Evidence for Programmatic Painting in Italy." *Marysas* 9
  (1961): 36.
Thucydides. *The Peloponnesian War.* Translated by Rex Warner.
  Harmondsworth, England, 1966.
Tillyard, H. J. W. *Agathocles.* Cambridge, 1908.
Tlatli, Salah-Eddine. *La Carthage punique. Étude urbaine.* Paris,
  1978.
Trente ans au service du patrimoine. Tunis, 1987.
Trousset, P. *Recherches sur le "limes tripolitanus."* Paris, 1974.
Trump, D. H. *The Prehistory of the Mediterranean.* New Haven,
  Conn., 1980.
Tylecote, Ronald F. "Metallurgy in Punic and Roman Carthage."
  In *Mines et fonderies antiques de la Gaule.* Toulouse, France,
  1982.
Vercoutter, Jean. *Les objets égyptiens et égyptisants du mobilier
  funéraire carthaginois.* Paris, 1945.
Vermaseren, Maarten. *Cybele and Attis.* London, 1977.
Virgil. *The Aeneid.* Translated by C. Day Lewis. New York,
  1953.
————. *The Aeneid.* Translated by W. F. Jackson Knight. London,
  1956.
Walsh, P. G. "Massinissa." *Journal of Roman Studies* 55 (1965):
  149–160.
Ward, Philip. *Sabratha.* South Harrow, England, 1970.
Ward-Perkins, J. B. *Roman Imperial Architecture.* New York, 1985.
Warmington, B. H. *The North African Provinces from Diocletian to
  the Vandal Conquest.* Cambridge, 1954.
————. *Carthage.* London, 1960.
Weinfeld, Moshe. "The Worship of Molech and of the Queen of
  Heaven and Its Background." *Ugarit-Forschungen* 4 (1972):
  133–154.
Weinstein, J. "The Egyptian Empire in Palestine: A
  Reassessment." *Bulletin of the American Schools of Oriental
  Research* 241 (1981): 1–28.
Wellard, James. *The Great Sahara.* New York, 1965.
Wells, Colin. "L'Afrique à la veille des invasions arabes." In

L'Afrique romaine, edited by Colin Wells, 87–105. Ottawa, 1982.

Wentker, H. Sizilien und Athen. Heidelberg, Germany, 1956.

Wertime, Theodore, and James D. Muhly. The Coming of the Age of Iron. New Haven, Conn., 1980.

Wheeler, Mortimer. Roman Art and Architecture. New York, 1964.

Whitaker, Joseph. Motya, a Phoenician Colony in Sicily. London, 1921.

White, K. D. Greek and Roman Technology. Ithaca, N.Y., 1984.

Whittaker, Charles. Land and Labour in North Africa. Berlin, 1978.

Whittaker, C. R. "The Western Phoenicians: Colonisation and Assimilation." Proceedings of the Cambridge Philological Society 200 (1974): 58–79.

Wightman, Edith. "The Plan of Roman Carthage: Practicalities and Politics." In New Light on Ancient Carthage, edited by John Griffiths Pedley, 29–46. Ann Arbor, Mich., 1980.

Wolff, Samuel. Maritime Trade at Punic Carthage. Ph.D. diss., University of Chicago, 1986.

Yacoub, Mohamed. Tunisian Mosaics. Washington, D.C., 1967.

———. La Musée du Bardo. Tunis, 1970.

———. Chefs-d'oeuvre des musées nationaux de Tunisie. Tunis, 1978.

Yoffee, Norman, and George L. Cowgill, eds. The Collapse of Ancient States and Civilizations. Tucson, Ariz., 1988.

Index